One Hundred
Great French Books

D1316191

ONE HUNDRED GREAT FRENCH BOOKS

From the Middle Ages to the Present

◆ ◆ ◆

LANCE DONALDSON-EVANS

BlueBridge

To Mary, Catherine and Andrew,
and in memory of Lorna Evans

Published by

BlueBridge

An imprint of
United Tribes Media Inc.
240 West 35th Street, Suite 500
New York, NY 10001

www.bluebridgebooks.com

LIBRARY OF CONGRESS CATALOGING-IN-PUBLICATION DATA
Donaldson-Evans, Lance K.
One hundred great French books : from the Middle Ages to the present /
Lance Donaldson-Evans.
p. cm.
Includes bibliographical references and index.
ISBN 978-1-933346-22-9
1. Best books—France. 2. Best books—French-speaking countries. 3. French imprints—Translations into English. 4. French literature—Stories, plots, etc. I. Title.
Z1035.2.D66 2010
011'.73—dc22
2009049070

Cover design by Angel Guerra

Cover art top: Eugène Delacroix (1798–1863), Liberty Leading the People, *1830.
Louvre, Paris. Photo credit: Réunion des Musées Nationaux / Art Resource, NY*

Cover art bottom: Auguste Renoir (1841–1919), The Reader, *1874–1876,
Musée d'Orsay, Paris. Photo credit: Scala / Art Resource, NY*

Text design by Cynthia Dunne

Printed in the United States of America

10 9 8 7 6 5 4 3 2 1

CONTENTS

◆ ◆ ◆

INTRODUCTION

◆ ◆ ◆

Despite occasional squabbles, France and America have always admired each other. Indeed, without the support of Louis XVI of France and the marquis de La Fayette, who fought in the War of Independence, the United States of America might not have been born as a free and independent nation. The French influence on the United States has been felt in many less dramatic ways as well, and exchanges between the two countries have always been numerous. For example, the layout of Washington, D.C., was designed by Frenchman Pierre L'Enfant, and the Statue of Liberty was the creation of his countryman Frédéric Auguste Bartholdi. Benjamin Franklin, Henry Adams, and Thomas Jefferson all spent time in France, as have countless American authors, artists, students, and other visitors ever since.

Of course the French influence on Canada has been even more dominant, and has continued more or less unabated since French explorers first set foot on what is now Canadian soil—today's Montréal has more French speakers than any other city in metropolitan France except Paris. For a time the vast territory known as La Nouvelle France (New France) extended as far north as Hudson Bay, east to Newfoundland, and cut a swathe across the continent to what is now the Louisiana coast. Even today, on a modern map of North America, one can trace the French influence from north to south through the proliferation of place names of French origin: Montréal (Mont Royal), Detroit (from the French word *détroit*, meaning strait), Prairie du Chien (Prairie of the Dog) in Wisconsin, all the way south to Baton Rouge (Red Stick) and New Orleans ("old" Orléans being in France). So while North America doesn't quite bear the imprint "Made in France," the importance of the French political, economic, and cultural impact across five centuries cannot be stressed enough.

French literature, too, has long been an inspiration to North American readers and authors, for the very good reason that it is one of the great literatures on the planet and would surely be offered World Heritage status if such a category existed in the literary sphere.

Literary works written in French began to appear in the Middle Ages.

Until the invention of printing in Europe in the 1450s (many centuries after its invention in China), literature was primarily transmitted orally by traveling minstrels and troubadours who went from court to court, castle to castle, town to town in order to sing or recite publicly the great stories of battles, love, and chivalry that enthused their audiences. Handwritten books and manuscripts did exist, but there were few copies of each work, and they were usually only available to the rich. And since few outside the church were fully literate, these hand-copied books and manuscripts could only be read by a small, educated group. However, it is in this handwritten and hand-copied form that all literature prior to the mid-fifteenth century has come down to us. When the printing press began to spread across Europe (arriving in France in the 1470s), a predominantly oral culture gradually gave way to a written culture, as more and more people learned to read (and could eventually also afford books). It is only during the past century that our written culture has been in decline again, as visual culture has become more and more prominent in our daily lives.

One of the first literary texts in French of which we have a written record is the late-eleventh-century *Song of Roland* (*La Chanson de Roland*). It is with this founding text that *One Hundred Great French Books* begins, not simply because this is one of the "firsts," but because it has aged well and can still provide the pleasures of a good story, unforgettable characters, and epic struggles. From *The Song of Roland* we move in chronological order—mostly according to the date given to a manuscript, or the first date of the original French publication of a work, or the year of a play's first performance—through the ages until we reach our own time.

For convenience's sake, French literature is usually categorized according to the period during which it was written. Literature in French begins in the Middle Ages, the earliest-known literary manuscript in Old French being a late-ninth-century poem of twenty-nine lines in praise of St. Eulalia. But only in the High Middle Ages literature in French begins to be produced in quantity. The Middle Ages as a literary period in French extends to the last years of the fifteenth century. French Renaissance literature covers approximately the sixteenth century. The seventeenth century is the age of French classicism, while the eighteenth century corresponds to the Enlightenment. The late eighteenth and the first part of the nineteenth centuries usher in romanticism, which is followed by symbolism (in poetry) and realism and naturalism in works of prose. The twentieth century is associated with movements such as

Dada, surrealism, and "the new novel" (*le nouveau roman*). Of course, these classifications are not engraved in stone and are susceptible to many variations and combinations.

At this stage, I need to make clear what this book is, and, perhaps even more importantly, what it is *not*. Foremost, it is not an introduction to the *best* one hundred French books. Such a list would be impossible to establish as anything more than a highly subjective popularity competition. So the emphasis needs to be on the title word "great," because each work selected (and of course the selection is, by necessity, subjective) is a great book in its own right. Since I am a professor of French literature, I must also stress, in the interest of full disclosure, that this book is not addressed to specialists of French literature, but rather to the general reader who is interested in learning about, or renewing acquaintance with, some of the most important and intriguing "French" books. And in order to be agreeable to readers who either have no knowledge of the French language or who prefer not to read these books in the original French, one of the key criteria for this selection was that all books featured had to be available in an English translation, either in print form or on the Internet.

I should also warn you that this book has a hidden agenda. Not simply an introduction to one hundred French books, its aim is to whet your appetite to read or reread some or all of the works presented in the following pages. Each entry provides an overview of a work, together with some information about its author (when known) and the context in which it was written. While this book can be read in a linear fashion, or even in a single sitting, it is just as accessible in small sections, one or two at a time (and not necessarily consecutively). It is in some fashion what we might call a Reader's Guide. However, since it is difficult to do justice to a "great" work in just two pages, only some of the obvious qualities of each work can be highlighted. The next step is for the individual reader to explore the subtleties and many delights of the texts that beckon her or him. If you feel like reading a captivating book, this one will give you a hundred (and more) suggestions as to where you could begin.

While many of the books presented here belong to what we might call "high" literature (although I believe all of these are very accessible to any reader), I have also included a number of detective stories, the amusing comic series *Astérix*, the journal of the great painter Delacroix, the reminiscences of the movie director Jean Renoir (son of the painter Auguste Renoir), and a spiritual treatise by François de Sales.

The title of this book is *One Hundred Great French Books*, but it could as well be titled "One Hundred Great Books Written in French." Although a majority of the authors featured are women and men of French nationality, I have also included a number of authors who were born outside metropolitan France but for whom French is a primary language. So you will encounter writers not only from France but also from the Caribbean, Canada, Belgium, Switzerland, and African countries. It is a testimony to the vibrancy and appeal of the French language that many great "French" works have been written by those who do not necessarily hold a French passport.

A word about translations: When I began to work on this book, I was surprised to learn that quite a number of what I consider to be great books in French either have not (yet) been translated into English or were translated many decades ago, so that these translations are no longer in print. This has of course influenced the choice of books to be included. On the other hand, some of the better-known books I present are available in several different translations. I decided that, when quoting from the original, I would do all the translations myself, since the main purpose of providing a quotation is to give the flavor of the work concerned and not to promote a particular translation. A list of the works, together with available English translations, is given at the end of this book.

Lovers of poetry will note that my list of great works in French is somewhat short on poetry. This is not a reflection of the current preference for prose over poetry but simply a result of the relative scarcity of translations of poetry (and translating poetry is certainly the most difficult task any translator has to face). Even an excellent translation of a prose work can never quite capture the full flavor of the original, and a great deal of wonderful poetry is quite simply untranslatable, except at the most prosaic of levels—and who wants to read prosaic poetry?

Choosing one hundred books from the great store of French literature was far from easy, and there are many others that I would have liked to include. Suggestions for further excursions into literature in French are given briefly in the Afterword. Even so, there are of necessity many omissions. If you don't find a particular book you are seeking here, I apologize, but I can promise that you will find many others that are worthy of your attention. I hope that the books I have selected will interest you, fascinate you, make you reflect, and, in some instances, even inspire you. But I hope above all that you will enjoy them and participate in what Roland Barthes has called *le plaisir du texte*, the pleasure that comes from reading a great book and being stirred to the core by it.

I wish to thank my children Catherine and Andrew and the many friends who have expressed their interest in this book. I am also grateful to my colleagues Joan DeJean, Lydie Moudileno, and Gerald Prince who have allowed me to pick their brains at various times. My thanks go also to Amy Ralston for her invaluable help in preparing the index. I am particularly grateful to Jan-Erik Guerth of BlueBridge who conceived the idea and who has been generous with his help and encouragement right from the inception of this book. To my wife, Mary, I owe a huge debt of gratitude. She has been immensely supportive, providing not only moral support and encouragement, but also tirelessly reading and rereading my text and making many valuable and insightful suggestions. Her keen editorial eye—and pencil—have greatly improved the book both in style and substance. It would have been much the poorer without her help and expertise.

The Song of Roland

La Chanson de Roland (ca. 1095)

◆

Turoldus?

O n a rugged mountainside in the Pyrénées lies the dying knight
Roland, the nephew of the great Charlemagne. He contemplates
the wild landscape, strewn with the bodies of slain soldiers from the
rearguard of the French army, victims of an ambush set by Saracen soldiers in collusion with another of Charlemagne's knights, the resentful
Ganelon (who is another uncle of Roland yet also his bitter rival). But
Ganelon is not the only culprit; Roland also bears a heavy responsibility for the defeat of the French army. Overly confident of his military
prowess, he refused to sound his famous horn, Oliphant, to summon
reinforcements until it was too late. The battle scenes are described
in gruesome and bloody detail. For example, when Olivier, Roland's
close friend, engages one of the Saracen knights in battle, "he breaks
his shield adorned with gold and precious stones and strikes his head
so hard that his eyes fly out and that his gray matter spills out and covers his feet." However, this is a Christian epic and therefore contains
numerous spiritual and miraculous elements. When Roland, confess-
ing his sins to God and repentant of his former pride, breathes his last,
his soul is transported directly to heaven by angels. His death and that
of the French soldiers will be subsequently avenged by the patriarchal,
godlike Charlemagne, who calls on God not to allow the sun to set to
give him time to avenge the death of his knights and soldiers.

Before being written down in manuscript form toward the end of
the eleventh century, *The Song of Roland* circulated for decades as oral
literature, performed in public by roving troubadours who recited or
sang it. The name Turoldus is mentioned in the last line of the manuscript, but it is not clear whether he is the author or simply a scribe or
performer of the poem. Recounting events and legends that took place
three centuries earlier, the epic centers on what was in fact a minor
battle that took place in 778 between the rearguard of the Frankish
king Charles (who did not become the emperor Charlemagne until the
year 800) and a group of Basque fighters, who were in fact Christian. In
historic documents, the death of Roland is recorded in a single sentence
without further elaboration, but legends about him quickly sprang up,

and in the late eleventh century (probably around 1095, when the First Crusade was proposed), these legends became the basis for this founding epic of French literature: Charles becomes Charlemagne, the Holy Roman emperor and also king of the French (even though France as we know it did not exist in the eighth century). In the spirit of the First Crusade, and perhaps to serve as a kind of recruitment propaganda for it, the minor battle is expanded to become a gigantic crusade, pitting Christians against Saracens (Muslims). A typical comment from the Christian knights is, "Christians are right and pagans are in the wrong." Likewise, when the Saracen knights are described, the account is tempered with phrases such as "What a splendid knight he would be, if only he were a Christian." Racial and religious tolerance are in short supply in this epic. A biblical symbolism underlies the story, with Ganelon playing the role of Judas, betraying both Charlemagne (who reminds us of the biblical patriarchs with his long white beard and his purported age of over two hundred years) and Roland, who is portrayed as an almost Christlike figure, despite some human failings. The defeat of Charlemagne's reargard by the overwhelming enemy force (400,000 Saracens against 20,000 French) is then avenged by the emperor, who, with the help of God, wins a decisive victory that is presented as that of Christendom over Islam. The final section of the epic deals with the judgment of the traitor Ganelon who—after a suspenseful trial in which he is almost acquitted—is finally condemned to death. And a particularly horrible death it is, for he is drawn and quartered. One horse is attached to each of the traitor's limbs and all four horses are sent galloping off in different directions, literally tearing him apart. "All his sinews are torn asunder and his arms and legs are ripped from his body. Ganelon dies like a cowardly traitor should die. It is only just that any man who betrays his brother should not live to boast about it." Let the squeamish reader beware—the medieval audience loved blood and gore!

The Song of Roland shares much of the gruesomeness we can still find in modern epic action movies. It is likewise dramatic, full of colorful description, and has well-delineated and psychologically uncomplicated characters. This exciting epic captures the fervent but often intolerant and fanatical spirit of the Crusades, and its subject is also, sadly, remarkably relevant to today's political and religious struggles. In many ways, it can be read as a morality play for our own time.

TRISTAN AND ISEUT

Tristan et Iseut (ca. 1160-70)

◆

Béroul/Thomas (Twelfth Century)

In its portrayal of passionate and fatal love, the Tristan legend was one of the most popular tales in the Middle Ages. Indeed, so profound is its appeal to the imagination that it continues to survive in various forms to this day, leaving its mark on literature and music, and more recently on the cinema. Since the legend was first adapted to the screen in 1909, during the silent era, it has inspired fourteen more films—the most recent, *Tristan and Isolde*, was released in 2006.

The first two written versions of the legend, produced by two different authors, Béroul and Thomas, appeared in the latter part of the twelfth century. Virtually nothing is known about the authors themselves and precious little about their sources, although we know the legend is of Celtic origin. Béroul and Thomas locate the story in Cornwall and in Brittany, where even today many inhabitants of the region speak both French and Breton, a Celtic dialect. A tale of irresistible passion and adultery, the story of Tristan and Iseut (or Isolde) has been seen as the archetypal Western love narrative. The Swiss writer Denis de Rougemont theorized that the legend of Tristan and Iseut is the origin of what has become an obsession of Western literature: unhappy, tragic love, most often adulterous in nature. Only parts of these two earliest versions of *Tristan and Iseut* have survived. With lots of blood and gore, the version by Béroul (about 4,000 lines) is considered to be the more primitive, almost certainly predating that of Thomas (some 3,000 lines), which is more courtly and refined.

The basic legend is this: the hero, Tristan, is the nephew of King Mark of Cornwall. When King Mark decides to marry, he chooses the beautiful blonde Irish princess Iseut, who had cured Tristan of a poisoned wound in a prelude to the main story. Once the marriage is arranged, Tristan is sent to Ireland to collect the bride-to-be. To ensure the success of the marriage, Iseut's mother, skilled in the magic arts, has prepared a love potion that her daughter and King Mark are to drink on their wedding night. By mistake, Tristan and Iseut drink the potion during their journey back to Cornwall, and this causes them to fall hopelessly in love. Interestingly, in the Béroul version the potion is only effective for three years, whereas in Thomas's it lasts forever. The rest of the story graphically recounts their attempts to overcome the many obstacles that are put in the way of their love. Restlessly propelled by their magically induced passion, the lovers are easy targets for the slander of King Mark's courtiers, whose behavior causes the couple to be forcibly separated several times in the story. Surprisingly, the lovers enjoy the favor of the common people and the help of God. For example, when Tristan is captured by King Mark's soldiers and is being led to his execution, he asks to pray at a wayside chapel at the top of a cliff. His captors allow him to enter alone. His miraculous escape reads like a precursor to similar scenes in a modern spy thriller as his clothes act as a primitive, but effective parachute: "Tristan moves swiftly to the window behind the altar. He removes it and jumps out, preferring this death to being publicly burned [. . .] The wind fills his clothes and cushions his fall [. . .] He lands softly on the sand, while his captors still wait for him outside the church. He is free. God has been merciful to him." After many similar escapes, he is finally banished to Brittany by Mark. Tristan marries Iseut of the White Hands, whose name and beauty obviously remind him of Iseut the Blonde, but the marriage remains unconsummated. When Tristan is again grievously wounded, he sends for Iseut the Blonde so that she might cure him once more. A signal (similar to that of the classical Greek tale of Theseus's return to his father) has been arranged: if Iseut is aboard the ship coming to his rescue, a white sail will be hoisted; if she is not, the sail will be black. Apprised of the plan, Iseut of the White Hands spies the ship on the horizon, white sail hoisted, and because she is jealous lies to her gravely ill husband about the sail's color. On hearing this news, Tristan promptly dies of despair, and when Iseut the Blonde disembarks to find her one true love dead, she succumbs to a broken heart. The two lovers are buried alongside each other, and from their graves grow a vine and a rose that intertwine as a sign that they are now reunited in death.

The idea of irresistible love that encounters repeated obstacles and finds fulfillment only in death is still capable of firing our imagination and tearing at our emotions. Seduced by the notion of fatal love and carefully guided by the narrative skill of Béroul and Thomas, we identify with the young couple, the handsome Breton warrior and his beautiful blond lover, prototypes of Romeo and Juliet and many others who, like them, succumbed to a fatal passion.

LAIS OF MARIE DE FRANCE

Lais de Marie de France (ca. 1160-78)

◆

Marie de France (1154-1189)

"What's in a name?" When that name is Marie de France, the answer unfortunately is "everything," since this is basically the only personal information we have about France's first known female poet. We know a bit more about her literary output. She composed a version of some of Aesop's fables (*Fables*), twelve lais (short narrative poems concerning the vagaries of love), and *Saint Patrick's Purgatory* (*L'Espurgatoire Seint Patriz*). It is at the end of the manuscript of the *Fables* that she identifies herself somewhat laconically: "I shall give my name for the sake of posterity: Marie is my name and I am from France." Ever since this name was attached to her work by a sixteenth-century literary historian, there has been a flurry of speculation about Marie de France. Because during her time women were rarely as educated as she clearly was, and because women did not usually write poetry, some believe that the author was in fact a male using a female nom de plume. But the consensus today is that the poet was indeed a woman, and the fact that scholars have become aware of a small number of female troubadours who were active during the Middle Ages supports this belief. As for her name, Marie de France, normally the preposition "de" followed by a place name indicates nobility in French, and "de France" is usually reserved for members of the royal family. However, it can also refer simply to origin, and it is now generally supposed that de France was writing in England, perhaps at the francophone court of Henry II (who was a Plantagenet of French origin), and this would explain why she uses the nomenclature "de France." Either way, Marie de France was almost certainly of aristocratic origin, since this would have been the only way she could have acquired her considerable education. We also know that her accomplishments aroused jealousy in the heart of at least one male poet of the time: Denis Piramus, who was active at the court of Henry II and Eleanor of Aquitaine and who wrote *The Life of Saint Edmund the King*, cast aspersions on de France's poetry, claiming that "Lady Marie [. . .] wrote in rhyme and composed the verses of the lais, which are not true at all." Suffice it to say that the mystery surrounding the author of the lais will remain profound unless some new information comes to light.

If we can't say much about the poet, we can say a great deal about her poetry. The lais are a graceful and artful reworking of contemporary medieval stories, some of Breton origin, others inspired by more general narrative material of the period. All concern love, and the theme of extramarital love is paramount. However, not only is adultery *not* condemned, in most cases it is taken for normal practice. In some ways her treatment of this theme resembles that of other writers influenced by the tradition of courtly love (or *fin'amour*), but her representation does not involve the complicated rules and arduous service courtly lovers had to observe. There are many fairy-tale and fantastical elements in Marie's lais that should appeal to readers today who love these elements in works like *The Lord of the Rings, The Chronicles of Narnia,* and other best-selling fantasy. Some of her tales are quirkily bizarre. For example, *Bisclavret* narrates the adventures of a knight who disappears for three days every week to assume the form of a werewolf. He becomes human again when he puts his clothes back on. Upon discovering his secret, his wife decides a different husband is in order and transfers her affection to another man. Together they steal the husband's clothes so that he cannot return to his human state, allowing the lady to be married to her new lover. One day, while hunting, the king comes across the werewolf, who behaves with such charm that he adopts it/him as a pet. Only once does the creature behave violently, attacking his former wife when she appears at court and biting off her nose. Obliged to confess her transgression, the wife produces her former husband's clothes, enabling him to become a handsome knight again. The woman and her new husband are banished, go on to have many children, but all are born without a nose. This is a strange story indeed.

In another lai, *Yonec,* a beautiful young woman who has been forced to marry an older man who keeps her locked away, finds a young lover when a hawk, appearing at her window, is transformed into a handsome knight. If this story, like *Bisclavret,* tells of adultery, transmigration between species, and savage acts of cruelty, the outcome is very different, for here the wife's transgression meets with approval.

Because of their violence and bloodshed, some of these tales are not for the faint-hearted, but they do open a fascinating, if romanticized, window onto medieval life, and the questions they raise about love and adultery are echoed in the popular culture of our own day.

YVAIN, OR THE KNIGHT OF THE LION

Yvain ou le Chevalier au lion (ca. 1175-81)

◆

Chrétien de Troyes (ca. 1135-1183)

Humor is not something we normally associate with stories of the Knights of the Round Table, unless of course we're thinking of *Monty Python and the Holy Grail*. However, *Yvain*—and indeed many of Chrétien's works—recount rip-roaring knightly adventures, seasoned with some delightfully tongue-in-cheek comedy. Although chivalric romances often deal with the courtly love of a knight for a higher-born, married noblewoman, Chrétien breaks from the pack by celebrating married love in this work, in which the rival for Yvain's affection is not another woman, but rather the temptations of the knightly life.

We know almost nothing about Chrétien himself, except that he was in the service of two noble patrons, Marie of Champagne and Philippe of Alsace. His major poems, *Erec and Enide* (*Erec et Enide*, ca. 1170), *Cligès* (ca. 1176), *Yvain* (ca. 1175–81), and *Lancelot, or the Knight of the Cart* (*Lancelot ou le Chevalier de la charette*, ca. 1175–81) reveal him to be a highly educated cleric who knew both old Greek romances and the Celtic tales that had become wildly popular in medieval Europe. His last poem, *Perceval, or the Story of the Grail* (*Perceval ou le Conte du Graal*, ca. 1181), which remained unfinished, explores not earthly but spiritual love, delving into the mystical aspects of the Arthurian legend of the quest for the Holy Grail.

Yvain begins at King Arthur's court, where Calogrenant, a young knight, recounts an adventure that ended in his humiliation. Coming across a magic fountain, he was challenged by a fearsome and powerful knight who easily defeated him in a jousting match, and rode off with his horse. Arthur's knights decide to avenge their comrade, but Yvain, Calogrenant's cousin, preempts their quest by stealing away from the company to confront the enemy knight on his own. Proving the stronger of the two, he routs his adversary, who, mortally wounded, turns tail and gallops toward his castle, with Yvain in hot pursuit. But this castle is equipped with an ingenious double gate that can entrap someone trying to enter the castle in the narrow space between the two portcullises. The stricken lord of the castle passes through both gates, but his men drop the two portcullises, equipped with razor-sharp blades on their bottom edge, just as Yvain tries to enter the castle. The inner portcullis cuts off his horse's head, while the outer one removes the poor animal's hindquarters, leaving the hapless knight in a ridiculous posture, astride the remains of his steed, trapped like a rat. The lord of the castle succumbs to his wounds and his men come looking for his killer. Meanwhile, Lunette, a resourceful young woman in the service of the dead knight's wife, rescues Yvain by giving him a ring that can make him invisible, so that the dead knight's soldiers are unable to find him, and the whole scene takes on a farcical air as they play a kind of reverse blind man's bluff in their attempt to locate the invisible Yvain. Meanwhile, Yvain glimpses the grieving lady of the castle, Laudine, falls in love with her and, with the help of the resourceful Lunette, successfully woos and marries the widow. When Arthur's knights arrive on their mission of vengeance, to their surprise they find Yvain in charge of the castle. Although his marriage is only a week old, Yvain is persuaded by his friend Gawain to return to Camelot to maintain his knightly skills. Laudine reluctantly agrees, but only on condition that Yvain returns to her within the year. But Yvain, totally absorbed by knightly activities, forgets his promise and, after the year is up, receives a message from his wife, informing him that he is no longer welcome to return. Aghast at his thoughtlessness, Yvain goes mad with shame and takes to living like a hermit in the forest. One day, coming upon a lion and a dragon engaged in mortal combat, he intervenes in favor of the lion by killing the venomous dragon. The gratitude of the lion transforms the fierce animal into a faithful, doglike companion. Cured of his madness and accompanied by the lion, Yvain embarks upon a series of adventures that constitute the principal part of this narrative. In the end, Yvain is reconciled with Laudine, and the couple then lives happily every after, the state of matrimony having regained its rightful place in Yvain's life.

Despite all its fairy-tale elements, *Yvain* can be seen by readers today as a parable of our contemporary concern to find an appropriate balance between the exigencies of personal and professional lives, a concern that Chrétien had already addressed in his chivalric romance *Erec and Enide* (where, as the title hints at, the hero forgets his knightly duties and becomes totally consumed with domesticity). *Yvain* is also notable in presenting a strong, resourceful, and highly intelligent woman in the person of the servant Lunette. This amusing and absorbing tale, with its numerous twists of plot and character, provides us with illuminating proof that the preoccupations of the Middle Ages are not nearly as far removed from our own as we might think.

AUCASSIN AND NICOLETTE

Aucassin et Nicolette (Early Thirteenth Century)

◆

Author unknown

I s there such a thing as musical comedy in the Middle Ages? Not quite, at least not in the modern sense of the word. However, there exists, surprisingly, a charming work in French that anticipates many of the characteristics of the genre that still reigns supreme on Broadway. This is the short *chantefable* (literally, a tale with songs) *Aucassin and Nicolette*. An amusing parody of the medieval romance genre, it contains both story (in prose) and songs (in verse, and preceded by the musical notations for the tunes to which the words are to be sung). In 2005, this medieval gem was indeed transformed into a musical comedy titled *Chasing Nicolette*. Adapted for the stage by Peter Kellogg and David Friedman, this off-Broadway comedy captivated its twenty-first-century audience with its humor and its unexpectedly relevant love story of a young Christian knight hopelessly in love with a young Saracen woman.

The anonymous author of the original medieval tale plays with all the conventions of the typical courtly romance. Traditionally, it is the knight who rescues the passive damsel, whereas in this narrative the young woman shows herself to be as brave and resourceful as her lover. Too often, Christians and Muslims were deadly enemies, but here a Christian nobleman has fallen in love with Nicolette, a Saracen now converted to Christianity, but of Saracen origin nonetheless. A former slave, rescued and adopted as godchild by the viscount of the city of Beaucaire, Nicolette is not deemed a suitable match for her admirer, Aucassin, whose stern father, the count of Beaucaire (and therefore the viscount's superior), insists that his son marry within his class. When the lovesick and tearful Aucassin refuses to obey, the count orders Nicolette to be banished from the city. But the viscount, unbeknownst to the count (or to Aucassin), merely locks his goddaughter up in a secret room in his castle. Meanwhile, Aucassin continues to weep in most unknightly fashion in his own quarters, and, when the city comes under attack, agrees to help defend it only on condition that his father allows him to see Nicolette again. When the count agrees, Aucassin shows his mettle and helps save the city, but the count does not keep his promise and, when his son persists in his desire to see Nicolette, places him in "protective custody." The resourceful Nicolette manages to escape from her secret room and discovers the location of her beloved's prison, informing him that she intends to flee. She takes refuge in the nearby forest, building herself a hut in the hope that one day Aucassin will pass through and find her.

The count believes that Nicolette has indeed permanently disappeared and releases his son, who immediately sets out to look for his beloved. Soon he is reduced to tears once more. "Aucassin traversed the forest, spurring on his steed. Don't think that the brambles and thorns spared him, oh no, not at all. Blood flowed from his arms, his side, his legs [. . .] so much so that one could have followed the trail of blood he left behind. But he was so preoccupied thinking of Nicolette that he felt no pain. However, after searching the forest all day without finding any trace of her, he began to weep." After an ironic episode in which he is reproached for his tears by a peasant, he continues his quest and finally locates Nicolette. They flee together but are shipwrecked, captured by roving Saracens and then separated during a violent storm. Miraculously, Aucassin arrives back in Beaucaire where he is recognized and made count, his parents having died during his three-year absence. Nicolette is deposited on the shores of Carthage (most probably Cartagena, Spain, part of the Moorish empire in the Middle Ages) where she discovers that she is the local king's daughter, kidnapped and sold into slavery when she was a small child. Her Muslim father wants his daughter to marry a king of the same faith, but she refuses and returns to Beaucaire disguised as a male minstrel. There, in Aucassin's presence, she sings a ballad recounting their love. Overjoyed, he asks the bard to find Nicolette and persuade her to return to Beaucaire. Nicolette quickly departs, changes out of her masculine garb, and returns as the beautiful woman she is. Aucassin can finally dry his unmanly tears, the couple weds, and lives (of course) happily every after.

Illustrating that the Middle Ages was not always the grim, humorless, and intolerant period it is sometimes made out to be, this tongue-in-cheek tale, with its multicultural elements and the strong role it accords the female protagonist, will strike today's readers as particularly timely. *Aucassin and Nicolette* reminds us that love can overcome the barriers of intolerance and prejudice and that a Christian nobleman and a Saracen princess can indeed find happiness together.

THE ROMANCE OF THE ROSE

Le Roman de la Rose (ca. 1225-78)

◆

Guillaume de Lorris (Thirteenth Century)/
Jean de Meun (died 1305)

If printing had been in existence in thirteenth-century Europe, *The Romance of the Rose* would have been a runaway bestseller. One of the most popular texts of the Middle Ages, there are over three hundred manuscript copies of it extant, many lavishly illustrated. The *Romance* influenced other writers as well: Chaucer created a version in English, while in France in the sixteenth century Clément Marot produced his own variant. The interpretation of this sprawling text provoked much discussion for centuries, particularly when its misogynistic elements were attacked by Christine de Pizan in 1399. The polemic, which continued right into the Renaissance, was called the Debate about Women (*La Querelle des femmes*; see also page 13).

Virtually nothing is known about Guillaume de Lorris, author of the first part. As for the second author, Jean de Meun, also known as Jean Clopinel (or Chopinel), the only biographical information we possess on him is that he translated a number of important medieval texts from Latin into French and that he died in 1305. De Lorris is the author of the first 4,058 lines of the poem (and an anonymous author added a 78-line conclusion to this first version), which dates from approximately 1225 to 1240. Then some thirty to forty years later, the poem was taken up by Jean de Meun, who amplified it by adding a whopping 17,644 lines.

One of the many fascinating aspects of this text is the discrepancy between the tone and spirit of the two parts. While some modern scholars have postulated the unity of these two, most readers agree that this is indeed a strange marriage. The poem begins in a fairly traditional way, with the narrator recounting a dream which he says the God of Love instructed him to record in a book that would be titled *The Romance of the Rose* and would contain the complete Art of Love. "In my twentieth year, when Love takes hold of young people, I was fast asleep one night, when I had a dream [. . .] which I want to recount in a poem [. . .] that contains the whole art of love." This was a nod to two very popular works in the Middle Ages, *Ars amatoria* (*The Art of Love*) by the Roman poet Ovid and Andreas Capellanus's twelfth-century *De amore* (*About Love*), the latter being the theoretical work on which "courtly love" was based. In his dream, the first-person narrator, also called the Lover, undertakes a journey in which he comes across a garden surrounded by walls. Here he meets the God of Love and his attendants and, after gazing into the Fountain of Narcissus, falls in love with a rose growing in the middle of the garden. This poem is an allegory, with the Rose obviously representing the Lady and female virginity, surrounded and protected by various characters, including Danger, Fear, and Shame. With the assistance of Venus, the Lover manages to kiss the Rose, but Jealousy intervenes and sequesters the Rose in a tower to protect her from the Lover. So far, we have an interesting, but not atypical courtly poem. However, Jean de Meun's long addition is of a quite different order. Whereas de Lorris's style is courtly and aristocratic, de Meun is much more down-to-earth, more cynical, satirical, and even humorous. He centers his text on a series of speeches given by such characters as Reason, Wealth, Nature, and the Old Woman, the latter being the Guardian of the Rose in this part of the poem. Instead of concentrating on pure love (courtly love), Jean de Meun deals with all forms of love and injects a heavy dose of eroticism into the poem. He also paints a very misogynistic portrait of women, for with her cynical, practical advice to young women the Old Woman reveals the wiles the female sex uses to seduce men: "If a girl has a beautiful neck and a fair bosom, she should ask her tailor to make her dresses with a décolletage which reveals at least six inches of appetizing skin both in front and behind." The Lover finally manages to breach the enclosure protecting the Rose, and after a highly eroticized description of his penetration into this inner space, he succeeds at last in plucking the purple rose from the rosebush, at which time he awakens. The dream may be over, but the Lover is satisfied. Although de Meun continues the allegorical mode adopted by his predecessor, he introduces into the poem an encyclopedic summa of contemporary knowledge, sometimes in a parodic vein. He also indulges in a satire of the morals of his time, exposing such things as the corruption of the clergy, a trait that we normally associate with the Renaissance rather than with the Middle Ages.

The Romance of the Rose gives us a lively picture of the intellectual ferment of the thirteenth century, in all its complexity and contradictions. Except for a few passages that can mire the reader in pedantic detail, this seminal text is surprisingly readable, highly informative, and often great fun.

THE BOOK OF THE CITY OF LADIES

Le Livre de la cité des dames (1404-5)

◆

Christine de Pizan (ca. 1363–ca. 1430)

Christine de Pizan, one of the most intriguing writers in all of French literature, is generally acknowledged to be among the very first women in Europe to earn her living by writing—quite an accomplishment in the late Middle Ages. Born in Venice around 1365 to a professor who taught astrology there and in Bologna, she was about three years old when her father was appointed court astrologer to the French king Charles V, and moved his family to Paris. De Pizan, brought up in prosperous circumstances at the royal court, married Etienne de Castel, a royal secretary who encouraged her to continue the education that had probably begun under her father's tutelage. It is known that Charles V had an excellent library, and it was possibly thanks to this resource that de Pizan received an education that was unusually broad for a woman at this time. Upon the death of Charles V in 1380 her father, having lost his position at court, became impoverished. Ten years later Christine de Pizan's husband died, leaving her to support their three children, a niece, and her own mother, who had also become a widow. Although de Castel had left his estate to his wife, the settlement of his will was delayed because of a legal tangle that took almost fourteen years to resolve, and she resorted to writing in order to support her family. She began her career by composing lyric poetry that, although it may have contained some autobiographical material, was on the whole fairly conventional. She authored numerous other works including *The Tale of Joan of Arc* (*Ditié de Jehanne d'arc*, 1429) and *Christine's Vision* (*Lavision Christine*, 1405), but her first truly original writing was her *Epistle to the God of Love* (*Epistre au Dieu d'Amours*, 1399), in which she adopted a feminist position against Jean de Meun, whose long addition to *The Romance of the Rose* she criticized for its misogynistic portrayal of women. This was the first salvo fired in what would become known as the Debate about Women (*La Querelle des femmes*), a literary battle which was waged for two centuries between those who saw woman as an imperfect and sinful creature, responsible for the Fall in Eden, and those who viewed her as a superior being (no need to point out on which side de Pizan positioned herself). Interestingly enough, the vast majority of the other protagonists in this debate were men, fairly equally divided between pro- and contra-women factions.

Perhaps her best-known work, the *City of Ladies* is part of her polemical approach to this question, and is in essence a rewriting of Boccaccio's *De mulieribus claris* (*About Famous Women*). Whereas her predecessor had included both virtuous and evil women in his list of well-known women of mythology and antiquity, de Pizan chooses only virtuous women as examples for women of her time. She does this in order to counter the misogynistic arguments to be found in Boccaccio, those she had previously criticized in Jean de Meun, but also to respond to the charges of another virulently misogynistic text, *The Lamentations of Matheolus*. De Pizan tells how one day, when she was sitting in her study surrounded by books, she came upon this particular work and was distressed at the negative portrait it painted of women. She was filled with self-doubt and began to "detest herself and the entire feminine sex, as though we were monstrosities in nature." The rest of her book, in typical medieval fashion, recounts a dream, rich in allegory, in which she is visited by three goddesses: Reason, Rectitude, and Justice. Christine is asked to construct a literary city in which virtuous women may reside. Each of the foundation stones will represent a famous woman of antiquity, the first being Semiramus, who oversaw the construction of the buildings and gardens of ancient Babylon. All the other women forming the foundations of the city are known for their physical strength, normally considered a masculine attribute. It is the goddess Reason who helps Christine to construct this strong foundation. The city walls and buildings, which represent womanly virtues, are the domain of Rectitude, while Justice will put the finishing touches to the city by building roofs and towers and by decorating the buildings with gold. It is also she who will select those women who are worthy to become citizens of this female Utopia. When the city is complete its gates are opened to its queen, the Virgin Mary, who enters, accompanied by female saints and martyrs. The city will henceforward become a place of refuge for women in need of protection and of moral and spiritual support.

This remarkable work makes a case for women's equality, both physical and intellectual, not only by showcasing the accomplishments of women of the past, but also by championing women's education and arguing in favor of their capacity to adopt roles of leadership in government and in society in general. We can truly say that in this City of Ladies, women rule.

THE TESTAMENT

Le Testament (ca. 1461)

◆

François Villon (ca. 1431–ca. 1463)

"Where are the snows of yesteryear?" ("Où sont les neiges d'antan?") may well be François Villon's most famous line, as he laments both the fading of youth and beauty and the brevity of life. Writing at the end of the Middle Ages, Villon is the first of a long line of French *poètes maudits*, an expression we could translate freely as bad-boy poets. A thief and possibly a murderer, Paris-born Villon was variously known as François de Montcorbier or des Loges. He was brought up in poverty by his mother after the death of his father, but had the good fortune to be adopted by a professor of canon law, the cleric Guillaume de Villon, whose name the future poet took, presumably out of gratitude. During his years of study in Paris, Villon was involved in what was, at the time, typical disorderly conduct by students, and in 1455 he mortally wounded a priest during a street brawl, apparently in self-defense. Accused of murder nonetheless, Villon fled Paris but returned six months later. At Christmas 1456, he and two accomplices stole the considerable sum of five hundred gold crowns from the College of Navarre. After this caper, he was obliged to head once more for the provinces, where he began to compose his first great poem, the *Lais* (*Lais*). Meanwhile, one of his partners in crime denounced him and he was obliged to lie low, probably associating with a notorious criminal gang known as the *Coquillards* (the Shells). The year 1461 found him in prison in Meung-sur-Loire, but by good fortune he was released during a visit of King Louis XI to the town. It was during this period that he began work on *The Testament*. The following year he was arrested and jailed in Paris at the Châtelet prison (nowadays the name of a very busy Métro station) but managed to arrange his release. Then, mysteriously, we lose all trace of him after he was sentenced to be "hanged and strangled" for his participation in a street brawl, but—just as mysteriously—he was freed, being sentenced to banishment from Paris for ten years.

Villon has captured the imagination of countless generations of readers, not only because of his unorthodox and troubled life, but also thanks to the graphic realism and universal themes of his poetry. He infuses traditional medieval forms with the force of his personality, as he writes about love and betrayal, suffering and death, and his own personal trials and tragedies. His two long poems, the *Lais* and *The Testament*, appear to be partly autobiographical and—presented as mock wills—they enable the poet to take revenge on the "beneficiaries" he names in them. For example, in Stanza LXXIII of *The Testament* he attacks Thibault d'Aussigny, the bishop of Orléans who was responsible for his imprisonment at Meung-sur-Loire, by ironically thanking him for his hospitality:

> Thank God and Tacque Thibaut
> Who gave me so much cold water to drink [. . .]
> And fed me with the fruits of anguish.

The irony is all the more acerbic since Villon deliberately confuses the good bishop with Tacque Thibaut, a notoriously unpopular homosexual companion of the duke of Berry.

However, perhaps his most famous poem is his epitaph, also known as the "Ballad of the Hanged." Here he imagines himself after his execution, still dangling from the gibbet, addressing those still alive with a plea for their understanding:

> My brothers who survive us
> Do not harden your hearts.
> If you feel pity for us,
> God will take pity on you.
> You can see us hanging here, five or six of us.
> Our flesh, which we indulged too much when alive,
> Has long since rotted and been devoured,
> We, the bones, are all that remains
> Fast turning to dust and ashes [. . .]
> The rain has washed us clean [. . .]
> Magpies and crows have pecked out our eyes [. . .]
> Take care that you don't end up like us
> And pray that God will forgive us all.

The lucid, unsentimental tone of the poem strikes directly at our common humanity and at our all too ready propensity to judge others without taking into consideration the individual circumstances which may have caused their downfall. This lesson, expressed so poignantly and graphically, is as relevant today as it was when Villon penned it over five centuries ago.

THE FARCE OF MASTER PATHELIN

La Farce de maistre Pierre Pathelin (ca. 1464)

◆

Author unknown

The farce, with its plays on words, verbal misunderstandings, and its use of slapstick is still a staple of comedy, whether on stage, at the movies, or on television. Charlie Chaplin, Jerry Lewis, the Three Stooges, or television programs like *Three's Company* and *Monty Python's Flying Circus* are just a few of the examples of this genre that have appeared in the modern era. Although one can find connections with the comedies of ancient Greece, the modern farce is most closely related to short plays that appeared in the fifteenth century in Europe. The precise origin of the term "farce" has not been definitively determined, but one theory is that it evolved from short comic interludes that were performed during long religious plays, to give some comic relief to the public who watched these dramas for three or four hours at a time. In French *farce* means stuffing (as in the stuffing of a turkey), and the theatrical farce would have been something stuffed in between the divisions of a religious play. The farce then evolved into a separate short play, destined to amuse the public without any attempt at moralizing.

Whatever the origins of the genre, the longest and most complete example we have from fifteenth-century France is the delightful *Farce of Master Pathelin*. This play, which takes about an hour to perform and is much longer than the typical farce of the period, has a small number of characters and is based above all on verbal humor, the principal theme of the play being deceit and the use of cunning to best the unwary—a typical subject of farce. The title character is a street lawyer who has no official legal training and few clients. Clothes were a very expensive item at the time, and both Pathelin's clothes and those of his wife, Guillemette, are in rags. The wily Pathelin decides to use his native cunning to procure new ones. He goes to visit a cloth merchant, Guillaume Joceaulme, and, after flattering him, succeeds in persuading the merchant to let him take home a piece of cloth on credit. Pathelin promises to pay the merchant's asking price, which is higher than the going rate, and offers to serve him dinner at his house when he comes to collect. Each is delighted at the end of this first episode, Pathelin because he has managed to procure *gratis* enough material to allow him and his wife to dress respectably again, Guillaume because he thinks he has made a large profit and will get a hot meal as a bonus. Guillemette and her husband concoct a scenario to convince Guillaume, when he comes for his payment, that Pathelin was not—indeed *could* not have been—the person who took the cloth originally. The scene in which Guillaume confronts Pathelin—who is in bed feigning illness—is quite hilarious, with the latter pretending to be delirious and raving on in several different languages. Rabelais and Molière took note of this and used similar techniques in their works to great comic effect.

In a separate incident, Guillaume discovers that his shepherd, an apparently naive peasant named Aignelet (literally, little lamb), has been stealing his sheep. He takes him to court but when Aignelet hires Pathelin as his lawyer, Guillaume undermines his case by continually confusing his lawsuit against Aignelet with his grievance against Pathelin. To up the comic ante, Pathelin has instructed his client to act simpleminded and to answer the judge's every question with a loud "Baaa!" This tactic and the plaintiff's confusion lead to a dismissal of the case. However, in a classic "deceiver/deceived" scenario, Pathelin himself becomes a victim, for when he asks Aignelet for his fee, the shepherd answers "Baaa!" and runs off, leaving the cunning Pathelin the victim of his own trick.

The play relies for its effect not only on situational comedy but also on verbal pyrotechnics and simple repetition. For example, when Guillaume visits Pathelin and finds him apparently sick in bed, every time the merchant raises his voice in anger, Guillemette shushes him with a *plus bas* (speak more softly)—because Pathelin is supposed to be ill. The repetition of "Baaa!" by Aignelet achieves the same effect in the courtroom scene. Pathelin impresses when he resorts to using different languages and finally Latin to convince the naive merchant that he is delirious once more. And at court Pathelin uses his verbal agility to gain the sympathy of the judge, who treats him as an equal, unlike the incoherent Guillaume who is unable to articulate a logical argument. All of these techniques have become part of the repertoire of farce, and it is surprising to find them already so fully developed in fifteenth-century France. Today's readers will not only find themselves laughing out loud at the antics of the various characters of *Master Pathelin*, but will also recognize this play as the great-great-grandparent of the movie comedies and TV sitcoms we love to watch.

Lyric Poetry of the French Renaissance

(1525-86)

◆

Clément Marot (1496-1544), Joachim Du Bellay (1522-1560), Pierre de Ronsard (1524-1585)

The cultural phenomenon known as the Renaissance that began in Italy in the fourteenth century was late in coming to France, in part because the French had been engaged in the deadly Hundred Years War with England until 1453. It was only late in the fifteenth century and above all in the sixteenth century that France began to emulate the renewal of interest in the culture, art, and literature of ancient Greece and Rome that was already under way in Italy. Although the French Middle Ages produced outstanding poetry, some of it inspired by classical models, the sixteenth century is the time when lyric poetry flourished in France. Three of the greatest practitioners of the "new" poetry were Clément Marot, Joachim Du Bellay, and Pierre de Ronsard.

Marot, born in the southern city of Cahors in 1496, was a real pioneer in the new direction poetry was to take. The son of the poet Jean Marot, he moved to Paris, where he enjoyed the patronage of Marguerite de Navarre and of her brother, King François I. Marot was also attracted to the Reformation that was sweeping across Europe, and had to flee France several times because he was accused of being a Lutheran (as Protestants were then called). He never officially converted, but his case was not helped by the fact that his paraphrases of the Psalms were put to music and adopted by the Calvinist church. Sadly, Marot died in exile in Turin in 1544. His poetry is varied in tone and subject. Outside of French Protestant circles, he is best known as the author of light, often sensual love poems, which sometimes parody Petrarchan themes, such as the rondeau in which the poet proposes a bargain to the husband of his beloved: since the poet has won the lady's heart, while the husband enjoys only her body, the poet "magnanimously" offers to change places with him, so that he can enjoy the pleasures of physical intimacy. In addition to this light verse, Marot also wrote much serious poetry and a great deal of satirical verse, aimed at the legal system and the narrow-mindedness of Catholic theologians of his time.

Unlike Marot, Du Bellay and Ronsard were from the nobility (Du Bellay's family was one of the most prominent in France). Originally from the Loire Valley, the two were distant cousins and were educated in Paris at Coqueret College, whose principal taught them Greek and Latin literature. Du Bellay began his career as a writer with a polemical document entitled *Defense and Illustration of the French Language*, which was a call to arms to encourage French authors to realize the full potential of French by writing works that were inspired by the great works of the past, but would go beyond them to new heights of excellence. His first poetry, *Olive*, was a collection of love sonnets influenced by Petrarch, but his best works are two sonnet sequences, the *Antiquities of Rome*, a poetic meditation on the past grandeur of the Roman Empire and on its decadence, and the *Regrets*, which recounts the day-to-day frustrations and the homesickness that he experienced during his sojourn in the Eternal City as secretary to his cousin, who was a cardinal of the Catholic church. In one of his most moving poems, he sees himself as an exile in Rome, forgotten by his mother country, France:

> Alas, your other sheep don't lack nourishment,
> They do not fear the wolf, the wind, or the cold,
> And yet I am not the worst of the flock.

Ronsard, who took holy orders, was to become known as the Prince of Poets. The central figure in a group of seven French poets that he named the Pléiade (after the star constellation the Pleiades), he began his career by emulating Greek and Latin poets—in particular Pindar and Horace—in his *Odes*, then composed hundreds of love poems dedicated to a number of different women. He had a wonderful sense of the musicality and phonetic richness of the French language and exploited the carpe diem motif in some of his better-known pieces to encourage his readers to take advantage of the moment. He also wrote a series of philosophical poems and part of an epic, but his most famous poem is undoubtedly "Mignonne allons voir si la rose . . ." ("Oh my Lovely One, let us go and see if the rose . . ."), in which the poet, by pointing out to a young woman that the petals of a lovely rose admired that very morning had fallen by evening, invites her to take advantage of her beauty to love him before it disappears.

Twenty-first-century readers who enjoy poetry will find the creations of these three "greats" in turn moving, thought provoking, charming, amusing, and graceful, even if the "message" of certain of the love poems is tainted with a sexism unfortunately typical of the age.

PANTAGRUEL

(1532)

◆

François Rabelais (ca. 1483 or ca. 1494-1553)

Rabelais is a name that even today conjures up all sorts of associations: grotesque and coarse humor, gigantic intellectual appetite, and overindulgence in sensual pleasures of all types. It has given us the adjective Rabelaisian, one of the few authors' names used outside a purely literary context. Indeed, when we think of Rabelais we imagine a jolly, ribald fellow with a bottle of wine in one hand, a wench in the other.

It comes as a major surprise to many readers to learn that this larger-than-life figure was a monk and an evangelical (in the Renaissance sense of someone who wished to reform the Catholic church from within). It was probably Rabelais's father, a native of the picturesque Loire Valley and a respected lawyer, who directed his son toward a religious vocation. First becoming a Franciscan, then a Benedictine monk, Rabelais finally left the cloistered life without official permission but was never defrocked, even though he subsequently fathered two children by a Parisian widow. After studying medicine at Montpellier, he became a resident physician in the principal hospital of Lyon, where he wrote *Pantagruel,* the first volume of his comic history of a family of giants.

Giants were a hot topic in the popular literature of the time and, perhaps as a joke or to earn a little extra cash, Rabelais decided to write a sequel to a contemporary best-selling book, the *Gargantua Chronicles,* which featured the exploits of a French giant who became one of King Arthur's knights. In his parody of this book, Rabelais invented a son for Gargantua, choosing the name Pantagruel for this protagonist of his own narrative. Pantagruel, who (unlike the hero of the *Gargantua Chronicles*) hails from the mythical country of Utopia, comes to France in order to pursue his education. After visiting several provincial universities, he arrives in Paris to study at the Sorbonne and meets and befriends a charming but disreputable character called Panurge, a rogue and a trickster who succeeds in impressing the giant. It is in fact Panurge who occupies center stage for most of the rest of the book, as he bedazzles the giant and other characters with his linguistic skills (he speaks more than a dozen foreign languages) and with his ability to get the better of his adversaries by sheer cunning. After a series of comic adventures in France, Pantagruel is recalled to Utopia by his father to help repel a foreign invasion. Of course Pantagruel, aided by his new best friend, is victorious, and peace is restored to the homeland after a series of mock-heroic battles. Because of his irreverence toward the religious and academic establishment, Rabelais deemed it prudent to publish his book under a pseudonym, Alcofrybas Nasier, an anagram for his own name. Alcofrybas is both the narrator of the work and also appears as a character in certain episodes. In one famous chapter, in order to take shelter from a passing rain shower, he takes refuge in Pantagruel's gigantic mouth, where he finds a new world: "The first person I came across here was a man who was planting cabbages. Amazed, I asked him: 'My friend, what are you doing?' 'I'm planting cabbages.' [. . .] 'Jesus,' I said, 'this is a new world.' 'No,' he replied, 'it's certainly not new [. . .]'" An amusing parody of contemporary travel narratives, this chapter pokes fun at the parochialism of Europeans who thought they were superior to the newly discovered peoples of the Americas.

   Pantagruel was condemned by the Sorbonne for "obscenity," which at the time meant "indecency" and "filthy language." Rabelais followed this first book with a "prequel" in 1534, *Gargantua*, in which he rewrote the original *Gargantua Chronicles* in a comic mode. He penned two more books—usually known simply as the *Third* and *Fourth Books*—narrating the continuing odyssey of Pantagruel and Panurge. Mysteriously, nine years after the author's death, a *Fifth Book* appeared in print, but its authenticity has never been established beyond reasonable doubt.

   The work of Rabelais, a physician who believed in the curative value of laughter, is still a fun read, and its comedy runs the gamut from coarse "toilet humor" to sophisticated irony and satire. Rabelais delights in the ambiguity and richness of language, and his love of wordplay is typically French. As one of the great writers of world literature, he has inspired many authors both within France (Balzac, for example) and beyond its borders (James Joyce, among others). While certain of the questions he addresses with great comic verve are local and historical, most will still manage to surprise and amuse the twenty-first-century reader with their modernity and profundity. Perhaps today's reader will even find *Pantagruel* therapeutic, since it was Dr. Rabelais's firm belief that laughter is the best medicine, a remedy he provides in great abundance.

THE TORMENTS OF LOVE

Les Angoysses douloureuses qui procedent d'amours (1538)

◆

Hélisenne de Crenne (Marguerite Briet?) (Sixteenth cent.)

Part chivalric romance, part love story, this work has been hailed as the first *roman sentimental* (the French term for a novel about passionate love) in European literature. Although there is not universal agreement about the attribution of this work, it is generally considered that Hélisenne de Crenne is a pseudonym chosen by Marguerite Briet, a minor noblewoman about whom little is known. This novel was long read as the thinly disguised autobiography of a young married woman's irresistible love for another man, although more recently the autobiographical aspect has been discounted since we know so little of Marguerite Briet's life (even assuming she was the author). Born in Abbeville, Picardy, between 1500 and 1515, Briet lived until approximately 1560. She married Philippe Fournel de Crasnes (also spelled Crenne) and they had one son. She eventually separated from her husband. In addition to the *Torments*, two other fictional works are attributed to her: *The Personal and Invective Letters* (*Les Epistres familieres et invectives,* 1539), which has the distinction of being the first epistolary novel in French literature, and *The Dream of Madame Hélisenne* (*Le Songe de Mme Hélisenne,* 1540). One year later, she published her own very free translation of the first four books of Virgil's *Aeneid.*

The Torments of Love is divided into three parts, the first apparently so different in tone and subject from the second and third that some modern editions of the work present only part 1. The novel is, according to its preface, a cautionary tale warning its readers—particularly female readers—against the destructive power of passion. After such a conventional beginning, we are surprised to discover the constantly shifting moral perspectives of Hélisenne's narration of her love story. At times she seems to be roundly condemning her own passion in the most traditional, moralistic terms. At other times she appears to be enjoying her illicit love—in spite of her promises of fidelity to her husband, she schemes to find pretexts to approach her lover, Guenelic, a handsome but lowborn, immature young man who often treats her with indifference. However, since Hélisenne herself does not hesitate to lie to him as well as to her husband, she quickly marks herself as an unreliable narrator and undermines any confidence we may have in the "truth" of her narrative. When her husband scolds her for her adulterous love, she describes her reaction: "I began to weep and to bitterly condemn my outrageous folly. However I was not really repentant, but simply angry at myself for not being more discreet in my behavior, whereas he thought I was taking his words to heart."

In parts 2 and 3, both of which represent a complete departure from part 1, the work morphs into a chivalric romance, starring Guenelic and improbably recounted by Hélisenne in the first person, i.e., "speaking in the person of her beloved Guenelic." These later parts also thwart readers' expectations by including another preface, in which Hélisenne modifies the view she had previously given us of her beloved: here she claims that her earlier suggestion that Guenelic was lowborn merely meant that his social status was lower than hers. She now describes him as a young knight who sets forth on a chivalrous quest to find and liberate his lady, Hélisenne, imprisoned by her husband to prevent her infidelity. After a series of knightly adventures, Guenelic—accompanied by his friend, the knight Quezinstra—discovers the location of Hélisenne's prison and engineers her escape. However, this hazardous enterprise exacts a heavy toll on Hélisenne, who dies expressing Christian repentance. Guenelic, overcome with grief, also succumbs, expressing his own contrition. However, the novel reserves one last surprise for us when Quezinstra, left to contemplate the lovers' lifeless bodies, is visited by a dazzling figure with golden wings, seemingly an angel, but who in fact is Mercury. The Christian perspective disappears as this pagan god leads Quezinstra on a tour of Hades, revealing the lovers' final destination, the Elysian Fields—Hades' most upscale neighborhood. Beside Hélisenne's body, Mercury finds a book in which the hapless woman has recorded the story of her love and entrusts it to Quezinstra who publishes it—and here we return to the moralistic tone of the *first* preface to the novel—in order to protect its readers against lasciviousness and to teach them to fix their gaze on eternal rather than transitory things.

The Torments of Love is a strange, yet compelling book that resembles a hall of mirrors, now seeming to be one thing while at the next instant transforming itself into something unexpected. While remaining firmly anchored in its century, it does anticipate the manipulation of narrative techniques and the moral relativism of many modern novels. Little known outside academic circles, this dynamic, hybrid work merits a much broader audience.

SONNETS

(1555)

◆

Louise Labé (ca. 1520–1566)

The following lines are from one of the best-known poems by the most famous female poet of the French Renaissance:

> Kiss me again, kiss me once more, just go ahead and kiss me,
> Give me one of your most delicious kisses,
> Give me one of your most amorous kisses,
> And I'll reward you with four that will burn your lips like hot coals.

Born in Lyon sometime between 1516 and 1523, Louise Labé was the daughter of a rope maker and thus belonged to a social class which did not usually bother to educate its women (and often not its men, either). Perhaps because her mother died when Labé was very young, her father apparently sent her to a nearby convent school, where she learned to read and write not only French, but also Italian and Latin. She married within her social class but somehow managed to break into the very active literary circles of Lyon. We know little about her life, in spite of what may be autobiographical references in some of her poems. However, because these references are implicit rather than explicit, and because authors have a tendency to romanticize their own lives, it would be unwise to accept these as solid facts. We do know that it was around 1552 that she began to write poetry, some of which was in circulation in manuscript form (as was customary in those days) before it was finally published in 1555 and then again in 1556. John Calvin, among others, found her poetry to be shocking, calling her *plebeia meretrix* (a woman of ill repute). After the death of her husband, she certainly had a relationship with the Lyonese banker Thomas Fortini, and she was to die in his house after a long illness in 1566. The scandal provoked by Labé's life and poetry in the sixteenth century was still reverberating as recently as the mid-twentieth century, when the plan to name a girls' school in Lyon after her was scuttled because it was believed that such a name might encourage bad morals on the students' part. Happily, today Lyon does have a high school, open to both girls and boys, that bears her name. Now *that* is progress!

What so perturbed many of her contemporaries was that Labé dared to write openly about female sexual desire. Also, writing in general and writing poetry in particular were seen primarily as male occupations at the time. For the tiny minority of women who were sufficiently educated to indulge in this activity, it was deemed acceptable to treat religious or moral subjects. However, if love was evoked, it was expected to be of the chaste variety, or better still to be confined to the maternal or divine love arenas. But Labé had the audacity to write like a man, to express in extremely sensual language her own carnal desire, and then to publish her poems for all to read.

Her poetry also represents a challenge to the typical, male-authored love poetry of her age. Refusing their stereotyped, hyperbolic praise of female beauty, Labé ridicules its vacuity by her matter-of-fact treatment of the question "What makes a man attractive to a woman?"

> What makes a man worthy of love? Is it how tall he is?
> Is it the color of his hair or the beauty of his complexion?

She insists that she does not need to use this overblown and insincere rhetoric, since her desire for her beloved is so intense that such inflated language can in no way enhance it.

Some doubt has recently been shed on the authenticity of her poetry. A French scholar, Mireille Huchon, has proposed that Labé's poems are in fact the work of a group of male poets who wanted to play a literary joke by attributing poems they composed to Louise Labé. This theory has encountered skepticism, as it seems unlikely that such a prank could have remained a secret for some 450 years. However, whether Labé's poetry was authored by her or by a group of men using her name (and there is no doubt that there was a historical Labé), these poems stand on their own merits, and the suggestions of literary intrigue and conspiracy only enhance their reputation. The linguistic directness of her poems and their overt sensuality still resonate with today's readers and are a powerful expression of female desire:

> I live, I die: I am on fire, I'm drowning.
> I have a high fever, while wracked with chills [. . .]
> I laugh and I cry at the same time [. . .]
> I go from being a withered flower to blossoming anew.
> The fickleness of Love is to be blamed [. . .]

THE HEPTAMERON

L'Heptaméron (1559)

◆

Marguerite de Navarre (1492-1549)

One might not expect a Renaissance princess to pen a collection of short stories that is at times bawdy, yet that is exactly what Marguerite de Navarre did. The sister of King François I, Marguerite was fully engaged in the intellectual and political life of her country, and later became a queen herself when she married the king of Navarre, at the time a small independent realm in the Basque country between France and Spain.

After she had already written religious poetry and plays that had incurred the wrath of the church because of their reformist themes, Marguerite de Navarre decided to try her hand at something entirely different: the creation of a French equivalent of Boccaccio's highly successful fourteenth-century collection of Italian tales, the *Decameron*, consisting of one hundred stories, divided into ten days and told by ten different narrators. De Navarre did not live long enough to complete her work, so the title *Heptameron* (meaning, "seven days") was the brainchild of one of her editors, who wanted to take advantage of the popularity of Boccaccio's work by giving hers a similar name, but a name which indicated that the book did not contain the full complement of one hundred stories—there are in fact only seventy-two tales.

However, while attempting to capitalize on the reputation of the *Decameron* (already during the Renaissance, publishers did everything possible to ensure good sales), the *Heptameron* claims to be different from the earlier work by relating only true stories, which makes them not simply entertainment but exemplary moral tales. While there are certainly many real-life tales in Marguerite de Navarre's work (the characters' names having been changed to protect the innocent), the contention that all are drawn from reality needs to be taken with a grain of salt—de Navarre in fact recycles a number of narratives inspired by fictional sources such as medieval French romances and folk tales, although she always gives them a realistic veneer. Unlike the *Decameron*, which had three male and seven female storytellers, the *Heptameron*'s narrators are five men and five women, all from the French nobility. These nobles, who had been indulging in that very French pastime of taking the waters in a spa town in the Pyrénées (Cauterets, which still exists), are isolated by a devastating flood and must seek refuge in a nearby monastery. To pass the time they decide that for ten days each of them will recount a "true" story, each story being followed by a discussion of the events and characters presented (an early predecessor of today's book clubs), an important innovation with respect to the *Decameron* itself. With few exceptions, the vast majority of the stories center on the theme of love and (in)fidelity, presented from both masculine and feminine points of view. A story about an unfaithful wife is countered by another featuring a wayward husband, women's wiles are exposed alongside masculine deception, etc. There is, as might be expected given the female author, a pro-women bias in most stories. In the eighth story, when a lecherous husband tries to sleep with his wife's chambermaid and cuckolds himself because he "shares" the prize with his best friend, not realizing his wife has substituted herself for the maid in the darkened bedroom, the husband is ridiculed: "When he had made love to her [his wife], not for as long as he wanted to, but only as long as he was able, his potency being only that of an old married man [. . .]"

Surprisingly, the attitudes and opinions of the narrators do not always correspond with traditional gender lines. The sexist attitudes we expect from the men are often crudely expounded by the two male narrators Hircan and Saffredent, whereas Dagoucin, another of the men, is more sympathetic to the women characters in the stories than some of the female narrators. Varying in length from two to over twenty pages, the stories provide fascinating insights into Renaissance attitudes about various forms of sexual experience. Although "virtuous" love is presented as the ideal, Marguerite de Navarre deals with everything from brutal rape to the purest of spiritual love, and the tone varies from the crudely comic to the highly tragic. One topic not addressed overtly is homosexuality, although some readers have discerned homoerotic elements in certain stories.

Besides investigating different forms of love, these tales, in their great variety, also criticize many aspects of Renaissance society. For example, they tax the clergy with lust and hypocrisy and denounce the aristocracy for viewing marriage as a purely commercial transaction. In confronting these issues so publicly, they deal boldly with moral and ethical questions that are still relevant today—double standards, clerical abuse, the meaning of "true love"—all the while appealing to one of our most basic human traits: the love of a good story.

ON MONSTERS AND MARVELS

Des monstres et prodiges (1573)

◆

Ambroise Paré (ca. 1509-1590)

Humankind has been fascinated by the unusual and the monstrous ever since antiquity, and our modern age has not changed in this respect. Frankenstein, Dr. Jekyll and Mr. Hyde, circus freak shows, Yeti, Bigfoot, and the Loch Ness Monster can still hold sway over our imaginations. The sixteenth-century surgeon Ambroise Paré shared this interest, and at the very dawn of the scientific age he wrote, as part of his voluminous medical treatises, a book devoted to perceived human and animal deformations, complete with illustrations. Typical of the time, we find in it a mixture of science and mythology, of actual and legendary "monsters," but what sets it apart from its predecessors is the scientific interest the author demonstrates for the *causes* of the existence of these strange creatures. Interestingly, the word "monster" was not originally pejorative, deriving as it does from the Latin *monstrum*, which simply designates something marvelous or prodigious, often seen as a divine portent. Paré adheres to this in the first sentence of his introduction where he describes monsters as "things appearing outside the course of nature (usually a sign of some future misfortune)." Among the nonscientific phenomena responsible for the existence of monsters, he first lists "the glory of God" and "the wrath of God." Discussing the last of thirteen "causes," he attributes their presence to the work of "demons and devils." With this interpretation he belongs to a tradition that goes back to antiquity. However, his other causes depart from such traditional explanations: he focuses on such matters as birth defects and devotes considerable attention (with attendant illustrations) to what we now call conjoined twins, cataloguing the various permutations he has seen of, or read about, this particular deformity. His scientific explanation—"too much seed"—may seem naive to us today, but his power of observation is not, and unlike his predecessors he does not equate such unusual births with any divine prognostication. He also looks at examples of individuals who have changed sex when male or female organs have appeared belatedly, and in such cases, as in those of dwarfism or children born lacking limbs or other body parts, he believes the cause is most probably "insufficient seed," again based on the rather rudimentary medical knowledge he had at his disposal. Other causes of "monsters" in his view are the narrowness or smallness of a mother's womb, and hereditary diseases.

Paré extends his investigation to the animal kingdom, and here again we encounter a mix of fact and legend, since he gives examples of creatures that are half human and half animal (like a centaur) because of the "mingling of seed." He shows us pictures of three-headed sheep and of marine animals such as the shark, the crocodile, and the whale, as well as of mermaids and other mythical creatures. He also has a most interesting section on beggars who counterfeit birth defects to solicit money, telling of one beggar who appropriated the severed arm of a dead man and, by tying one of his own arms behind his back, pretended that this rotting arm was part of his own anatomy. Since Paré still believed that what is manifest in the microcosm (the human or animal body) is a reflection of what happens in the macrocosm (the universe as a whole), he also examined natural wonders such as the eruption of volcanoes and the appearance of comets in the sky (in his age they were still considered to be some kind of divine portent).

The importance of On Monsters and Marvels is partially due to Paré's focus on observation rather than authority. In addition, the fact that he wrote in a colloquial style and in French rather than Latin made his book accessible not only to the intellectual elite, but to anyone who was literate (a small but increasing number of the population at that time). Indeed, his medical colleagues criticized him for making medical knowledge accessible to women and girls.

Besides being a most interesting author, Ambroise Paré was a pioneer in medicine. Born in Laval and trained as a barber-surgeon (considered by the physicians of the era to be the lowest echelon of the medical profession), he served first in the French army and was then appointed royal surgeon to four successive French kings. Among other accomplishments, he pioneered a more effective treatment for gunshot wounds, until then cauterized in a most painful way with a red-hot iron or hot oil. Paré replaced this barbaric treatment with a dressing consisting of a salve of his own invention after he had noticed that the wounds treated by this method healed faster and did not afflict additional pain on the wounded. Modest about his successes, he adopted as his motto, "I dress the wounds; God cures them." Ambroise Paré is often considered to be the father of modern surgery, and On Monsters and Marvels is a thought-provoking read to this day.

HISTORY OF A VOYAGE TO THE LAND OF BRAZIL

Histoire d'un voyage faict en la terre du Brésil (1578)

◆

Jean de Léry (ca. 1534–ca. 1613)

"This book is sheer magic [. . .] The non-specialist should read it as a literary work and as an extraordinary adventure novel." So wrote the noted ethnographer Claude Lévi-Strauss about Jean de Léry's account of his journey to Brazil. However, Lévi-Strauss also considered this book to be one of the ancestors of modern ethnography—"the first model we have of an ethnological study"—which is no small praise from a man who was one of the foremost specialists in his discipline. While Léry's work is hardly the first travel journal by a Frenchman, it differs from its predecessors by being an eyewitness account supported by a factual approach—whereas previous works had tended to mix the observations of the author with often legendary or mythological accounts from other sources, in particular the writings of the ancient Greeks and Romans. Renaissance writers, even when writing about the present, almost always looked to the past, particularly to antiquity, to help explain what they saw around them.

Although the sixteenth century spawned a considerable number of travel accounts in French, France was not at the forefront of the first great wave of explorations. It had been the Portuguese who had pioneered the sea route around the Cape of Good Hope to the riches of India and beyond, and the Spaniards who, after the accidental discovery of the "New World," had exploited their find and set up their colonies there. The French were decidedly Johnny-come-latelies to the exploration business. Although Verrazano did make a series of voyages for King François I as early as 1521, discovering the East Coast of the United States and the site of New York City, no colonies were established as a result of his expeditions. Cartier sailed to Canada in 1534, but his attempt to set up a colony there was unsuccessful. The same was true for Villegagnon in Brazil (1555–60) and Ribault and Laudonnière in Florida (1562–64). If these expeditions can all be deemed failures at establishing France as a major colonial power (that would not happen until the following century), the men who undertook them did awaken their compatriots' interest in the strange world that had been "discovered" across the Atlantic Ocean.

Jean de Léry was among those intrepid souls who made the long voyage to Villegagnon's French colony in Brazil, called France Antarctique (France in the Southern Hemisphere), on an island in Guanabara Bay, Rio de Janeiro. Villegagnon was a Catholic nobleman who had shown interest in, and tolerance for, those of the "new religion"—the Calvinists. As tensions between Protestants and Catholics were worsening in the years leading up to the Wars of Religion (1562–98), Admiral Coligny, a Protestant leader, asked Villegagnon to set up a colony in Brazil which would be a haven for those seeking relief from religious persecution and an example of religious tolerance for all of France. It was to this colony, established in 1555, that Jean de Léry traveled in 1556, and when the religious quarrels that had driven him from France were carried over to the colony in 1558, he undertook a perilous return voyage in a leaky ship across storm-tossed seas which almost sank her.

Léry, a shoemaker of humble origin, was born in La Margelle, Burgundy, in 1534. Converting to Calvinism and eventually becoming a pastor, he recorded his journey to and from Brazil, intending to publish it on his return. Delayed by his involvement in the Wars of Religion and by the temporary loss of his manuscript, publication of the first of ultimately six editions finally took place in 1578. A remarkable portrait of the indigenous people with whom he came in contact in the New World, Léry's account of their customs, their dress, their interaction with the European settlers, their cannibalism, and their religion makes for captivating reading even today. Unlike other colonizers, Léry made no attempt to convert the Tupinamba Indians during his stay, considering them "unconvertible." While there was much he admired about their civilization, he was also quite aware of its deficiencies—although he considered these shortcomings no worse than those of contemporary Europeans. It was this neutral attitude that gave him the intellectual distance to be able to judge the Tupinambas dispassionately, and which inspired Lévi-Strauss to speak of the "freshness" of his observation and the modernity of his reporting. Léry's secret, according to Lévi-Strauss, was that he had managed to get "inside" the natives ("to get into their skin," as the French expression has it) and to communicate this experience in a clear-eyed, straightforward manner. Indeed a remarkable achievement for a sixteenth-century shoemaker who became a Protestant minister as well as a kindred spirit to a modern ethnographer.

THE ESSAYS

Les Essais (1580-95)

◆

Michel de Montaigne (1533-1592)

"Que sais-je?" ("What do I know?") So wrote Michel de Montaigne in his modestly entitled work *The Essays*. It is surprising and even humbling to consider that this admission of the limits of knowledge was made by an author whom Orson Welles called "the greatest writer of any time," one whom Shakespeare read when composing *The Tempest*, one who inspired Descartes, Pascal, and Jean-Jacques Rousseau. Montaigne was certainly no ignoramus. He had spent a great deal of his life studying philosophy, history, and law; had twice been elected mayor of Bordeaux; and had occupied important administrative positions in the Bordeaux law courts before that. Despite or perhaps because of his education, he had come to see human reason and learning as limited and imperfect tools in the quest for truth. Indeed, Montaigne's famous motto may be regarded as a plea for humility: far from making us arrogant, learning should make us realize that reason has its limits and must not overreach itself.

The search for knowledge is at the heart of Montaigne's work. After suffering the deaths of his beloved father and his best friend, Etienne de La Boétie, Montaigne sank into a depression that was only exacerbated by the bloody Wars of Religion between French Catholics and Protestants. Having torn France asunder since 1562, these wars were to continue until after his death. In 1571, Montaigne cloistered himself in the library of his small château east of Bordeaux to read and meditate upon works of philosophy, history, and literature. Taking notes as he read and then amplifying them, he fashioned them to become *The Essays*, "essay" being used in its original sense of "test, trial, or experiment."

The object of these "experiments" is Montaigne and what one might term his selfhood. Realizing how difficult it is to obtain any sort of profound knowledge of the world outside his own being, Montaigne decided to concentrate on himself, not in a narcissistic way but in order to know himself as completely as possible. He believed that this knowledge would help him not only to live his life more fully but also to analyze the behavior and psychology of other people, since each of us contains within ourselves "the entire form of the human condition."

When he retired to his library in 1571, Montaigne claimed that he was not melancholic by nature, but he was certainly suffering from a form of melancholy that we would call situational depression today. While we should beware of simplifying as complex and rich a work as *The Essays*, we can view it, on one level at least, as the ancestor of the modern self-help book, literally *self*-help because it enabled Montaigne to overcome his depression and gain a new appreciation for life. *The Essays* are, among other things, Montaigne's "writing cure," undertaken during an era that did not have recourse to talk therapy or antidepressants, and his work may be seen as an early attempt to deal with a psychiatric illness not yet fully understood.

His essays, 107 in all (the shortest fills only 1 page, the longest 184 pages), cover a wide range of subjects: how to face loss, illness, old age, and death; the value of friendship; how to educate children; the acceptance and understanding of people and cultures different from our own. In his essay "About Cannibals," dealing with the peoples of the newly discovered Americas, he shows remarkable tolerance: "Now, from what eyewitnesses have reported to me, I can find nothing 'barbaric' or 'savage' about the native people of Brazil, unless by 'barbaric' one simply means 'whose customs are different from ours' with no pejorative connotation."

While each essay reveals some aspect of Montaigne's character and philosophy, each one also teaches us to look at ourselves and at others in a new way, to recognize our strengths and weaknesses, and, in true humility, to accept and love life on its own terms. Montaigne sums up this attitude with wry humor in the concluding words of his final essay, "About Experience": "It is no good trying to make ourselves taller than we really are by walking around on stilts, for even on stilts, we are still dependent upon our own human legs. And even if we're seated on the highest throne in the world, we're still just sitting on our own behinds." This self-deprecating humor is Montaigne in a nutshell: through the acceptance and enjoyment of his own humanity he finds the path to serenity and happiness.

AN INTRODUCTION TO THE DEVOUT LIFE

Introduction à la vie dévote (1609)

♦

François de Sales (1567–1622)

S ometimes described as the greatest Catholic "self-help" book ever, the *Introduction to the Devout Life* is not just for Catholics. It went through more than forty editions in the lifetime of its author and has remained one of the best-loved Christian devotional classics of all times, but one which can be read with interest and profit by people of many different faiths—and by those who wish to gain insight into one of the most influential spiritual figures of the late sixteenth and early seventeenth centuries. One of the main reasons for its lasting popularity is that it was one of the first devotional treatises to be written for lay people, rather than for the clergy. François de Sales believed that those who lived in the workaday world could—and indeed should—also have access to an intense and meaningful spiritual life, and his *Introduction* sets out in detail how this can be accomplished. Another reason for the remarkable success of this work is its pleasant, readable style. François de Sales is sometimes described as the Smiling Saint, and his gentleness and geniality are apparent in almost every sentence of this work. Third, the book is divided into sections that can easily be read and assimilated. It began as a series of letters addressed to a noblewoman, Madame de Charmoisy, dubbed Philothea (Lover of God) by the author, who was her confessor. The *Introduction* is divided into five parts: the first shows how to transform one's initial desire to lead a pious life into a continuous daily practice; the second teaches how prayer and the sacraments lead to communion with God; the third describes how to practice virtue in the world while still leading one's ordinary existence; the fourth is about resisting the everyday temptations we encounter; and the fifth part instructs how to practice devotion using various specific exercises that can "refresh one's soul."

In his preface, de Sales informs his readers that, although he is presenting the same doctrine as his many predecessors, he is not doing so in the same way, and he gives the example of Glycera, the flower girl painted by the famous ancient Greek painter Pausias who was able to make a great number of different bouquets using the same blossoms. He describes the novelty of his approach in the following way: "Those who have written about devotion have almost all destined their advice to those removed from interaction with the world, or at least have taught a form of devotion which is meant to lead the reader to remove him- or herself from the world. My goal is to instruct those who live in towns, in households, at court and who are obliged to lead a regular life on the outside [. . .] how to live in the world without being contaminated by it." He warns that this is not an easy task, but the step-by-step instructions he provides and the practical, down-to-earth details he gives demonstrate that the ultimate goal of leading a devout life is far from impossible. It simply demands discipline, perseverance, lucidity, and willingness to concentrate on the inner life.

François de Sales was born into an aristocratic family in Savoy in the beautiful French Alps. He received a Jesuit education at the College of Clermont in Paris, intending to become a magistrate. During this time he suffered from depression after having had discussions on predestination, since he was convinced he was one of the damned. When he was suddenly freed from this fear while praying in a church, he made a vow of chastity, although he continued with his legal studies at Padua in Italy. Upon completion of his doctorate there, he was admitted as a lawyer before the senate of Chambéry in Savoy. His doting father had already selected his future wife and was distressed when François informed him that he intended to take holy orders. It was only after the intervention of several prominent members of the clergy that his father accepted his son's new vocation. Savoy, then an independent state, was a region torn by religious strife because of the proximity of the Protestant stronghold of Geneva. François de Sales undertook, at considerable personal risk, a series of missions in the area with the intent of converting (or reconverting) Protestants to the Catholic fold. Appointed bishop of Geneva in 1602, he had no access to the principal city of his bishopric, whose Cathedral of Saint Peter had become a Calvinist church. Instead he resided in Annecy, south of Geneva, and it was there in 1607 that he founded the convent of the Visitation of the Blessed Virgin, which exists to this day. In Lyon, where he had been obliged to accompany the court of Savoy on a visit in 1622, de Sales suffered a stroke two days after Christmas, dying the following day.

His *Introduction to the Devout Life* is an excellent demonstration of his talent for down-to-earth, practical advice on leading a devout life, and although of particular interest to those of the Christian faith, it has much appeal for anybody interested in spiritual matters.

DISCOURSE ON METHOD

Discours de la méthode (1637)

♦

René Descartes (1596-1650)

One of the best-known philosophical statements in the world has to be "I think, therefore I am" ("Je pense, donc je suis"). A disarmingly simple affirmation, it marks the beginning of a new philosophical outlook that has had a dramatic and profound influence on Western thought from the seventeenth century onward. This statement was made by René Descartes, whose name gave rise to the adjective Cartesian, a word used both in mathematics—for Descartes was also a brilliant mathematician—and in a more general sense to describe logical, reasoned thought. Even today, the French still like to think of themselves as supremely Cartesian.

Descartes was born near Tours, in La Haye, a town that subsequently changed its name to Descartes in his honor. Descartes, like so many French authors in prerevolutionary France, was educated by the Jesuits. After completing a law degree at Poitiers, he decided to travel and study "the great book of the world." Moving first to Holland in order to join the Dutch army, he later went to Bavaria, where he also enlisted in the army. On November 10, 1619, in freezing weather in Neuburg, Bavaria, he had a kind of epiphany after spending an entire day deep in thought in a room heated by a porcelain stove. It was then that he hit upon the idea of formulating a new method of inquiry. After still more travels across Europe, he returned to Paris but decided that its many distractions were not conducive to philosophical reflection. Thus he set off for Holland once again, where he would spend the next twenty years elaborating his philosophical doctrine. Writing first his *Treatise on the World*, he decided against publishing it when Galileo was condemned by the Vatican in 1633, because Descartes was expressing sympathy for the Italian astronomer's ideas. His *Discourse on Method* was actually conceived as the preface to three scientific works, *Dioptrics*, *Meteors*, and *Geometry*; he followed these works with *Meditations on First Philosophy* (*Méditations métaphysiques*, 1641) which—by questioning Aristotle's authority—attracted sharp criticism. His last philosophical work, published in Latin, was *Principles of Philosophy* (1644); it was here that "I think, therefore I am" ("Cogito, ergo sum" in Latin) first appeared. By this time his reputation was so great that he was invited to the Swedish court in Stockholm by Queen Christina, but the harsh climate and the queen's habit of summoning him at 5 a.m. for philosophical discussions took their toll, and it was in Stockholm that he died of pneumonia in 1650.

One of the many striking features of the *Discourse* is that it is one of the first philosophical texts to appear in French rather than Latin. It is also presented as a first-person narrative, tracing the stages of Descartes's intellectual evolution. He begins by telling us that what he studied at school did not help him in his search for truth, and that as he matured, he decided to replace book learning with observation of the world and of himself. It was during the revelation he received in the heated room in Neuburg that he decided to ignore the knowledge he had previously acquired and to start from zero. He proposed four basic principles (to himself), which seem unproblematic today but which were revolutionary at the time because they challenged all authority.

The first principle was "never to accept anything as true that was not obviously and clearly so [. . .]" The second was "to divide each problem into as many small parts as were necessary" (so that one could solve a series of small problems in order to solve the overall problem). The third was "to order my thoughts so that I proceeded from the simplest questions to the more complex ones [. . .]"; and the fourth principle was "to make a complete list of all the elements of a problem so as to ensure that I missed nothing." Descartes's starting point was he himself, and he concluded that since he was capable of thinking and questioning, he could be certain of his own existence. And he used a similar argument to prove the existence of God: since Descartes, an imperfect mortal, could conceive of a Perfect Being, such a Being must exist. So in spite of his new philosophy based on radical doubt, Descartes adopted a conservative view on religion and morality and proposed three basic rules to live by: to obey the laws and customs of his country, including those of the religion "in which God gave me the grace to be instructed from my childhood"; "to be as firm and resolute in my actions as possible"; and "to try to master myself rather than attempting to master the course of events [. . .]"

Such are the basic principles on which Descartes's method is founded, and many of them are valid even today. However, his challenge to philosophical authority opened the floodgates for others to go much further than he did in their questioning of accepted wisdom, leading to a radical interrogation and revision of philosophy, politics, the social order, and, of course, religion. *Cogito, ergo sum* announced a whole new world order.

THE CID

Le Cid *(1637)*

◆

Pierre Corneille (1606–1684)

While France may not have one towering playwright like Shakespeare, it is not lacking in distinguished dramatists. Indeed, seventeenth-century France witnessed the rise of theater as the preeminent literary form thanks to the talents of the three greatest dramatists of French culture: Corneille, Molière, and Racine.

Born in Rouen in 1606, Corneille studied law (as did Molière), and he practiced the legal profession from 1628 until 1651, all the while pursuing his career as a dramatist. In 1662, he moved to Paris with his wife and children, by this time a well-established and highly popular playwright. Corneille was discreet about his private life, but we are well acquainted with his career in drama, which began with a comedy, *Mélite*, in 1629, and concluded with a tragedy, *Suréna*, in 1674. Between the two, he composed a large body of work encompassing comedies, tragicomedies, and tragedies, including *The Comic Illusion* (*L'Illusion comique*, 1635), *Horace* (1640), *Cinna* (1641), *Polyeucte* (1642), *The Liar* (*Le Menteur*, 1644), and *Rodogune* (1645). His big breakthrough as a playwright was the staging of the tragicomedy *The Cid*, which won the hearts of the Parisian public in 1637.

Of solid bourgeois stock, Corneille, ironically, is in his plays the spokesman for what one might call the aristocratic ideal. His protagonists are exemplary, noble not just by birth but in their actions, men and women who can certainly find themselves torn between love and duty but who have the strength of character to choose duty when these two imperatives collide. This is certainly well illustrated in *The Cid*, probably to this day his best-known play. Spain was very much in vogue in the 1630s in France, so it is not surprising that Corneille chose a Spanish subject. Rodrigo Diaz de Vivar, called the Cid, was a legendary eleventh-century warrior and a favorite subject of Spanish authors. Corneille based his own interpretation of the popular hero on a 1618 play, *The Youthful Deeds of the Cid*, by the Spaniard Guillén de Castro. No doubt Corneille saw in the nobility and courage of the Cid the ideal of the French nobleman he wished to promote in his own drama.

Particularly appealing to the audiences of Corneille's play are the two lead characters, Don Rodrigo and Chimène, who are destined to be married. Their happiness is short-lived, however, as in the first act their fathers quarrel over an honor that Rodrigo's father, Don Diego, has been given by the king. Chimène's father, Count Gomez, furious because he believes the honor should be his, slaps Don Diego's face. This insult, according to the Spanish code of honor that also existed in France until 1626, could only be avenged by a duel—but since Don Diego is an old man, he is no match for Count Gomez and thus asks his son to fight in his stead. As a loyal son, Don Rodrigo must obey, and he kills Chimène's father. Chimène, too, is noble and strong and although she cannot fight Don Rodrigo herself, she is bound to defend her father's honor by avenging his death.

> My good name and that of my family are at stake and I must
>   take vengeance
> And however much my love pleads to the contrary
> Any excuse is shameful to a noble spirit [. . .]
> To uphold my name and end my pain
> I must pursue him, do away with him and follow him in death.

So instead of love conquering all, we are presented with a case of honor conquering all. The king attempts to persuade Chimène to forgive the man she loves, but she persists in seeking justice and chooses a nobleman to fight him on her behalf. After Don Rodrigo prevails, the king again asks her to pardon him (the more so since, in the meantime, the Cid has won a great victory over the Moors), giving Chimène a year to mourn her father before the couple is supposed to be married.

The Cid, although it does not represent any violence on stage, is an extremely lively play, and even if we witness no actual duels, we enjoy the verbal sparring of its characters. And the battle between honor and love that is waged in the hearts of these two evenly matched "opponents" is still fascinating to contemplate. The important role played by the king also reflects the political realities of the time. One of the goals of Cardinal Richelieu, the prime minister of Louis XIII, was to make the king "absolute in his domain"—a goal only fully realized during the monarchy of his successor, Louis XIV, but one for which Richelieu was already striving in the early years of Corneille's career as a dramatist.

The Letters of Madame de Sévigné

(1646-96)

◆

Marie de Rabutin-Chantal, Marquise de Sévigné (1626-1696)

L etters have been a principal means of communicating news since antiquity, and the seventeenth century witnessed a burgeoning of letter-writing in France due to the concentration of political, cultural, and intellectual power in Paris and Versailles, and the concomitant desire of the provincial nobility to be informed of the latest news (and gossip) from the capital. Of the few newspapers that already existed the *Gazette de France* appeared only weekly, while the *Mercure galant* was first a weekly, then a monthly paper (the first daily, the *Journal de Paris*, arrived much later, in 1777). Letters thus filled an important gap in the circulation of information, a role greatly facilitated in the 1600s by improvements in the French postal system that carried letters from Paris to the south in as little as five days, not all that much slower than "snail mail" today.

One of the most prolific of these letter writers was Marie de Rabutin-Chantal, Marquise de Sévigné, whose epistolary production opens a fascinating window onto important historical and cultural events of the time, while revealing what the life of a noblewoman in France was like under the Ancien Régime. Had the Internet been available to her, the marquise would surely have become a blogger, for although publication of her letters only began in the year of her death, her correspondence was almost certainly not a private affair—it was quite customary for the recipients of letters to circulate them among a wide group of friends.

De Sévigné, born in Paris into the upper echelons of the French aristocracy, was orphaned at an early age. Raised by various family members who ensured that she would receive a sound education, she married the marquis de Sévigné, an inattentive and philandering husband, in 1644. She bore him a son and a daughter, becoming a widow seven years later when her husband was killed in a duel over another woman. Refusing various offers of marriage, she devoted herself to her children's upbringing, dividing her time between Livry in the Île-de-France, Les Rochers (her château in Brittany), and Paris, where she resided for a time at the Hôtel Carnavalet (now part of the Museum of the History of Paris). During her sojourns in the capital, she was in contact with some of the leading lights of her time, including Nicolas Fouquet, the famous financier and finance minister, and the authors Marie-Madeleine de La Fayette and François de La Rochefoucauld. Extremely attached to her daughter, Françoise, de Sévigné suffered the anguish of separation when Françoise married the comte de Grignan and moved to Provence. De Sévigné traveled south on three occasions to spend several months with her beloved daughter, and it was during her third stay that she died of smallpox.

De Sévigné is a brilliant stylist and a keen observer of contemporary life. Indeed, her accounts are sometimes the only independent source we have for important historical events that she either witnessed herself or heard about from those who had been there. In her correspondence with the marquis de Pomponne, for example, she gives an eyewitness account of one of the high-profile cases of her era: the trial of Fouquet, accused (probably unjustly) of misappropriating State funds, after he imprudently organized an opulent festival in honor of Louis XIV at his own magnificent château, Vaux-le-Vicomte, in 1661. The party was so extravagant that it awakened the king's suspicions as to the source of Fouquet's wealth. In her letters, Sévigné presents an entirely favorable portrait of the former finance minister's dignified behavior and wit during his trial, which ended with his being sentenced to life imprisonment.

Other letters deal with the scandalous Poisons Affair (*l'Affaire des poisons*), in which members of the court were implicated in the deaths of certain nobles, believed to have been poisoned. She also relates the suicide of the famous chef Vatel, who impaled himself on his sword when he believed that the supply of fish for a banquet he was preparing for Louis XIV was going to be woefully inadequate. Tragically, fresh supplies arrived shortly after his death.

Besides giving attention to these high-profile affairs, de Sévigné reports with verve on the day-to-day events of her own life: seeing Racine's play *Esther*, watching a house burn to the ground, witnessing a childish fight between two noblemen. She also writes movingly about her immense sadness at her physical separation from her daughter. Her letters are a way of filling the loneliness of her days at Les Rochers with imaginary conversations with Françoise.

De Sévigné's letters, greatly admired both for their content and style during her lifetime, have never lost their appeal, not only for the general reader but even for some of France's greatest writers. Proust considered her correspondence to be a literary masterpiece, no minor endorsement from one of the great authors of all times.

THE MISANTHROPIST

Le Misanthrope (1666)

◆

Molière (Jean-Baptiste Poquelin) (1622-1673)

I t wasn't easy to have a career in the theater in seventeenth-century France. The competition between rival theater companies was fierce, and while theater had finally managed to become "respectable" as an art form, actors themselves were, paradoxically, still considered by the church to be creatures of the devil and were treated as outcasts.

Molière is the nom de plume of one of the greatest writers of comedy in world literature: Jean-Baptiste Poquelin. The son of a Paris merchant, he studied law, but in 1643 gave up the legal profession to collaborate with members of the Béjart family in founding a theatrical company, the *Illustre Théâtre* (the Illustrious Theater). It was at this time that Jean-Baptiste added "de Molière" to his name, then dropped all of it except for "Molière." After struggling in the highly competitive Parisian market, the Illustrious Theater, heavily in debt, left the capital in 1645 to spend thirteen years as a traveling company. Thanks to the fact that during this time the company attracted the attention of some high-ranking nobles, in 1658 it was able to return to Paris where Molière and his troupe found favor with no less a patron than Louis XIV. From this period date his plays *The Ridiculous Pretentious Ladies* (*Les Précieuses ridicules*), *Sganarelle*, and *School for Wives* (*L'École des femmes*). However, Molière ran afoul of the religious faction at court with plays like *Tartuffe*, whose title character was a pious hypocrite, and *Dom Juan*, a libertine aristocrat. At around the same time he wrote a much less contentious play, *The Misanthropist*, and then went on to compose a series of comedies and *comédies-ballets*, including *The Bourgeois Nobleman* (*Le Bourgeois gentilhomme*, 1671), that had song-and-dance routines—distant ancestors of the modern musical comedy. The last of these was *The Imaginary Invalid* (*Le Malade imaginaire*, 1673), in which Molière played the leading role. Tragically, it was during the fourth performance of this play that Molière fell ill on stage and was transported back to his house, where he died the same night.

First performed in 1666, *The Misanthropist*, which has no obvious religious dimension, bears witness to Molière's desire to avoid the censorship problems that had plagued *Tartuffe* and *Dom Juan*. Alceste, the protagonist, is a paradoxical figure who refuses to conform to the social hypocrisy he sees all around him in Parisian high society and decides to be completely frank with everyone. His intention is to become a one-man truth squad, sparing no one. Ironically, Alceste has fallen in love with the beautiful young socialite Célimène, a coquettish, sharp-tongued woman who is precisely the sort of person he usually criticizes. When his friend Philinthe reminds him of this inconsistency, Alceste, although he knows that he should be courting either the kind-hearted Eliante or the strait-laced Arsinoé, confesses that he is powerless over the dictates of his heart. Actually, our truthful misanthropist is not consistent with his principles on several occasions. When another friend, Oronte, approaches him to ask his opinion of a sonnet he has penned, Alceste at first tries to avoid expressing his negative judgment of the poem by reporting a conversation he pretends to have had with someone else who had consulted him for the same purpose:

> Oronte: What do you find objectionable in my sonnet?
> Alceste: That's not what I am saying. I was telling the other fellow how many people have ruined their reputation by writing bad poetry.
> Oronte: Do I write badly? Do I resemble them?
> Alceste: That's not what I am saying [. . .]

However, when he finally does speak frankly to Oronte, he makes an enemy of the aspiring poet. As the play progresses, Alceste is repeatedly disappointed by the hypocrisies of his fellow humans, including Célimène, and in the closing moments of the play he storms off the stage to go into self-imposed exile, while Philinte and Eliante make plans to dissuade him from this enterprise.

Despite his many noble qualities, Alceste is usually played as a comic character who makes us laugh because of his excessive idealism and his absolute refusal to compromise. However, some modern productions have presented him as a dramatic, even tragic, figure, a tendency that diminishes the impact of the truly comic episodes in the play. Molière has the marvelous talent of identifying the tipping point between virtuous behavior and foolish intransigence, and Alceste, even though he often has the moral high ground, usually appears simply petulant and contrarian. But regardless which interpretation of his character we adopt, we do feel empathy for Alceste, for we have all known the feelings of betrayal and self-pity that he portrays for us onstage. Whether to laugh at ourselves or to take ourselves seriously—*that* is the question!

FABLES

Fables (1668-94)

♦

Jean de La Fontaine (1621-1695)

What can every child schooled in the French educational system recite by heart? It is certainly not the equivalent of the Pledge of Allegiance, since France has no such oath. Probably not the words of the French national anthem, *La Marseillaise*, either. Rather, it is La Fontaine's fables that schoolchildren have been learning for the last three centuries. But while the fables are indeed exquisitely written, the cynical view of life they present—revealing the egotistical underpinnings of human behavior—seems a curious choice for the elementary school curriculum. Like many fairy tales and even nursery rhymes, they are much more appropriate for adult readers.

Most of the fables are derived from the work of earlier writers such as Aesop, but La Fontaine was a master at encapsulating the wisdom of the past into a memorable poetic form. The very first in the collection, "The Cicada and the Ant" ("La Cigale et la fourmi") is adapted from Aesop and teaches a lesson of industriousness and self-sufficiency. The cicada symbolizes the happy-go-lucky person who has spent the summer enjoying herself without a thought for the coming winter. The ant has been busy all summer long accumulating a food supply, so that she is prepared. As it gets cold the cicada is forced to ask the ant for food. When the ant sarcastically asks how the cicada has been spending her time, she replies:

> "Night and day for passers-by
> I sang whenever I had the chance."
> "You sang for them all? My, my!
> Now you can just go ahead and dance!"

The message is certainly a practical one, but this fable does not promote feelings of compassion and understanding for the needs of others, which would have been a worthwhile lesson for young children.

La Fontaine himself would no doubt be surprised to learn that his fables have been taught to children all along. Born in Château-Thierry, not far from Paris, he was originally destined for the priesthood but decided to pursue the study of law in Paris instead. In 1647 he got married, but he was by all accounts a neglectful husband. His first literary work, *The Eunuch* (*L'Eunuque*, 1654), was a comedy inspired by the play of the same name by Terence. It was not long before La Fontaine became part of the Vaux-le-Vicomte literary circle under the patronage of Nicolas Fouquet, the finance minister, whose magnificent castle and lifestyle were to arouse the jealousy and suspicion of the young Louis XIV (see also page 42). Despite these connections, La Fontaine's finances were often on shaky ground, and three years later, the duchess of Orléans took him under her wing. His *Stories and Tales* (*Contes et nouvelles*), published in 1665, won him fame and considerable notoriety, since they recounted in verse the raciest tales from such prior works as Boccaccio's *Decameron*. The first version of the *Fables* (the first six books) appeared in 1668, to be followed in 1678–79 by a new edition containing five more books; a twelfth book was added in 1694. After the death of the duchess of Orléans in 1672, La Fontaine acquired several other patrons, including Madame de Sablière and Madame de Montespan (one of Louis XIV's many mistresses), and was finally elected to the Académie française in 1684. In 1692, he fell gravely ill and, after being converted by Abbot Pouget, he denounced his *Stories and Tales* as too lascivious. He did recover from his illness and died a pious death three years later.

Although La Fontaine published other poetry as well as several plays, he is best known for his fables. A keen observer of humanity, he does not hesitate to make some guarded political commentary in certain fables. "The Animals Sick from the Plague" presents a group of stricken animals attempting to appease the wrath of Heaven, which they see as the source of their malady. Their leader, the lion (a symbol of the king?), suggests that each one confess his most grievous sins; and the animal judged the most sinful will be sacrificed in order to save the others. The lion owns up to having eaten many sheep and even a shepherd or two. The fox (the wily courtier?) excuses the lion and proclaims that to eat such stupid animals is no sin at all and, as for the shepherds, they were guilty by association. Each animal confesses to similar sins but always manages to attenuate their gravity. The last animal to speak is the lowly donkey, who admits to having eaten a few blades of grass from a neighbor's field. The other animals pounce on him, declaring this a heinous crime, and he is sacrificed "for the common good." The moral is that, in law, the rich always go free, while the poor end up paying—a cynical and pessimistic conclusion which, unfortunately, still seems as valid today as in seventeenth-century France.

THOUGHTS

Pensées (1670)

◆

Blaise Pascal (1623-1662)

"Pressure applied at any point on an enclosed fluid is transmitted uniformly and undiminished throughout that fluid." Physics buffs may remember this principle from their high school days, but it is not some arcane discovery that is irrelevant for the rest of us, for it impinges on many aspects of our daily lives. Anyone who rides in a motor vehicle or flies in a commercial airliner, for example, depends on this principle that governs the workings of anything hydraulic (brakes, aircraft controls, etc.). So who was the brilliant scientist who discovered this principle? None other than Blaise Pascal, born in Clermont-Ferrand in the Auvergne. Pascal was not only a great scientist—he repeated Toricelli's experiment with the mercury barometer and thus helped perfect the instrument still used by meteorologists today—but also a great mathematician who invented a sophisticated "arithmetic machine," the ancestor of today's calculator. Oh yes, and he also set up the first public transportation system in Paris with his "five-pennies-a-ride" coaches. One would expect that when a man with such a versatile and inventive mind decided to put down his thoughts on paper, they would be of a scientific or technological nature. Yet the *Pensées*, published posthumously, are anything but that. They are a fragmentary collection of notes that he jotted down over the course of the last decade of his life, as the basis for a book he intended to write, an "Apology for the Christian Religion."

Pascal was a deeply religious man who experienced a dramatic conversion experience as he crossed the Seine near Paris on the night of November 23, 1654. It was a night of "fire" that caused him such intense emotions—he wept "tears of joy"—that he felt compelled to record the experience on a piece of parchment (the "Memorial") which he had sewn into his doublet so that it was always next to his heart. Pascal was strongly influenced by the austere Catholic movement called Jansenism, whose followers firmly believed in St. Augustine's rigorous interpretation of predestination. Close to Calvinists in theology, if not in religious practice, they based their beliefs on the notion that God only reveals himself to the limited number of saved souls chosen from all eternity (the Elect). The Jansenists reacted sharply to the lax Catholic practices of the day, and Pascal wrote a polemical work, *Provincial Letters* (*Lettres provinciales*, 1656–57), that attacked the Jesuits for their complicity in this laxity. Jansenism upheld a doctrine that tended to promote in its disciples a metaphysical anguish that some have seen as a precursor to that of existentialism. This anguish, caused by the belief that salvation depended entirely on the grace of God—whose designs no human being could know in this life—might have been expected to lead to passivity, but it did not. Even if good works did not earn salvation for the believer, they were a sign of God's grace and so, paradoxically, Jansenists (like Calvinists) practiced them in the hope that their actions identified them as God's Elect. Uncertainty about the religious status of individuals did not prevent evangelization. Hence, in Pascal's *Pensées*, there are many fragments that aim to persuade those practicing loose living to seek God. One of the famous arguments Pascal proposed to the libertines who were proliferating in French society in the seventeenth century was the idea of the wager (*le pari*), a particularly appealing idea to a social class for whom gambling was often a passion: "Calculate your winnings and losses if you wager on the question of God's existence: if you win, you win everything; if you lose, you lose nothing at all." Because of his Jansenist outlook, Pascal paints the human condition in somber tones. Humans are seen as miserable creatures, infinitesimally small parts of the universe, self-preoccupied and bored, always seeking distraction. They are like reeds (*roseaux*), bending to every wind, and yet, because of their God-given intellect, they also have an innate grandeur: they are thinking reeds (*des roseaux pensants*). As a scientist, Pascal does not dismiss reason as incompatible with faith; in fact he believes that "to cure humankind's contempt for religion, we have to prove that religion is not contrary to reason." However, logical thinking is not the only path to knowledge, for as he states, "we know the truth not only through reason but also through our hearts." And this leads to one of his best-known insights: "The heart has its reasons that reason cannot understand."

Today, although Pascal is no longer considered a major religious thinker, the beauty of his prose and the profundity of his thought make him one of the most admired stylists and thinkers of French literature. His finely articulated description of the greatness and misery of the human species still manages to capture the paradox of the human condition—our uneasy suspension between the bestial and the divine.

PHAEDRA

Phèdre (1677)

◆

Jean Racine (1639–1699)

The youngest of France's holy trinity of dramatists (with Corneille and Molière), Racine exemplifies the minimalist French classical dramatic ideal: unity of plot (no distracting subplots); unity of time (action limited to a twenty-four-hour period); and unity of place (a single locale). Inspired for the most part by the Greek and Roman tragedies of antiquity, his plays feature noble protagonists, usually mythical, legendary, or historic. However, in contradistinction to Corneille who depicts human beings as they ought to be, Racine prefers to present them as they are, with all their basic human flaws.

Born in the French provinces and orphaned while very young, Jean Racine was schooled by the Jansenists of Port-Royal, outside Paris, an austere Catholic movement that believed in a strict doctrine of predestination that offered salvation only to a small number of the Elect (see also page 47). It was here that Racine acquired the knowledge of Greek and Latin that introduced him to the plays of classical antiquity. However, his interest in the theater did not sit well with the Jansenists and he soon rebelled against their condemnation of it.

His career as a dramatist began in 1664 with *La Thébaïde*, followed by a series of tragedies (and one comedy) culminating in *Phaedra* (1677), arguably his best and certainly his most famous play. The same year, he was named to the prestigious and well-remunerated position of King's Historiographer, abandoning the theater until his later years, when he composed two biblical dramas. By the time he had written *Phaedra*, he had already been reconciled with the Jansenists and had authored a number of religious poems, perhaps as a way of atoning for the dissolute life he is purported to have led during his earlier years.

Phaedra portrays the final hours of its eponymous protagonist, a mythological figure who had all the cards stacked against her. Her mother, Pasiphaé, daughter of the Sun, betrayed her husband, Minos, king of Crete, by having sexual intercourse with a bull—a union that produced the Minotaur, half man, half bull. Feeding this monster presented a problem, since it ate only human flesh. King Minos's solution was to demand a yearly tribute of young men and women from the less powerful Athens, whose inhabitants finally sent Theseus, their king, to put an end to the practice by slaying the monster. He successfully accomplished his mission thanks to the help of Phaedra's sister, Ariadne, who provided him with magic thread that enabled him to find his way out of the labyrinth built to confine the Minotaur. While Theseus might have been expected to marry Ariadne now, the ungrateful hero married Phaedra instead.

When the curtain rises these events have already taken place, and Theseus is absent, pursuing yet another amorous adventure. Meanwhile, Phaedra has fallen in love with her stepson, Hippolytus, the fruit of another of Theseus's affairs. She confesses her passion to her companion Oenone:

> I'm no longer only a victim of the love which courses through
>   my veins,
> I'm a victim of Venus herself, who is in full possession of me.
> My unholy passion fills me with terror
> And life is as hateful to me, as my love is heinous.

However, unable to resist her overwhelming desire for Hippolytus, Phaedra first tries to seduce the shy young man, who, unbeknownst to Phaedra and contrary to his father's wishes, is in love with an Athenian princess, Aricie. When Theseus (who was rumored to have died) unexpectedly returns, Phaedra, having discovered that she has a rival for Hippolytus's affection, is consumed with jealousy and falsely accuses Hippolytus of having tried to seduce her during her husband's absence. Theseus calls on the gods to avenge him, a prayer they answer only too quickly by causing his son's violent death, which is recounted but not represented on stage, in conformity with French classical norms. Stricken with remorse, Phaedra takes poison and, before dying, confesses her treachery to Theseus, who is left on stage to contemplate the destruction wrought on his household by his tragic blindness (and indirectly because of his womanizing).

The power of this tragedy derives above all from the futile struggles of Phaedra, desperately trying to retain her purity but caught in the vise of her own flawed heredity. In spite of herself, she has become a monster, engulfed in an illicit passion for her stepson and tortured by the fact that one of her ancestors is the Sun, whose blinding light illuminates her guilt. Phaedra's plight is a universal one: she demonstrates the dreadful impact the forces of heredity, passion, and guilt can have on human behavior and on the human soul.

Maxims

Maximes (1678)

◆

François de La Rochefoucauld (1613-1680)

The French have always had a gift for animated and witty conversation, and a dinner party with French friends is usually a very lively affair. This aspect of the French character was particularly in evidence in the salons of the seventeenth and eighteenth centuries. Although the salon, an aristocratic discussion group that met regularly to converse about matters of literary and social interest, existed before this period, it was during the seventeenth century that these institutions became a mainstay of French culture, thanks to the influence of prominent noblewomen who presided over them and stressed the importance of the art of conversation and of witty repartee. Both were especially important at the royal court.

The *Maxims* of La Rochefoucauld are part of this tradition. However, they are much more than a simple collection of bons mots. Taken as a whole, they are a cynical and pessimistic analysis of human behavior that lays bare the true motivation behind our conduct, and demonstrates that we have changed little over the centuries. La Rochefoucauld, born in Paris as the prince de Marcillac and later becoming the duc de La Rochefoucauld, belonged to one of France's most illustrious families. He distinguished himself by his bravery when he began military service in 1629 in Italy, but then became involved in a number of political intrigues in which—unfortunately for him—he was always on the losing side. He backed the queen and queen mother against Cardinal Richelieu, for example, and participated in the Fronde, the revolt of the nobles against the monarchy when Louis XIII died and was replaced by the boy king Louis XIV. In 1652, during one of the skirmishes of this struggle, he was shot through the head and almost lost his sight. Disillusioned and disgraced, he retired to his estate to convalesce and reflect. It was during this period that he wrote his *Memoirs* and, in 1665, a first version of the *Maxims*. After his return to Paris later that same year, he began to frequent the literary salons of such prominent women as Mademoiselle de Scudéry, Mademoiselle de Montpensier, and Madame de Sablé, and established friendships with Madame de Sévigné and with Madame de La Fayette, author of *The Princess of Clèves*. Thanks to his contacts with this cultivated milieu, in which conversation played such an important role, he was inspired to continue work on the *Maxims*, polishing and expanding them. He published an edition of five hundred maxims in 1678; fifty more were published after his death in 1680.

Most of the maxims are quite short and pithy, although there are a number that extend over several pages. Analyzing human behavior as largely motivated by *amour-propre* (self-esteem or pride) and self-interest, La Rochefoucauld contends that pride makes "men idolaters of themselves and tyrants of other men if they have the means to be so." He also remarks that *amour-propre* is "the greatest flatterer of all [. . .] more skillful than the most skilled man in the world." He expresses great skepticism as to the motivation behind virtue. From his admittedly jaundiced perspective he observes, "We only blame vice and praise virtue because it is in our interest to do so." In his view, *amour-propre* and self-interest give rise to other negative qualities, such as pride and vanity: "If we had no pride, we wouldn't complain about other people being proud" and "We'd rather hear people bad-mouthing us than not talking about us at all." As for our virtues, they are usually just "vices in disguise," and indeed "we would often be ashamed of our most noble acts, if people knew what really motivated them." Even friendship is suspect: "What men call friendship is usually only undertaken for company's sake, for mutual interest, for an exchange of favors; it is in the final analysis just a transaction in which our own self-esteem hopes to gain some advantage."

Although La Rochefoucauld doesn't hold a very high opinion of human nature, he does stress the importance of humility and lucidity, which can counteract the negative forces motivating much human behavior: "Humility is the real proof of Christian virtues: without it, we keep all our faults, since they are simply concealed by pride, which hides them from others and from ourselves."

If we are humble and lucid, it is possible to avoid the traps set for us by our *amour-propre* and self-interest. And so in the final analysis, La Rochefoucauld is much more than a creator of pithy and memorable sayings, he is a moralist who sees through, and reveals, the shams that pass for virtue in his (and our) society. His definition of virtue is one we should all take as a model: "True virtue is doing in private what we make such a show of doing in public."

THE PRINCESS OF CLÈVES

La Princesse de Clèves (1678)

◆

Marie-Madeleine Pioche de La Vergne de La Fayette

(1634-1693)

In fairy tales beautiful princesses often meet handsome princes and live happily every after, but this rarely happens in real life—or even in most fiction. The protagonist of this novel may share some of the characteristics of the fairy-tale princess—she is the most beautiful, the most virtuous, the most desirable woman around—yet her story is no fable and there is no happy ending.

In seventeenth-century France, the novel as a genre was still in its infancy. Before this era, narratives took the form of epics, romances, and short stories. It was only at the beginning of the 1600s that Honoré d'Urfé published the five-volume *L'Astrée* (a novel in the pastoral tradition), and in the mid-1600s that Madeleine de Scudéry produced massively long novels like *Clélie* (in some of its editions amounting to ten volumes), which were wildly popular at the time but whose length and complexity attract few readers today.

Marie-Madeleine de La Fayette changed all this with her radically new conception of the novel. Born in Paris into an aristocratic family, she soon became part of the city's literary circles. Indeed, she had her own literary salon, the members of which included many of the cultural luminaries of the era, among them La Rochefoucauld, with whom she developed a close friendship. He collaborated with her on *The Princess of Clèves* and, although it has been suggested that he might be its real author (the fact that it was first published anonymously—a not unusual occurrence at the time—may have given rise to this speculation), it is to La Fayette that the novel is attributed.

She is the author of works including *The Princess of Montpensier* (1662), *Zayde* (1670), and *The Comtesse de Tende* (which appeared posthumously in 1724), but her best-known book is *The Princess of Clèves*, a historical novel that differs markedly from its antecedents by the relative simplicity of its plot. Primarily interested in the psychology of her characters, La Fayette presents them in such a true-to-life fashion that the line between fact and fiction is hard to discern. Her protagonist, for example, is an invented character, but meshes seamlessly with the many historical figures also incorporated into the narrative. Although the novel is set in the court of Henri II in sixteenth-century France, the amorous and political intrigues which form its backdrop could just as easily be taking place at the court of Louis XIV. The story is straightforward: a beautiful young noblewoman from the provinces, Mademoiselle de Chartres, accompanied by her protective mother who has inculcated into her daughter the dangers of passionate love and the importance of virtue, arrives on the Paris social scene. Mother arranges an advantageous marriage for her daughter with the prince of Clèves. Although she is not in love with him, Mademoiselle de Chartres obeys the dictates of duty, and the marriage is successful, if not exactly happy, until she meets the handsome young duke of Nemours at a ball: "The duke of Nemours was so astonished by her beauty that, when he approached her and when she curtseyed, he couldn't help showing his admiration. When the two began to dance, there was a murmur of approval in the ballroom." After this chance encounter, the two become deeply enamored of each other. The princess of Clèves struggles mightily against her passion, and in a scene much discussed by contemporary readers she confesses to her husband her feelings for Nemours, at the same time pledging never to give in to this illicit love. Unfortunately, precisely because he now realizes that his wife can never return the passionate love he feels for her, Clèves is stricken with jealousy and is so tortured by what his wife has told him that he dies. If this were a fairy tale, the young lovers would now be free to wed, but the princess, afraid that Nemours's passion may not last, and wary of the effects that love has had on her own soul, retires from Parisian society to spend her last years in solitary retreat in order to seek *repos*, rest and repose from the storms of passion.

While contemporaries of La Fayette most probably saw the novel as an examination of marriage and of relations between the sexes, today we are fascinated by the finesse with which the author dissects the psychological workings of love in her protagonist's heart. (Interestingly enough, this novel was the talk of the 2009 Paris book fair, with people wearing badges proclaiming they had read the book: "J'ai lu *La Princesse de Clèves*.") Demonstrating a profound knowledge of human psychology, La Fayette often astounds us with her pre-Freudian insights into the princess's thoughts and actions. Her innovative technique gives *The Princess of Clèves* a surprisingly modern cast and reveals new possibilities for the novel as a genre.

PERSIAN LETTERS

Lettres persanes (1721)

♦

Charles de Secondat,

Baron de la Brède et de Montesquieu (1689-1755)

While the eighteenth-century thinkers known as *les philosophes* (the philosophers) were far from being the only instigators of the French Revolution, their writings certainly helped to undermine the crumbling edifice of the Ancien Régime. Louis XIV's seventy-two-year-long reign came to an end in 1715 and was followed by the regency of Philippe d'Orléans; Louis's successor, Louis XV, was too young to rule in his own right until 1723. In reaction to the moralistic austerity of the final years of Louis XIV's reign, the regency was characterized by its gaiety, sexual liberties, and fiscal irresponsibility. This was the period of the Mississippi Bubble, when fortunes were made and lost. It was also the beginning of a long period when thinkers and writers began to question the French political system, and with it the very base upon which French society was constructed.

Montesquieu was a young nobleman from the Bordeaux region who studied law in Bordeaux and Paris. Due to the death of his parents, he was brought up by his rich uncle who left him his fortune, the office of president of the Bordeaux law courts, and the barony of Montesquieu. (This experience was an excellent preparation for his most ambitious work, *The Spirit of the Laws* [*L'Esprit des lois*], published in 1748.) Montesquieu was one of the first to criticize his society, and he did so in the *Persian Letters*—which he published anonymously—by adopting the tried and true technique of creating a fictional foreigner who travels to France and whose surprise at what he sees lays bare the inconsistencies and absurdities of French society. Since the latter part of the seventeenth century, the French had been fascinated by the Orient, and in particular the Middle East. Montesquieu introduces two travelers from Persia into France, recording the reactions of these exotic foreigners through their exchange of letters with their compatriots back home. This book is at once a kind of travel journal and an epistolary novel, recounting not only the story of what happens to the tourists in France but also what transpires in the harem which Usbek, one of the two Persians, has left behind. However, the rich and somewhat jaded Usbek and his young companion, Rica, are not just casual tourists: they spend a total of nine years in France and are, perhaps in spite of themselves, influenced in their turn by the culture they are observing, so that they are able to recognize and criticize the faults of their own culture as well.

When Usbek and Rica first arrive in Paris they are impressed by the height of the buildings. Used to the single-story buildings of Persia at the time, the six-story edifices of Paris seem enormous (Rica describes them as "six houses, one on top of the other") and, as the Persians put it, "when everyone comes down into the streets, it gets frightfully congested." Of course, their appearance and dress provoke the interest and even the astonishment of the Parisians who stare at them from their windows and surround them every time they go out into the bustling streets. However, when Rica tires of the attention and begins to wear European clothes, he discovers that now nobody pays attention to him, unless the question of his origin happens to come up. Then the reaction of the French is damningly ethnocentric: "Ah, so you are Persian? How extraordinary! How can anyone be Persian?" The Persians' comments on French politics and society are similarly amusing yet pointed: they describe the king of France as "a powerful magician, because he is able to make his subjects think what he wants them to think." But the king is trumped by an even greater magician, the pope, who can make people believe that "three equals one, and that the bread one eats at mass is not bread, nor the wine, wine." An interesting aspect of Montesquieu's technique in the *Persian Letters* is that on one hand the Persians' observations reveal the ridiculousness of certain French customs and institutions—while on the other hand the rigid model of Persian society we see in the authoritarian rule that Usbek has set up in his harem is not held up as an ideal to which the French should aspire. The most politically revolutionary aspect of the *Persian Letters* is the frame of mind the book inspires, for it encourages questioning and analysis in accordance with the dictates of reason and nature. For example, Usbek's favorite concubine, Roxane, has worked to transform the despotic harem into "a place of delights and pleasures" during his absence. However, when she is caught in the arms of a young man who found his way into the harem, the eunuchs who rule the harem kill him, causing her to make the ultimate sacrifice to affirm her freedom: she takes her own life. As she lies dying, she writes to Usbek to inform him of her revolt: "I may have lived in servitude, but I have always been free. I have reformed your laws in accordance with those of nature, and my mind has always been independent."

MANON LESCAUT

(1731)

◆

Antoine-François Prévost (Abbé Prévost) (1697-1763)

Like Rabelais, Prévost was a man who was not always faithful to his vows. However, unlike Rabelais, he paid a price for his transgressions since he was obliged to spend six years in exile in England and Holland after leaving his Benedictine monastery in Paris in 1728 without permission. Having finally regularized his position with the church, he returned to France, although he was briefly banished again in 1741, before being allowed to regain his native country. In spite of his turbulent life, Prévost (who came from the very north of France) was an extremely productive author and translator. *Manon Lescaut* (an abbreviation of the full title, *Story of the Knight Des Grieux and of Manon Lescaut/Histoire du chevalier des Grieux et de Manon Lescaut*) is the work for which he is chiefly remembered today; it is the last volume of his seven-volume *Memoirs and Adventures of a Nobleman* (*Mémoires et aventures d'un homme de qualité*), which he wrote from 1728 to 1731. This was followed by *The English Philosopher* (*Le Philosophe anglais ou Histoire de monsieur Cleveland*, 1731–39) and *Story of a Modern Greek Woman* (*Histoire d'une Grecque moderne*, 1740), among other works.

The principal story of *Manon Lescaut* is introduced by the nobleman who is the protagonist of the overall, seven-volume novel. The nobleman meets Des Grieux and listens as the latter recounts his life. Des Grieux's account is the love story of two adolescents, he (Des Grieux) of noble parentage, she (Manon Lescaut) of much more lowly lineage. Although class is one obstacle to their love, the biggest impediment is money (or lack thereof): *Manon Lescaut* is one of the first French novels to have this as a major theme. The young lovers initially meet by accident when Des Grieux, spying Manon as she emerges from a stagecoach in Arras, is immediately captivated by her. "She appeared charming to me, who had never given a thought until now to the fair sex, nor had looked attentively at any girl. I, whose wisdom and level-headedness everyone admired, was in an instant totally smitten." A naive and serious young man who is on his way to join a Catholic religious order, the Knights of Malta, Des Grieux had up until this point "never even thought about the differences between the sexes." Mustering up all his courage, he engages the beautiful Manon in conversation and learns that her family is sending her to a convent in an attempt to cure her "propensity for pleasure." Des Grieux persuades her to run away with him and set up house together, and the couple thus abandons family and friends, and Des Grieux his religious vocation. At first the young lovers' existence appears idyllic. However, Manon's extravagant tastes soon plunge them into debt, and their situation deteriorates rapidly. After Des Grieux discovers that his beloved is supplementing their dwindling income by selling herself as a high-class prostitute (she considers sexual fidelity to be a useless virtue when one is confronted with poverty), the couple resorts to other nefarious ways of making money, taking a downward path that leads to prison and finally to deportation to America for Manon. Des Grieux manages to find enough money to pay his passage on the ship that is transporting her and the other criminals to New Orleans. However, even in the New World the old troubles reappear, when her beauty attracts the prurient interest of influential men in the colony, although Manon is now no longer unfaithful to Des Grieux. To escape from these tribulations the couple flees into the Louisiana wilderness where, in a tragic final scene, Manon dies from exhaustion and exposure and Des Grieux desperately tries to dig a grave for her with his sword, a pathetic moment that reveals both his love and his degradation—the sword he uses to dig her grave is the symbol of his noble birth. Des Grieux is accused of having killed Manon, is acquitted but is so overcome with grief that he falls ill and hopes for his own death: "I continually invoked death and refused all attempts to heal me. However, Heaven, after punishing me so harshly, intended that my misfortune and punishment serve as a lesson. I was prompted to remember my noble birth and upbringing."

Manon has usually been seen as the archetypal femme fatale, capable of inspiring passionate love in members of the opposite sex and leading them to ultimate destruction. However, since this novel is recounted in the first person, we see her only through Des Grieux's eyes—and his narrative is really a confession, an exercise in self-justification, blaming his crimes and degradation on the overwhelming power of love. Some modern readers, interpreting the story from Manon's point of view, see *her* rather than Des Grieux as the real victim. Prévost himself presents his novel as a cautionary tale to warn his readers of the consequences of sacrificing everything to love and of the disastrous role money can play when added to the equation. Indeed, we only need to look at our daily newspapers to realize that this warning has lost none of its force.

LETTERS OF A PERUVIAN WOMAN

Lettres d'une Péruvienne (1747)

◆

Françoise de Graffigny (1695-1758)

What happens to a fictional Inca princess named Zilia when she is kidnapped by Spanish conquistadors, rescued by a French naval vessel, then transported to eighteenth-century France? A great deal indeed, much to the delight of the French reading public who made this novel one of the bestsellers of its century. The French during the Enlightenment were endlessly fascinated by tales that depicted the way in which foreign cultures reacted to their own. The representation of the exotic Other (Zilia), and the fact that this novel is a love story with a feminist and anti-colonial slant, explain its great popularity in its time. Although it subsequently fell out of favor, it was thankfully resurrected during the twentieth century.

Its author, Françoise d'Issembourg d'Happencourt, was born in Lorraine in 1695, taking the name "de Graffigny" from that of a family property when she married at the age of sixteen. Because her husband was both a spendthrift and a brute, she was eventually able to obtain a legal separation from him. She spent the latter part of her life in Paris, where she had moved in order to be part of the capital's literary scene. It was there that she published *Letters of a Peruvian Woman* in 1747, when she was in her early fifties. Her other great literary success was the play *Cénie* (1750). She also left a voluminous correspondence when she died in Paris.

Letters of a Peruvian Woman is an epistolary novel whose Peruvian narrator, Zilia, writes a series of letters from France to her beloved Inca fiancé, Aza, from whom she is separated when she is kidnapped. These letters are followed by five more addressed to Déterville, the French nobleman who had rescued her from the Spaniards and taken her to France. Her first letters recount her undying love for Aza and apprise him of her fate as she is transported to Europe. Since she can at first neither read nor write in French, she records her story and her reactions to French society by means of quipus, knotted strings that the Peruvians used mainly for mathematical purposes (although Graffigny presents them as a kind of writing). When Zilia learns to write French, she translates these quipus, thus creating the early letters of the novel.

During the voyage, Déterville falls in love with her, although he cannot communicate this to her until later, when she is able to speak French. Upon her arrival in France, Zilia reports on the snobbery of French society and describes the disdainful treatment she receives from Parisian women. Only Déterville and his sister, Céline, treat her with respect; Déterville engages a tutor to teach her how to read and write. Zilia's account of this enterprise gives the flavor of the work: "The Cacique [Déterville] brought me a savage from this country, who comes to teach me the language and the method they use here to give a kind of substance to their thoughts."

Déterville's mother is particularly cold to Zilia, because she doesn't want her son to marry (and certainly not a Peruvian), hoping instead that he will join a religious order so that his older sibling will inherit the entire family wealth. When Déterville is called to war, Zilia and Céline are sent to a convent. Here Zilia is instructed in the Catholic faith, but points out to her teacher the wide gap between Christian teachings—which she admires—and the hypocritical practices of French society.

Graffigny's use of an Inca princess to criticize French society resembles the strategy employed by Montesquieu in his *Persian Letters*, published several decades earlier. However, here the love interest drives the narrative. In the end, Zilia's fidelity to Aza goes unrewarded, and her integration into French society does not include her acquiescence to Déterville's desire to marry her. Much to the consternation of the original French readers, Zilia's independence and newfound wisdom seal her celibacy, a trait that many of today's readers see as the sign of a strong, "modern" woman. This does not prevent her from offering her friendship to Déterville, who has taken refuge in Malta. In her last letter, she writes: "Déterville, come and learn from me how to conserve the resources of your soul [. . .] Give up tumultuous feelings, which imperceptibly destroy our soul. You will find in my heart, in my friendship, in my feelings the remedy for the damage love has inflicted upon you." And so, at the end of this remarkable, woman-centered novel that does not bother itself with chronological consistency (the Spanish conquistadors' invasion of Peru took place in the early sixteenth century), an Inca princess who had landed in eighteenth-century France and evaluated the mores of its citizens instructs a French nobleman on the value of friendship. Friendship, in Zilia's opinion, is more priceless than love, since love is susceptible to the destructive force of passion.

MAN A MACHINE

L'Homme-machine (1748)

◆

Julien Offray de La Mettrie (1709-1751)

The eighteenth century did not lack for writers who thought outside the box. Rousseau and Diderot, among many others, questioned and criticized the contemporary political, social, and religious regimes and suffered censorship or even exile as a result of their intellectual boldness. However, La Mettrie exceeded them all in the subversive nature of his works and was banished not only from France (in 1746) but even from Holland (in 1748), a country known for its tolerance for new ideas. What was it about La Mettrie's philosophical thinking that made it anathema in two countries? The work that caused the banishment from France was his *Natural History of the Soul* (*Histoire naturelle de l'âme*), published anonymously in 1745, in which he examined the machine-like characteristics of animal behavior and then extended such mechanistic principles to human beings. Similar ideas had already been promulgated by Descartes in his early writings but were subsequently abandoned by the seventeenth-century philosopher as too dangerous. The English philosopher John Locke had then expressed comparable ideas at the end of the 1600s, but La Mettrie's work was nevertheless considered scandalous in France because of its atheistic materialism. He was forced to leave his native land for Leiden in the Netherlands, and it was there that he wrote his next treatise, *Man a Machine*, also an anonymous work (although anonymity was no real protection) that went even further than the *Natural History of the Soul*, antagonizing the usually open-minded Dutch and obliging its author to seek refuge at the court of King Frederick the Great in Prussia.

Man a Machine, a short, closely argued but very readable essay, is the most accessible introduction to La Mettrie's thought. Based on his medical experiments and his observations of his own physical and mental states, *Man a Machine* concludes that thought, emotion, and the soul itself are all physical products of the body and that the soul has no metaphysical dimension. He also compares the workings of the human body to that of animals, and in doing so bestows on animals a dignity they were previously denied, as he stresses the interconnectedness of all living natural forms. Animals are not the intellectual equals of man, but what separates the two is relatively little: "From animals to mankind, the transition is not enormous as any true philosopher will agree. What was man before the invention of words and the knowledge of languages? An animal of his own species, who possessed much less in the way of natural instinct than the other animals." La Mettrie also stresses the importance of happiness and sees metaphysics and any sort of religious speculation as impediments to this desirable state. Just as members of the animal kingdom do not indulge in such meditations, neither should we: "Do we know anything more about our destiny than about our origin? Let us surrender to complete ignorance [in these matters]; our happiness depends on it. He who adopts such a position will be wise, just, accepting of his fate, and as a result, happy. He will wait for death, neither fearing it, nor desiring it, cherishing life [. . .] and full of respect for nature."

La Mettrie was born in Saint-Malo, and after flirting with Jansenism, he decided to study medicine in Paris and Rheims. After completing his medical degree, he went to Leiden to do further study under the famous Dutch physician Hermann Boerhaave, some of whose works La Mettrie translated into French. Upon his return to Paris in 1742 he became an army doctor, and it was during an illness of his own, suffered on the battlefield, that he realized how his physical state affected the workings of his mind. This experience had a crucial influence on his subsequent writings, revealing to him the importance of the mind-body connection. Although he did finally find a safe haven in Prussia, his works did offend the ecclesiastical authorities in Berlin. It was only thanks to Frederick the Great's patronage that he was not expelled from Prussia. He died in 1751 of food poisoning after eating a pâté that had spoiled.

His atheistic materialism, which derived primarily from his studies in anatomy and physiology and from his belief that every organism aspires to happiness, made him an extremely influential figure both in his time and later. *Man a Machine* gives today's reader an engaging look at his pioneering intellect.

CANDIDE

(1759)

◆

Voltaire (François Marie Arouet) (1694-1778)

One of the most traumatic natural disasters of the eighteenth century occurred in Lisbon in 1755. A massive earthquake shook the city on All Saints' Day, followed by a huge tidal wave, killing an estimated 30,000 people. It was this event that inspired Voltaire's famous work *Candide*.

Born in Paris as François Marie Arouet, he decided in 1718 to henceforth call himself Voltaire (an anagram based on his family name). He belonged to the group of writers and thinkers known as *les philosophes* (the philosophers), who had undertaken a critical analysis of French society under the Ancien Régime. Although Voltaire was, in his time, the most popular playwright in France, with successes like *Oedipus* (1718), *Brutus* (1730), and *Zaïre* (the name of the play's principal character) in 1732, among many others, his theater is scarcely ever performed today. He was also a historian of note and composed a philosophical dictionary, the *Dictionnaire philosophique*, in 1764. Nowadays he is principally known for his bitingly sarcastic and often very funny philosophical tales such as *Zadig, Micromégas,* and *Candide.* Voltaire had a long and rather tumultuous career, during which he was exiled in England from 1726 to 1728, spent an unhappy three years at the court of Frederick the Great in Prussia, established himself first in Geneva, Switzerland, and then at nearby Ferney in France. There he became known as the Sage of Ferney. He used his pen to plead the cause of the persecuted, particularly those persecuted in the name of religion. After his long absence he finally returned to Paris in 1778 to general adulation, and died there the same year.

Candide is Voltaire's response to those who attempt to explain every event, including natural disasters, as a manifestation of divine providence. He particularly attacked the followers of the philosopher Leibniz, who had affirmed that, since the world was created by God, everything in it was the best it could possibly be, given the limitations God had imposed on the physical, natural world. For Voltaire, who was guilty of some oversimplification of Leibniz's position, such a philosophical stance was naive and actually served to justify evil in the world.

The complete title of his witty and profound book is *Candide, or Optimism* (*Candide ou l'Optimisme*), "optimism" from the Latin *optimum*, which means "the best" in the sense understood by Leibniz. Candide is the protagonist's name, meaning "naive and inexperienced" rather than "candid." The story begins in Germany at the castle of the baron of Thunder-ten-tronckh. Naively believing that theirs is the "best of all possible castles," the inhabitants include Candide (the servants suspect he is the illegitimate son of the baron's sister), Cunégonde (the baron's beautiful young daughter), and Pangloss, a pretentious windbag who is the young people's tutor. This mock earthly paradise is quickly shattered in the first chapter: "One day, Cunégonde, walking near the castle [. . .] saw Pangloss in the bushes giving a lesson in experimental physics to his mother's maid, a very pretty and docile brunette. As Miss Cunégonde was very interested in science, she breathlessly observed the experiment." When she attempts to teach Candide what she has learned, the two are caught in the act by the baron who ejects the young man from this Garden of Eden without his Eve. The source of the mischief, Pangloss, is also expelled.

There follows a breathless series of misadventures spanning half the then-known world, and throughout Candide persists in believing that everything is for the best in the best of all possible worlds. Among other catastrophes, Candide and Pangloss narrowly escape death when they arrive in Lisbon just as the 1755 earthquake is happening. Cunégonde and Candide see each other again briefly, only to be separated once more. Although Candide accidently discovers a utopian community, El Dorado, in the mountains of South America, he leaves it to continue his search for Cunégonde. The couple is finally reunited in Turkey, where, with other companions, they purchase and operate a small farm. This endeavor teaches them the value of hard work, which "spares them from three evils: boredom, vice, and poverty." Although the now syphilis-ravaged Pangloss continues to spout his optimistic nonsense, a wiser, more experienced Candide has come to the realization that humankind must create its own happiness. The famous last line of the book is by Candide: "Il faut cultiver notre jardin" ("we must cultivate our garden"), and the "we" cannot be overemphasized. We attain contentment by working together toward a common, achievable goal. This modest, down-to-earth collaboration is the nearest we can come to an earthly paradise, to our own little Garden of Eden. Although the lesson Voltaire wants to impart is not perhaps a lofty one, it is intensely practical and within the grasp of anyone who is willing to try it. This is Voltaire's own recipe for happiness.

Reveries of the Solitary Walker

Rêveries du promeneur solitaire (1782)

◆

Jean-Jacques Rousseau (1712–1778)

While there are certainly examples of a love and appreciation of nature in French literature before the eighteenth century, it is more usual to find it presented as a force to be feared and struggled against rather than as a beneficent one. The general respect for nature and all its workings that is prevalent today can be traced back to the late eighteenth century that spawned the Romantic movement, stressing the beauty of the natural world and the pleasures of communion with it. The writer who was the most important trendsetter in this respect was Jean-Jacques Rousseau. Although not considered a Romantic himself, he helped pave the way for this important literary and artistic movement.

Rousseau had already extolled the splendors of nature in his highly successful epistolary novel *Julie, or the New Heloise* (*Julie ou la Nouvelle Héloïse*, 1761; see also page 71) and had insisted on the superiority of the natural state over civilization in a number of other works. However, nowhere is his love of nature and his feeling of oneness with the natural world more palpable than in his *Reveries*, an unfinished work published posthumously in 1782 (together with part 1 of the *Confessions*). The last work Rousseau wrote, the *Reveries* is an exquisitely written piece expressing his search for self-knowledge. "I am undertaking the same project as Montaigne," he writes in the first of the ten *promenades* (walks), the name he gives to the ten sections into which the book is divided. "However my goal is the opposite of his, for he wrote his essays for others, whereas I am writing my reveries only for myself." Although it betrays a misreading of Montaigne, this statement does give the very personal flavor of Rousseau's work, even if he does suggest elsewhere in the same chapter that his book has a less private goal: "I am devoting the last days of my life to studying myself and preparing in advance the account that I will soon have to give of myself." The work's title and Rousseau's use of the words "reveries," "walker," and "walks" are significant, because the physical activity of walking was one of Rousseau's favorite pastimes and one which induced a state of reverie in him. It is interesting to note that one of the original meanings of the term "reveries" in French was "excursion" or "walk," so that *rêverie* and *promenade* are synonyms. He explains the melancholy feelings that prompted him to write this final work: "Here I am, alone on the earth, having no friend or companion but myself." His consolation for this feeling of isolation comes from his walks around Paris and in Switzerland and the meditations they inspire in him. In the famous "Fifth Walk," he reminisces about an almost mystical experience he had while staying on the island of Saint Pierre, in the Swiss lake of Bienne. In this bucolic setting he was able to engage in another of his favorite activities, collecting and examining different plants. At the end of the day, he would sit on the shores of the lake, and as he contemplated the movement of the water and listened to its sounds he was transported into a kind of trance, the ebb and flow of the lake becoming one with the movement of his own soul. Here, alone with nature, he was able to "experience the pleasure of his own existence without the intermediary of conscious thought." He literally let himself "go with the flow," and the resulting union with nature became his ultimate consolation for his personal anguish.

Jean-Jacques Rousseau was a complicated and multi-talented author. Born in Geneva, he left his hometown at the age of sixteen, settling first in the nearby French town of Annecy. He later became a French citizen. Having lost his mother shortly after his birth, he had a series of affairs with women who were fairly obvious maternal substitutes—he called one of them, Madame de Warens, *Maman*—before (and after) his marriage to Thérèse Levasseur. This unlikely life partner was an almost illiterate seamstress whom he first met in 1745 and by whom he had at least three, and possibly five, children, all of whom were placed in an orphanage. His irascible temperament and tendency toward paranoia alienated him from many of his contemporaries. The belief that he was the victim of a general conspiracy became in some ways a self-fulfilling prophecy. However, his psychological problems did not prevent him from writing brilliant and highly influential treatises on education (*Emile*, 1762) and on the social order (*Discourse on the Origin and Foundation of Inequality among Men / Discours sur l'origine et les fondements de l'inégalité parmi les hommes*, 1755; *The Social Contract / Du contrat social*, 1762), as well as one of the best-selling novels of the century, *Julie*, plus operas, the article on "music" for the *Encyclopedia* (see also page 76), and of course his *Confessions*, still considered a masterpiece in its genre. His educational theories were put into practice at the Rousseau Institute in Geneva, later directed by the famous child psychologist Jean Piaget. His feelings of humankind's essential unity with nature still resonate today with all who consider themselves lovers of the natural world.

DANGEROUS LIAISONS

Les Liaisons dangereuses (1782)

◆

Pierre-Antoine-François Choderlos de Laclos (1741-1803)

It is sometimes said that everyone has one good book in him (or her). Whatever the merit of this bit of folk wisdom, few authors can match Laclos's single book, *Dangerous Liaisons*, a witty, sarcastic perspective on the moral bankruptcy of eighteenth-century French aristocracy, still remarkably à propos in the sex-obsessed, materialistic world of contemporary Western society.

Dangerous Liaisons is a novel of seduction and betrayal in which love is often discussed but rarely felt, and in which, for the two principals, the marquise de Merteuil and Valmont, sexual liaisons are the most effective means of realizing their lust for power and domination. The novel is, among many other things, a war between the two of them, a war in which each individual sally is planned and executed with military precision, scarcely surprising since Laclos spent the greater part of his life in the French army. Born in Amiens, he trained to be an artillery officer with subsequent postings in the French provinces. He spent his leaves in Paris where he frequented literary circles, trying his hand unsuccessfully at poetry, a play, and the libretto for an opera that was panned after a single performance. Nothing in these early years indicated that Laclos was anything more than a dilettante—until 1778, when he started writing *Dangerous Liaisons* while stationed in Besançon. When published in 1782, it was an immediate success, provoking a scandal that was the talk of the Parisian salons and causing his army superiors to order him to remain at his most recent post in La Rochelle. Here he met Marie-Soulange Duperré, whom he dutifully married after they discovered that she was pregnant. He played a somewhat ambiguous role in the French Revolution, shifting alliances before finally attaining the rank of general in Napoleon Bonaparte's army, in whose service he died in Italy in 1803 of dysentery and malaria.

Dangerous Liaisons is an epistolary novel, a form much in vogue in the eighteenth century but now seriously out of fashion, although the popularity of e-mail and texting makes it seem very relevant again today. The two principal characters are aristocrats who are former lovers but who have since moved on, although their mutual attraction is not totally extinguished. Valmont is a notorious rake, while the marquise de Merteuil, although equally profligate, has managed to conceal her sexual conquests and to maintain an honorable reputation. The impetus for the story, told in a polyphonic way by a number of different letter writers, is Merteuil's desire to avenge herself on another former lover who is now seeking to marry a rich, young ingénue, Cécile Volanges. Merteuil offers Valmont sexual favors if he will participate in her revenge by seducing the virginal Cécile before her marriage. Valmont is at first reluctant, since he has found a new challenge—the virtuous, devout, married Madame de Tourvel. The fact that sexual conquest for him has little to do with sexual desire and everything to do with power is made quite clear in letter 6: "I will have this woman [Madame de Tourvel]; I will snatch her away from her unworthy husband; I will even dare to steal her away from the God she adores [. . .] I want her to maintain her faith in virtue, while sacrificing herself to me." Sexual conquest for Valmont takes on an almost metaphysical dimension.

Merteuil is equally cold and calculating, since Cécile's seduction will transform the innocent young girl into a hypocritical and dissolute woman of the world. However, the novel is steeped in a moral ambiguity that derives from the fact that the reader grudgingly admires the evil duo for their wit, intelligence, and sparkling linguistic virtuosity. In fact, we can't help being impressed by the way Merteuil has reinvented herself after the death of her husband, so that she can survive as a single woman in the patriarchal society of eighteenth-century France. Having mastered the art of total self-control, she has fashioned herself into a clandestine Delilah, exercising her sexual power over the many males she has secretly dominated: "How many modern Samsons have I succeeded in subjugating with my scissors poised over their locks of hair," she writes in letter 81, which contains a kind of proto-feminist credo. Even though both protagonists are unmasked at the end of the novel, their punishment, while serious, appears rather perfunctory. However, there is no "happily ever after," even for the virtuous characters. We might even remain more fascinated with the evil machinations of Merteuil and Valmont than satisfied by their downfall, particularly as the sexual politics they practice seem peculiarly modern, their powdered wigs notwithstanding.

THE MARRIAGE OF FIGARO

Le Mariage de Figaro (1784)

◆

Pierre-Augustin Caron de Beaumarchais (1732–1799)

Two of the best-loved operas of the comic repertoire, *The Barber of Seville* and *The Marriage of Figaro*, were inspired by the plays of Beaumarchais. Both plays were well received by Paris audiences, and the *Marriage*, conceived as a sequel to the *Barber* and featuring many of the same characters, was even a runaway hit, playing for sixty-eight straight performances, something almost unheard of at the time. Because it was written just a few years before the French Revolution (in 1781, but not performed until 1784), it is tempting to see in the play prerevolutionary tendencies. However, Beaumarchais was less a revolutionary than an opportunist, engaging in various ventures and undertaking missions for both Louis XV and Louis XVI. Two years after its first performance, the librettist Lorenzo da Ponte adapted Beaumarchais's play, and it became one of Mozart's most successful operas, *The Marriage of Figaro* (*Le Nozze di Figaro*).

Born Pierre-Augustin Caron, the son of a Parisian watchmaker, Beaumarchais invented a clockwork escape mechanism that vastly improved the accuracy of timepieces. The idea was stolen from him by the royal watchmaker, but he was eventually vindicated and awarded a position at Versailles where he became the harp teacher of Louis XV's daughters. Having married a rich widow, he inherited the property of Beaumarchais upon her death, and adopted the name of the property as his own. His first attempts at the theater—bourgeois dramas—met with no success, but when he turned to comedy the situation changed— dramatically! However, his activities were not limited to the literary, since he was throughout his life keenly interested in politics, playing an active role in helping the insurgents of the American Revolution. After the French Revolution began, his relationship with the new government was at times precarious, and he was forced to spend time in Holland, London, and Hamburg. When the Directory authorized his return to Paris in 1796, he produced his last play, *The Guilty Mother* (*La Mère coupable*, 1792), a sequel to *The Marriage of Figaro*, to considerable acclaim. Three years later, this colorful and multi-talented man died of a stroke.

At first, Beaumarchais had difficulty in staging the *Marriage* because of the important role he attributed to servants, who were represented as more intelligent and more resourceful than the aristocrats. The count in particular is portrayed as a hypocritical philanderer whose plans for the seduction of Suzanne are thwarted by a coalition of servants and his wife, the countess. When he had wed three years previously, the count had abolished the infamous *droit du seigneur* (the right of the lord to sleep with the brides of his servants on their wedding night), but now he hypocritically plots to seduce Suzanne, whose marriage to the servant Figaro is imminent. However, the count's lust is not the only thing threatening Suzanne's marriage, for Figaro has promised one of his debtors, an older woman named Marceline—who seems smitten with him—that he will marry her if he cannot repay her by an agreed-upon date. Despite Figaro's inability to pay and the count's evil intentions, everything works out in the end, thanks largely to a plot hatched by the servants and helped by one of those delightful recognition scenes so typical of French comedies. The count, caught in a humiliating trap, is chastened and promises to be faithful; Figaro and Suzanne are married and, just as in a modern musical comedy, the play finishes with a song-and-dance routine.

Perhaps the most "revolutionary" part of the play occurs in act 5, scene 3, when Figaro pronounces a soliloquy in which he rails against the privileges of the French aristocracy. Referring to the count, he complains, "No, my Lord, you won't have her [. . .] you won't have her. Just because you're a nobleman, you think you're a genius [. . .] Nobility, money, a high social rank, titles, all of these make a person proud. But what have you done to deserve so many rewards? You were born and that's all you've done. Apart from your birth, you're just an ordinary man; whereas I, by Heavens, lost in the crowd of commoners, had to use more brainpower and cunning just to stay alive than have been needed to govern the whole of Spain during the last hundred years." If not quite mount-the-barricades rhetoric, Figaro's lament is indeed rather bold at a time when social barriers were becoming more and more porous and when the traditional privileges of the nobility were being seriously questioned. However, *The Marriage of Figaro* is above all a comedy and a very successful one at that, whose fast-paced humor still charms and delights modern audiences.

PAUL AND VIRGINIA

Paul et Virginie (1788)

◆

Jacques-Henri Bernardin de Saint-Pierre (1737–1814)

Although the eighteenth-century French novel is usually associated with adultery, infidelity, and a libertine lifestyle, there is a counterpoint to this general tendency that appears in the latter half of the century, inaugurated in 1761 by Jean-Jacques Rousseau's mammoth epistolary novel, *Julie, or the New Heloise.* Rousseau's novel begins in a more traditional fashion with its heroine, Julie, falling in love with her tutor and becoming pregnant out of wedlock; but it ends surprisingly when Julie, now married to another man and with children, shows herself able to overcome the temptation to have a sexual relationship with her former lover when they meet again much later. Rousseau introduced both a strong moral tone into the sentimental novel of his age as well as a new appreciation for the beauty of nature. *Paul and Virginia* likewise exploits these twin themes; however, its setting is not the alpine beauty of Switzerland that Rousseau had chosen, but the much more exotic tropical island of Mauritius (called by its former name, Île de France, in the novel). Tropical islands had been brought to the attention of the reading public first by Daniel Defoe's *Robinson Crusoe* (1719), and then in France by the voyages of Louis Antoine Bougainville to Tahiti and other Pacific Islands. But it was Saint-Pierre's novel, with its exquisite descriptions of what he paints as a tropical utopia, that helped popularize this interest in such locales, an interest that has grown ever since. Saint-Pierre's Mauritius is a place of incredible beauty where nature supplies everything, a vision somewhat at odds with the reality he depicted in his 1773 account of his own three-year stint on Mauritius, *Journey to Île de France.* The various troublesome, tropical insects and the cockroach-infested houses he described in *Journey* disappear in the idyllic portrait he paints in *Paul and Virginia.* And into this idealized setting he places his characters, in a kind of utopian mini-society. United by coincidence in an isolated corner of the island are two French women, Madame de La Tour and Marguerite. The former, of aristocratic origin, had come to Mauritius with her husband to escape family censure in France, since she had married below her class. Marguerite, a peasant woman from Brittany, had been abandoned by her lover in France and, being pregnant, had left France to spare her family the shame of her condition. Madame de La Tour, whose husband had recently died of a tropical fever while on a journey to neighboring Madagascar, is expecting his child. The two women give birth on the island, the aristocrat to Virginia, the commoner to Paul, and despite their class difference they become firm friends and raise their children as brother and sister. Each of the women has a slave, a man (from Senegal) and a woman (from Madagascar), both presented rather unrealistically as happy in their service. The enslaved Africans are permitted to marry each other, thus creating for the reader an exemplary society in which distinctions of class and race are either suppressed or glossed over. Everything seems perfect—until Virginia begins to feel a sexual attraction to Paul, and although both mothers would eventually like to see their children marry, they do not wish this to happen before its time. A wealthy aunt of Virginia's who had treated her mother very harshly in the past seems to relent and asks her to send Virginia back to France. Madame de La Tour accedes to this request in the hope that Virginia will inherit the aunt's estate. Things end badly when Virginia is unable to integrate into French society. Her return to Mauritius is marked by a tragedy that calls into question the virtue so frequently touted in the earlier parts of the novel.

Born in Le Havre, Bernardin de Saint-Pierre was an engineer and botanist who, as a child, had traveled to Martinique with his uncle, a sea captain, and who had retained from this journey a love of travel to exotic places, further nourished by his reading of *Robinson Crusoe*. He spent the years 1768 to 1771 on Mauritius. In 1784 he published *Studies in Nature*, a pious three-volume work whose aim was to prove the existence of God through the wonders of the natural world. To a subsequent fourth volume he appended *Paul and Virginia*, which became one of the most influential French novels of its time as well as throughout the nineteenth century. He was married twice, to women considerably younger than he, and named the children born of the first marriage Virginie and Paul. Director of the Paris botanical garden (*Jardin des Plantes*) for a time, he was subsequently named professor of morals at the École Normale Supérieure. In 1807, as president of the Académie française, he gave a speech praising Napoleon, and his strong support for the emperor earned him a pension. He died in 1814.

Although today's readers may find the moralizing tone of certain passages of *Paul and Virginia* tedious, Bernardin de Saint-Pierre's masterpiece still impresses with its lush description of a tropical paradise and its story of tragic love.

JUSTINE

Justine ou les Malheurs de la vertu (1791)

♦

Marquis de Sade (Donatien Alphonse François de Sade)
(1740–1814)

The first psychiatrists were a literary lot. Sigmund Freud delved into Greek mythology and invented the terms "Oedipus complex" and "narcissism." Richard von Krafft-Ebing had the author Marquis de Sade in mind when he transformed the already existing "sadism"— derived from the marquis's name—into a clinical term, although it was originally defined in 1839 as a "horrible aberration of debauchery, and a monstrous antisocial system." De Sade was an extremely controversial but highly influential writer who has fascinated and revolted generations of readers, and whose novels and life story have been adapted to stage and screen. What makes de Sade interesting even today? Is it simply because of our prurient interest in sex and pornography, or is there another dimension to his work? Perhaps what intrigues us most about his writings is the way they flaunt conventional morality, and how they appear to promote the freedom from accepted modes of behavior.

Justine is a perfect example of these characteristics. The parents of the title character and her sister Juliette die, leaving their two daughters penniless and having to fend for themselves. Fifteen-year-old Juliette decides to use her beauty as a means of sexual and social conquest (her story is told in another of de Sade's novels, *Juliette*, published in 1797), while twelve-year-old Justine chooses virtue and religion as her guiding principles. At the beginning of the novel we find Justine telling her life story to a rich noblewoman she has just met, Madame de Lorsange, who, through a life of debauchery, has achieved wealth and respectability. Justine's pursuit of virtue, on the other hand, has propelled her from one catastrophe to another. Whenever she accomplishes virtuous actions she is robbed, repeatedly raped, and imprisoned by a seemingly endless procession of men and women for whom strange sexual practices are the norm. Yet in spite of everything, Justine maintains at least her inner purity and does not waver from her commitment to good. As she is ending her story, she and Madame de Lorsange realize that they are the sisters Juliette and Justine, and after a tearful reunion there is the promise of a happy ending, since Juliette takes her sister into her home and gives her the much-needed protection. However, in the midst of a raging thunderstorm Justine is struck by a bolt of lightning and is instantly killed. There is a "moral" ending since Juliette, finally repentant of her past life, enters a convent. Yet the overall message is that in this corrupt world vice prospers, while those who practice virtue must suffer. But *Justine* is also a novel of social criticism which lays bare the corruption and hypocrisy of society. The heroine's torturers are mostly from the aristocracy or the clergy, whose lifestyles are satirized. De Sade presents Justine's aggressors as perverted sexual addicts, which enables him to claim that this is a cautionary tale—although his perversity in describing the often monstrous sexual practices of the characters might also merely have been a ploy to placate the censors.

De Sade's biography suggests that much of what he describes in his work comes from personal experience. From an old, noble family, de Sade (who was born in Paris) married into money, but because of his scandalous conduct, which included attacks on prostitutes, his wife's family had him arrested and imprisoned several times. He spent twelve years in prison, first in the Château de Vincennes, then the Bastille, but was transferred to the insane asylum at Charenton just ten days before the storming of the Bastille. While in the Bastille, he wrote *The Hundred and Twenty Days of Sodom* (*Les 120 Journées de Sodome*), a work not published until 1904. He was released by the revolutionary government in 1790. The same year his wife took advantage of new legislation that permitted her to divorce him. He was incarcerated again because he was erroneously accused of conspiracy, barely escaping the guillotine before being released. When *Justine* was published anonymously in 1791, there was a public outcry and de Sade repeatedly denied having authored it. In 1795 he wrote *Philosophy in the Boudoir* (*La Philosophie dans le boudoir*), and in 1797 an expanded version of *Justine* appeared, published together with *Juliette* and titled *The New Justine or the Misfortunes of Virtue, Followed by the Story of Juliette Her Sister.* In 1801, Napoleon Bonaparte declared that *Justine* was an abominable book, and de Sade was rearrested and incarcerated before being returned to the asylum at Charenton, where he died in 1814. Although largely reviled during much of the nineteenth and early twentieth centuries, de Sade has since been rehabilitated, and despite the strong pornographic aspect of his work he has found champions both among male and female critics (the latter often seeing a moral dimension in his writings). Although not for the faint of heart or the weak of stomach, *Justine* introduces a writer who, love him or hate him, is impossible to ignore.

THE NUN

La Religieuse (1796)

◆

Denis Diderot (1713–1784)

To be a writer in France in the 1700s often meant to court danger. This was particularly true for authors who criticized the king, the state, or the church. Some French authors had their works published in foreign countries; others published in literary journals where it was less likely that they would be noticed by the authorities. Among these journals, perhaps the most important was *Literary Correspondence* (*Correspondance littéraire*), which commented on cultural events in Paris and included some original works. This particular magazine was an outlet for some of Diderot's most important writings, and it was here that an early version of *The Nun* first appeared in 1760. The first stand-alone publication of the work did not appear until twelve years after Diderot's death, due to the severity of French censorship at the time. But even as recently as 1966, during the Swinging Sixties, an elegant film adaptation of the novel by French director Jacques Rivette was banned by the French government. There followed a series of protests and a debate in the National Assembly that finally resulted in the lifting of the ban—under one condition: the title had to be changed from *The Nun* to *Suzanne Simonin, Diderot's Nun* (*Suzanne Simonin, la religieuse de Diderot*).

What was so scandalous about this novel that even a modern film adaptation would provoke such an uproar? First, it presented a criticism of convents and the fact that wealthy families often consigned second, third, and fourth children to these institutions in order to preserve intact the inheritance of the oldest. Second, it suggested that human freedom, even in indigence, was far preferable to the cloistered life, even if the latter often involved a material existence that could be comfortable, sometimes almost luxurious. Third, although the protagonist of the novel never actually loses her faith, the work criticized the behavior of some nuns in certain monasteries and could thereby be construed as a criticism of the church and of religion in general.

This controversial novel actually had its origins in a series of letters Diderot and his friends wrote to the socially conscious marquis de Croismare. The marquis belonged to their circle, and with these fictional letters they wanted to lure him back to Paris from his provincial estate. The letters were supposedly from a nun, Suzanne Simonin, who had fled her convent and was seeking a protector. The subsequent novel is in the form of Suzanne's memoirs, addressed to the marquis so that he might know the background of the person who had asked for his help. Diderot's fictional Suzanne is forced by her parents to enter a convent because, being the fruit of her mother's extramarital affair, she is illegitimate and has no right to the family inheritance. Her two sisters, less attractive and less intelligent than she, are married off. Suzanne attempts a public protest when she is to take her vows, and she is delivered back to her parents, only to be confined to her room—she has effectively exchanged one prison for another. She allows herself to be sent to another convent and experiences a series of harrowing events, including physical abuse, before being transferred to yet another institution where she is at the mercy of a somewhat insane lesbian mother superior. She manages to escape by climbing over the convent wall, but finds herself alone and penniless in Paris.

Diderot was one of the most prolific of the *philosophes*, whose works helped prepare the French Revolution. The son of a knife-maker in Langres, he was originally destined for the priesthood but began to lead a very bohemian life after going to Paris to continue his studies. There he wrote numerous dramas, philosophical works, novels, and short stories, including *Jacques the Fatalist* and *Rameau's Nephew* (both published posthumously), *The Indiscreet Jewels* (*Les Bijoux indiscrets*, 1748), and *The Illegitimate Son* (*Entretiens sur le Fils naturel*, 1757). However, he was best known as one of the principal editors of the massive *Encyclopedia* (*Encyclopédie*), seventeen volumes of text and eleven volumes of plates that encapsulated the ideas of the French Enlightenment. Although even Louis XVI read the immensely popular *Encyclopedia*, it was not the objective compendium of contemporary knowledge that it appeared to be, for it contained polemical articles, carefully concealed by a system of cross-references, which questioned the current political, social, and religious system of France. Some of the *Encyclopedia's* boldest and most revolutionary articles were written by Diderot. In his later years, he was greatly admired by Catherine II of Russia, who purchased his library in order to provide him with money and allowed him full use of it until his death. He subsequently spent time at the tsarina's court in St. Petersburg before returning to Paris where he died of a stroke in 1784. The work of a prodigiously talented writer, Diderot's *Nun* still has the power to affect us and to stir our emotion—either pity for the sad fate of Suzanne, or outrage for the impious way in which the cloistered existence is portrayed.

René

(1802)

◆

François-René de Chateaubriand (1768-1848)

The term "Romantic," when applied to an artist or writer, conjures up a picture of a mysterious figure in a black cloak, standing on a cliff overlooking a turbulent ocean or a foggy valley, with a somber castle, preferably Gothic, in the background. As one of the patron saints of French romanticism, Chateaubriand (whose name nowadays evokes a carnivore's delight supposedly created for this author by his chef) is in many respects the epitome of this vision of the Romantic. An aristocrat raised in the Gothic castle of Combourg, close to the storm-lashed coastline of Brittany, Chateaubriand was subject to the *mal du siècle* (the illness of the age), the deep melancholy and disgust with life felt by the Romantics, who actually cultivated these feelings since they expressed their disaffection with the bourgeois spirit of their age. This soul-sickness had already become immensely popular thanks to Goethe's novel *Sorrows of Young Werther* (1774), in which the melancholic hero takes his own life.

Chateaubriand led a long and varied life, frequenting literary circles in Paris as a young man, undertaking a journey to America in 1791, and subsequently returning to France when Louis XVI was arrested. Sickened by the violence of the Revolution, he joined the counterrevolutionary army in Koblenz, was wounded at the siege of Thionville, convalesced on the island of Jersey, and joined the émigré community in England. The death of his mother and his sister in 1798 led him to rediscover Christianity, and he began work on a defense of the Christian religion titled *The Beauties [Genius] of Christianity* (*Le Génie du christianisme*). After returning to France in 1800 he completed this work in 1802, incorporating in its structure two short novels, *Atala* (1801) and *René*. The two works were published in a separate volume in 1805. There followed a long period of intense political activity during which Chateaubriand continued to write historical, political, and literary works, including *The Life of Rancé* (*La Vie de Rancé*, 1844) and his autobiography, *Memoirs from beyond the Tomb* (*Mémoires d'outre-tombe*, published posthumously 1849-50). He died in Paris.

René is a slight work of some fifty pages, consisting largely of the protagonist's "confession" recounted to his two mentors in America, the blind American Indian Chactas and the French missionary Father Souël. René recounts his melancholy childhood, his close relationship with his sister Amélie, his travels to Greece and Rome, and his constant quest for solitude usually sought in the contemplation of nature. Like Young Werther, he is tempted to put an end to his life, but is dissuaded by his sister who comes to stay with him. As the weeks pass, he notices that she is becoming more and more ill at ease in his company. She proclaims her desire to enter a convent, and René, standing over her as she lies on a marble slab during the induction ceremony, overhears her confess the reason for her decision: she wishes to atone for the secret, incestuous love she has begun to feel for him. René, overcome with emotion, faints at this revelation and has to be carried out of the church. Tempted again by suicide, he decides instead to travel to America, where he receives a letter informing him that Amélie has died while ministering to the victims of a highly contagious disease. When Chactas offers René his sympathy, both are sharply rebuked by Father Souël who criticizes René for having believed that man is sufficient unto himself and for having neglected his relationship with God and with other people. René, in spite of his attempts to follow the priest's advice, fails to find the happiness he is seeking. The narrator, who had briefly introduced René's confession, closes the novel by reporting the deaths of René and his two mentors during a battle between the French and the Natchez tribe.

Although this somber tale went almost unnoticed when it first appeared, it later enjoyed a status equivalent to that of Goethe's earlier work. Chateaubriand's florid style was well-suited to describe René's self-indulgent sadness: "My complete solitude and the spectacle of nature soon plunged me into a state of mind that defies description." This state—Romantic melancholy—is seen by some critics as the forerunner of our modern angst. Indeed, modern-day Goths are in many respects the spiritual descendants of René. It is ironic that a work written to illustrate the deleterious effects of the passions on the human soul should be interpreted in a way quite contrary to the intention of the author. In fact, Chateaubriand later disavowed this unruly offspring: "If *René* did not already exist, I would not write it; if I could destroy it, I would: it has infected the minds of many young people, something I would never have predicted because it was written to cure this infection." However, the author's disclaimer did nothing to mitigate the damage, and *René* retains its power to this day.

ADOLPHE

(1816)

◆

Benjamin Constant (1767–1830)

Breaking up is hard to do! Such is the basic theme of *Adolphe*, a short novel that lucidly and somewhat cynically analyzes the many pitfalls of a love affair to which only one member of the couple is truly committed. Its author, Benjamin Constant, was certainly an expert on the subject, having been involved in numerous sexual relationships, including a particularly famous one with Madame de Staël, a major writer of the Romantic period who, like Constant, was a Swiss national. Born in Lausanne, Constant was raised by his father, his mother having died sixteen days after his birth. His father, a colonel in the Swiss army, entrusted his son's education to a series of private tutors in various European countries. After beginning university studies in Germany, the young Constant transferred to the University of Edinburgh where he discovered a taste for intellectual pursuits but also fell under the spell of gambling. He had his first love affair in Paris in 1785, and in 1789 he contracted his first marriage, which lasted only until he discovered his wife's infidelity three years later. His liaison with Madame de Staël began in 1794. He became very engaged in postrevolutionary politics and also wrote the very successful tragedy *Wallstein* (1807). His passion for Madame de Staël was beginning to cool, and their relationship became ever stormier until it came to an end in 1811, since Constant was simultaneously carrying on affairs with several other women. In 1816 he put the final touches to *Adolphe*. While continuing to write, he pursued a political career and was elected several times to the French parliament before his death.

Adolphe, the eponymous hero of Constant's novel, tells his story in the first person. Like Constant, Adolphe is brought up by his father, who treats him with indulgence but without great affection (since his mother is never mentioned, we assume that she must have died when Adolphe was very young). This paternal indulgence also extends to dalliances with women: "Engaging in amorous affairs does so little harm to them, and gives so much pleasure to us," he tells his son, which is quite ironic since Adolphe's subsequent affair will prove the contrary in both cases. It is when Adolphe notices how much joy a love affair brings to one of his friends that he decides to seek out a mistress, setting his sights on an older woman, Ellénore, the paramour of a family friend. Ellénore had demonstrated her devotion to her lover over the previous ten years, having had two children by him, and she had managed to be accepted into the aristocratic society of which he was a part. "Ellénore seemed to be someone who was worthy of my attentions," writes Adolphe with supreme egotism. However, because his natural timidity prevents him from making direct overtures to her, he decides to write to her. The passionate terms of his letters don't really reflect his true feelings, but he is so convinced by the power of his own rhetoric that he believes he is in fact falling in love. "The combats I had for so long waged against the defects of my character, my impatience at not having been victorious in these struggles, my uncertainty as to the outcome of my attempt to woo Ellénore, gave to my letter an air of agitation resembling that of love. Carried away by my style, I began to feel, as I finished the letter, something of the passion I had sought to express in the strongest possible terms." Ellénore at first refuses his advances but finally gives herself wholeheartedly to him, abandoning her lover and children, and in so doing sacrifices the good name and status that she had worked so hard to acquire. Adolphe is dismayed by her sacrifices, for he realizes that he doesn't really love her, his conquest having been motivated more by his own vanity than by love. The rest of the novel is given to the account of his largely unsuccessful and half-hearted efforts to disentangle himself from the liaison until, in the end, an event occurs which brings about Ellénore's death. Although the main narrative by Adolphe stops here, it is framed by two letters, the first telling how the story came to be published and providing the reader with information about the aimless and melancholy life Adolphe leads following Ellénore's death. The second letter confirms the veracity of the events recounted, and the publisher reveals that he knew Adolphe, whose character was the cause of his downfall and that of others. A typical narrative strategy of the eighteenth and early nineteenth centuries, these letters are a literary ploy whose goal it is to vouch for the authenticity of the tale and to provide a moral dimension, since we realize that Adolphe's repeated attempts to justify the actions of his youth are hollow and that Ellénore had become an excuse for his own failure to realize his ambitions. *Adolphe* is a penetrating psychological analysis of the dangerous mixture of hypocrisy and love as well as a typical portrayal of the egotistical romantic hero. Constant's contemporary Alfred de Musset wrote a play in which a woman dies because of a young man's fecklessness. The play's title, *Don't Trifle with Love* (see page 89), could serve as a fitting subtitle for *Adolphe*.

OURIKA

(1824)

◆

Claire de Kersaint, Duchesse de Duras (1777-1828)

Like many European countries, France was deeply involved in the slave trade. The Black Code (*Le Code noir*), the purpose of which was to regulate the conduct and punishment of slaves and to restrict interracial sexual relationships, was instituted in 1685 and was in force until the first official abolition of slavery during the French Revolution (1794). Slavery was reinstated by Napoleon in 1802, and although France abolished the slave trade once again in 1815, it continued unofficially on a smaller scale until the Decree for the Abolition of Slavery in 1848. Although black characters had appeared in French literature before *Ourika*, it is in this short novel that, for the first time, a black African is the central character and the principal narrator.

Claire de Kersaint was a member of the French aristocracy; her wealthy mother had grown up on Martinique. Born in Brest in 1777, Claire and her mother fled revolutionary France when her father was guillotined in 1793. After journeying to the United States, Martinique, and Switzerland, Claire settled in London in the French émigré community. It was here that she became friends with Chateaubriand and met the duc de Duras, whom she married in 1797. The duke and his wife returned to France in 1808 to live in the fairy-tale castle of Ussé in the Loire Valley. After the fall of Napoleon, the couple returned to Paris where the duchesse de Duras established one of its most important literary salons. Fascinated by the true story of a Senegalese girl who had been adopted and raised by an aristocratic family in Paris, she was encouraged by her literary friends to write about it. She used this story as the basis for *Ourika* and first published it privately in 1823, without using her name (which was often the case for aristocratic women writers). However, such was de Duras's reputation and status that everyone knew who had written *Ourika*, and it became a bestseller. Her novel *Edouard* was published in 1825, also without her name appearing on the book. De Duras had composed a first novel, *Oliver or the Secret* (*Olivier ou le secret*), in 1822, but as its subject was male sexual impotence, she judged it too controversial to be published during her lifetime and it did not appear until 1971, almost a century and a half after her death in 1828 in Nice.

The opening paragraphs of *Ourika*, recounted in the first person by a young doctor, tell how he was called to visit a sick nun in a Paris convent. He is surprised to discover that his patient is a black woman of refined manners and speech (this is early nineteenth-century France, which doesn't excuse but explains the doctor's racist reaction). She is suffering from an unknown malady, although she proclaims herself to be happy in her religious retreat, a refuge from the troubles of her former life. The doctor's diagnosis is that her illness is related to her prior chagrin, and he proposes that she recount her past to him in the hope that this will cure her. After much persuasion the nun, Ourika, reluctantly agrees, and her narration forms the principal part of the novel. She recounts how, at the age of two as she was being sold into slavery, she was rescued and brought to France by the governor of Senegal. He entrusts her to an aunt who will raise her in her own aristocratic household. She grows up with her new adoptive mother's grandson, Charles, who becomes like a brother to her. Her life is blissfully happy until, at age fifteen, she overhears one of her adoptive mother's friends expressing despair over her future: it will be impossible to marry her off except to someone beneath her station who would accept money to marry an African woman. Ourika's life is thrown into even deeper turmoil when, sometime later, the same woman accuses her of being in love with Charles, who is now married. Aghast at this accusation and realizing that her acceptance into this family as an apparent equal has been a sham, Ourika enters a convent. Her final reported words in the novel are meant for Charles: "Let me go to the only place where I am allowed to think continually about you." The doctor closes the novel with a few lines that report the failure of his "treatment"—Ourika has died soon after recounting her story.

The psychological portrait of a black woman in a racist society is finely drawn by de Duras in this story. What makes it all the more poignant is that the racism is of the "benevolent" paternalistic kind that, although well intentioned, gives no thought to the outcome of the initial "good deed." Adopting Ourika may have saved her from slavery, but she is now condemned to a kind of social limbo, unable to return to her own culture but also excluded from the normal role of a French aristocratic woman. *Ourika* is a cautionary tale that not only paints a moving portrait of an African woman living in a society from which she finds herself profoundly alienated, but also warns of the dangers of paternalistic attitudes in the realm of racial relations.

The Physiology of Taste

La Physiologie du goût (1825)

◆

Anthelme Brillat-Savarin (1755-1826)

No nation takes food more seriously than France, with its celebrity chefs, restaurant guides, and multicourse meals. The French reverence for gastronomy, already in evidence in the 1600s when the chef François Vatel committed suicide because of the late arrival of an order of fresh fish for the king, has not diminished today. Vatel's act of desperation has been repeated on several occasions by modern-day French chefs who were devastated at the thought of losing a coveted star in a prominent restaurant guide.

However, although food played an important role in French culture before the nineteenth century, the refined pleasures of the table were usually reserved for the upper echelons of society. It was in 1800 that the word *gastronomie* entered the French language and that the concept it defined took on a more democratic character. This change was due, above all, to the invention of a new kind of eating establishment, the restaurant, and to the fact that it was now considered acceptable and even desirable to go out to eat. There had always been eating-houses for those away from home, but until this period these establishments were frequented out of necessity rather than by choice.

The first gourmet chef of the modern era was Marc-Antoine Carême (1784–1833), employed by Napoleon I, among others. However, the first nonprofessional gourmet, the first real "foodie," was Anthelme Brillat-Savarin, whose *Physiology of Taste* made gastronomy if not quite a science then certainly an art form. Born in Belley, east of Lyon, he studied law and became deeply involved in the French Revolution as an elected deputy of the Third Estate in the Estates General in 1789. His birth name was Brillat, but a rich aunt promised him her fortune if he would take her name as well. Forced to leave France during the Terror, he found refuge first in Switzerland, then Holland, before a three-year sojourn in the United States. After his return to France in 1796, he was named a judge on the Appeals Court (*Cour de Cassation*), a post he held from 1800 until his death in February 1826, just a few months after his famous work was published.

The Physiology of Taste, which despite its title is not a medical treatise, does have some scientific pretensions, since it begins by analyzing our enjoyment of food. Brillat-Savarin finds the source of that enjoyment in the six senses—six, since he has added the sense of physical love, which he terms the genesaic (reproductive) sense. He also discusses the role of food in our enjoyment of life. The book's chapters, called *Meditations*, tip the reader off to the seriousness of the subject, and yet the general tone of the work is light, often amusing, whimsical, and idiosyncratic. We even encounter a few recipes, although the most interesting parts for today's reader will probably be Brillat-Savarin's numerous anecdotes and aphorisms: "Tell me what you eat and I will tell you who you are" (one of his most famous sayings); "Animals devour, mankind eats, but only the intelligent human being knows how to eat"; "The discovery of a new dish does more for the human race than the discovery of a new star." He defines gastronomy as "the science of all aspects of the human life which have to do with food" and asserts that "its goal is to ensure the preservation of the human race by providing it with the best possible food"—a laudable aim indeed. He also includes discussions of the properties and effects of various foods on the human body and psyche. The entry on truffles is typical: "Just the mention of the word 'truffle' is sufficient to awaken memories of love and good food in the fair sex and memories of good food and love in those of the male persuasion." However, he concludes that "the truffle is not an active aphrodisiac, but it can, under certain circumstances, make women more tender and men more affectionate." More general subjects are then examined, such as obesity and thinness—the latter being a disaster for women because "[their] beauty depends on [. . .] rounded contours," a view of female beauty typical of the nineteenth century. *The Physiology of Taste*, which also contains a philosophical history of cooking, concludes with an ode to Gastronomy, hailed as a new goddess, to whose worship we should all devote ourselves with the utmost enthusiasm.

This charming and at times irreverent book, although clearly of another era in its manner and some of its conclusions, gives us many valuable insights into the beginnings of the international preoccupation with good food and fine dining. However, its author takes great pains to distinguish between gastronomy and gluttony: "*Gourmandise* [by which he means 'gastronomy'] is the enemy of excess; anyone who gets indigestion from overeating, or drunk from overimbibing, can no longer claim to be a gourmet." Excellent advice for the countless food lovers among us.

THE RED AND THE BLACK

Le Rouge et le noir (1830)

◆

Stendhal (Henri Beyle) (1783–1842)

T*he Red and the Black*, one of the masterpieces of world literature, displays an ironic humor in its compelling description of French society under the Restoration of the French monarchy. During the preceding era, Napoleon had founded an aristocracy based on merit, and talented, ambitious men could succeed whether they were of noble birth or not. But with the reestablishment of the monarchy in 1815, commoners found themselves with few options for social advancement. Stendhal writes about his hero, Julien Sorel, who is of humble birth and born too late to take advantage of the opportunities the Napoleonic period would have given him: "Red signifies that, had he been born earlier, he would have been a soldier, but at the time he lived, his only option was to become a priest."

The Red and the Black is a coming-of-age novel in which we follow the dramatic social ascent of a young provincial who prefers reading books to working in his father's sawmill. The highly intelligent Julien Sorel, possessed of a prodigious memory, learns Latin under the tutelage of the village priest and is able to recite large portions of the Latin Bible by heart. His father despises his son's intellectual pursuits but allows him to accept a position as tutor of the two sons of the mayor of Verrières, Monsieur de Rênal. Although destined for the priesthood, Julien, a great admirer of Napoleon, is a passionate young man who—like a general planning a military campaign—decides to seduce his employer's attractive wife. His successful conquest, with all its twists and turns, is described in part 1 of this two-part novel, and it is here that the reader comes to know the simultaneously arrogant and timid Julien. After Madame de Rênal has finally succumbed to his carefully orchestrated seduction, he asks himself, "Did I forget to do anything that I owed it to myself to do? Did I play my role well?" Part 1 ends in the seminary in Besançon, where Julien has been sent after suspicions about his relationship with Madame de Rênal have forced him to leave the Rênal household. Having won the respect of one of the most fearsome priests at the seminary, l'abbé Pirard, Julien obtains with Pirard's support the position of secretary in an aristocratic Parisian household. Part 2 thus takes place at the home of the marquis de la Mole, who entrusts Julien with various missions on behalf of a cabal whose goal is to restore the privileges of the aristocracy and the church that had been abolished by the French Revolution. The marquis happens to have a romantic young daughter, Mathilde, who is fascinated by the young priest who is so different from the rather dull aristocratic suitors she had known until his arrival in the household. Stendhal's irony is evident in the passage describing the lovers' first meeting in Mathilde's bedroom, where she has challenged the priest to enter through her window at 1 a.m. Fearing a trap, Julien nevertheless obeys her orders but is surprised by the reception he gets. "She had decided that if he dared to come to her room with the help of the gardener's ladder, she would give herself to him. But never has anyone said such tender things in an icier and more polite tone [. . .] It was enough to make you hate love. What a lesson in morality for an imprudent young woman! Is it worth losing your entire future for such a moment?" The narrator's question is apt. When Mathilde becomes pregnant, the future of both young people becomes increasingly problematical in a society where crossing social lines is punished as a capital offense and where "losing one's head" is more than a metaphorical description of what happens when you fall in love. In an ironic final epigraph, Stendhal dedicates his novel "To the happy few."

Henri Beyle, who later took the name Stendhal, was born in Grenoble, a town he detested. His mother died when he was young and his relationship with his father was strained. Escaping Grenoble when he was accepted into the prestigious École Polytechnique in Paris, he went on to a military career in the Napoleonic armies. After Napoleon's defeat, Stendhal moved to Milan and became enamored of Italy. Here he remained until 1821, penning essays on composers, painters, and travel. Back in Paris, he began work on *Armance* (1827) and subsequently on *The Red and the Black*. After the political upheaval of 1830, when the last Bourbon king was overthrown, Stendhal was appointed French consul at Civitavecchia, near Rome, where he remained until shortly before his death from a stroke in 1842. His writing career had continued and his *Charterhouse of Parma* (*La Chartreuse de Parme*, 1839), set in Italy, and the unfinished novels *Lucien Leuwen* (1834–36) and *Lamiel* (1842), together with his autobiographical *Life of Henry Brulard* (*Vie de Henry Brulard*, published posthumously in 1890), have ensured him a prominent place in the literary canon. His biting wit still delights today's readers, and his ironic social commentary on the French Restoration period still strikes a chord in the twenty-first century.

THE HUNCHBACK OF NOTRE-DAME

Notre-Dame de Paris (1831)

◆

Victor Hugo (1802–1885)

More than just a great read, this novel is responsible for saving one of Paris's best-loved monuments, Notre-Dame Cathedral. Notre-Dame had fallen into a state of serious neglect after the Revolution, and in the first part of the nineteenth century the French found the Gothic style to be ugly. Hugo changed all that by highlighting the cathedral in his novel—indeed, in many ways Notre-Dame is the novel's principal character, as is evident in the original French title—and by giving a great deal of architectural information that transformed the taste of the day and eventually led to the restoration of the cathedral by the celebrated if controversial architect Viollet-le-Duc.

Like several other great nineteenth-century French novels, *The Hunchback of Notre-Dame* is known above all through its various movie adaptations. From the 1923 film starring the great Lon Chaney as Quasimodo (also played in later films by Charles Laughton and Anthony Quinn) to the animated Disney version of 1996, there has been no dearth of directors eager to tackle this novel. However, readers will come to see that no film adaptation can convey the full scope of a 600-page book, particularly one as rich as Hugo's opus. Set very precisely in the year 1482, during the reign of Louis XI of France and at the tail end of the medieval period, *The Hunchback of Notre-Dame* features a varied cast of characters whose roles are, somewhat surprisingly, not stable—they can change from hero to villain and vice versa. This makes them more complex, more realistic, and more human. The two central characters, aside from the cathedral itself, are Quasimodo, the hideously ugly bell ringer who lives in the tower of the cathedral, and the ethereally beautiful Esmeralda. Quasimodo, who at first seems to belong to the dark side, reveals inner qualities of heroism and virtue, belied by his exterior ugliness, and the love that he feels for Esmeralda is pure and noble. He was abandoned as a baby in the cathedral by a mother ashamed and alarmed at her son's physique, and was raised by the learned archdeacon Claude Frollo, who shows considerable compassion by adopting the unlovely orphan. The relationship between Quasimodo and the cathedral in which he was brought up is stressed by

Hugo: "Over time there had formed some indefinable link between the bell ringer and the cathedral [. . .] Notre-Dame had been for his development successively egg, nest, house, homeland, and universe." The novel's heroine, Esmeralda, who was raised by Gypsies, attracts men and makes women jealous because of her great beauty, but she has retained a pure heart. She becomes the sexual obsession of Claude Frollo, who pursues her relentlessly and attempts to rape her. She also wins the love of Quasimodo who protects her, rebelling against his guardian when Frollo attacks Esmerelda. Because of a misunderstanding she is accused of murder and sentenced to death. The dramatic ending contains no small share of surprises for the reader.

The author of this sad tale was the greatest representative of the Romantic movement in France. A larger-than-life character, Hugo tried his hand successfully at every literary genre and is known for his poetry, his plays (one of which, *Hernani*, revolutionized French theater in 1830), and, of course, his novels. Born in Besançon, he was the son of a general in Napoleon's army. With the preface to his play *Cromwell* (1827) he became the spokesman for the Romantic movement in the theater, while the preface to his collection of lyric poetry, the *Orientales* (1829), contained an ardent defense of the principle of artistic freedom. Hugo's novels, *Les Misérables* (1862; nowadays one of the most popular musicals ever), *The Toilers of the Sea* (*Les Travailleurs de la mer*, 1866), *The Man Who Laughs* (*L'Homme qui rit*, 1869), and *Ninety-Three* (*Quatrevingt-treize*, 1874) paint a sympathetic portrait of the lower classes, demonstrating their author's humanitarian concerns and interest in the political arena. In 1848 he supported the political aspirations of Louis-Napoleon, but later became a fierce opponent and went into voluntary exile on the Channel Islands. Although married, Hugo had a number of affairs, including one with the actress Juliette Drouet, who was both his lover and personal secretary for some eighteen years. The great tragedies of his life, however, involved his daughters: Léopoldine, who was accidentally drowned in 1843 (she inspired some of his most tender poetry), and Adèle, whom he had to commit to an insane asylum in 1872 (she became the subject of a touching film, *Adèle H.*, in 1975). Hugo finally left the Channel Islands for Paris where he resumed his political career, but with markedly less success than before. Continuing to write and to travel extensively, he succumbed to congestion of the lungs in Paris in 1885, and received a state funeral before his burial in the Panthéon. The grand old man was dead but his legacy lives on, and, in a way, the Cathedral of Notre-Dame de Paris is his true monument, thanks to this great novel.

DON'T TRIFLE WITH LOVE

On ne badine pas avec l'amour (1834)

♦

Alfred de Musset (1810–1857)

L ove and death are old partners in literature, but Musset gives this
relationship a new twist in this Romantic drama. Unlike classical French plays in which the mixing of genres was usually avoided,
Romantic theater in France threw out the old rules. Playwrights of the
period, influenced by their admiration for dramatists like Shakespeare
who had not hesitated to include comic scenes in some of the tragedies
(like the gravediggers in *Hamlet*), no longer respected the distinctions
traditionally observed in French classical drama. *Don't Trifle with Love* is
a play that, as its name suggests, illustrates in dramatic form the lesson
of a particular proverb. Musset wrote a number of such plays, including *You Can Never Tell* (*Il ne faut jurer de rien*, 1836) and *A Door Has
to Be Open or Shut* (*Il faut qu'une porte soit ouverte ou fermée*, 1845).
He had an unpromising debut as a playwright when his play *Venetian
Night* (*La Nuit vénitienne*) was booed on its first performance in 1830
at the Odéon Theater in Paris. This experience soured him on having
his plays performed, and for a time he chose to publish rather than stage
them. That changed in 1847 when his comedy *A Caprice* (*Un Caprice*)
was performed and well received, first in St. Petersburg and then at the
Comédie-Française in Paris. The spell had been broken, and Musset
was reconciled to the theater.

Don't Trifle with Love is a three-act play that begins on a comic
note as the chorus introduces the first of three buffoon-like characters,
Master Blazius. A cleric who is overly fond of the bottle, Blazius is the
tutor of the local baron's son Perdican, who is coming home after having completed his university studies. The baron's niece, Camille, is also
returning from being schooled in a convent, and she has a foolish governess, Dame Pluche, who vaunts her charge's purity and innocence.
The third buffoon, a glutton and a drunkard, is Father Bridaine, the
baron's chaplain. All three of these characters lend the first two acts
of the play a humorous and farcical tone. It had always been the baron's intention to marry his son to his niece, and he eagerly awaits their
meeting after a long separation. Perdican, a likeable and unpretentious
young man who wears his learning lightly, is happy to return to the

country home of his childhood and wants to renew the acquaintance of the peasants who live nearby and with whom he played as a child, among them the lovely Rosette. Camille, on the other hand, now quite priggish, greets Perdican very coolly. She has apparently been influenced by her companions in the convent, some of whom had retired there for life after suffering through unhappy love affairs. Soon the two young protagonists are engaging in verbal duels, she suggesting that he is a typical male who will never be able to remain faithful to one woman, he accusing her of being unrealistically idealistic and having her judgment warped by what she has heard in the convent. She announces her desire to return to the convent forever. He, in order to make her jealous but perhaps also partially because he is still nostalgic for the simple country life of his childhood, courts Rosette and even proposes marriage to her. In a final dramatic scene, Perdican and Camille admit their love for each other, and just when it seems that they will live happily ever after, they hear a cry from behind a curtain—and, for reasons that the reader will discover, their future happiness is shattered.

Alfred de Musset was one of the principal representatives of French romanticism. Although his Parisian family encouraged him to study either medicine or law, he informed them in 1828 that he intended to become a poet. The next ten years were a period of intense literary activity, devoted to composing poems like "The Secret Thoughts of Raphael" ("Les Secrètes pensées de Raphaël") and of course the play that turned him temporarily away from the theater, *Venetian Night*. He began a famous liaison with George Sand in 1833 and they left for Italy together, where Musset fell gravely ill. While he was being treated, George Sand had an affair with his doctor, and Musset, deeply affected by this betrayal, left for Paris as soon as he recovered from his illness. In 1834 he published the plays *Don't Trifle with Love* and *Lorenzaccio*. The year 1836 saw the publication of *The Confession of a Child of the Century* (*La Confession d'un enfant du siècle*), a semiautobiographical novel. Musset continued to write feverishly into 1838, producing more poems, such as "October Night" ("La Nuit d'octobre," 1838). In 1852 he was elected a member of the Académie française, and two years later he was named chief librarian of the ministry of education. He wrote his last comedy, *The Donkey and the Stream* (*L'Ane et le ruisseau*), in 1855 and died in Paris two years later. A prodigiously talented writer, he excelled in many different genres. *Don't Trifle with Love*, with its deft mix of lyricism, comedy, and tragedy and its loving evocation of the innocence of childhood and the beauty of the French countryside, remains one of his most popular plays.

OLD GORIOT

Le Père Goriot (1834-35)

◆

Honoré de Balzac (1799-1850)

Paris is a jungle, or at least that is what Balzac would have us believe in this novel dedicated to the naturalist Geoffroy Saint-Hilaire. In his fiction, Balzac classified and examined the various human types that in his view characterized the society of his day, and he did it with the zeal and eye for detail of a zoologist studying fauna in the wild. This project, which Balzac entitled *The Human Comedy* (*La Comédie humaine*), consists of over ninety novels and stories depicting more than two thousand different characters, many of whom figure in several of the works in the collection. Balzac was a monarchist, and his novels show great contempt for the capitalistic, bourgeois society that had arisen in France after the fall of Napoleon I.

Born in 1799 in Tours, Balzac led a frenetic existence. At the age of twenty he abandoned the study of law to become a writer, but initially without success. Although incurring heavy debts because of his failed business endeavors, he continued to write, and his breakthrough novel was *The Last Chouan* (*Le Dernier Chouan*) in 1829, retitled *The Chouans* (*Les Chouans*) when it was incorporated into *The Human Comedy* at a later date. There began a period of intense literary creation during which he composed the numerous works that became part of *The Human Comedy*, including *Eugénie Grandet* (1833), *Lily in the Valley* (*Le Lys dans la vallée*, 1836), and *Cousin Bette* (*La Cousine Bette*, 1846), to name just a few of the best known. Balzac had numerous love affairs and was fortunate to enjoy the patronage of a number of wealthy women. His most famous liaison was with a Polish aristocrat, Evelyne Hanska, an admirer who first made contact with him in 1832 and whom he finally married in 1850, just five months before his death in Paris.

The Paris of 1819, the year in which *Old Goriot* is set, is a highly stratified society. This is the period when the French monarchy was restored after the turmoil of the Revolution and the imperial ambitions of Napoleon Bonaparte, and while Restoration society is dominated by money, the social signifiers associated with the old aristocracy have not entirely disappeared. Eugene de Rastignac, a poor young student from the provinces, arrives in a Paris where the franc has become the new divinity. His aristocratic family, impoverished during the Revolution, has to make great sacrifices to give Eugene the opportunity to pursue his studies to become a lawyer. In this classic coming-of-age novel, Eugene at first applies himself to his courses, but quickly tires of living in the seedy Pension Vauquer. Watching luxurious carriages pass him as he makes his way on foot along the muddy streets of the capital, he is bitten by the desire for wealth and vows to climb the Parisian social ladder to enjoy the good life. Three characters give him advice on his journey. Two of them, fellow lodgers at the Pension Vauquer, are father figures. The sinister, calculating Vautrin (a master criminal, as it turns out), plays a Satanic role, tempting Eugene with a murderous scheme for acquiring instant wealth; the sad fate of Old Goriot, the over-indulgent father of two spoiled, rich society women, Anastasie and Delphine—who almost literally bleed their prosperous merchant father dry—nourishes Eugene's cynicism. The third character, a maternal figure whose worldview is ironically akin to that of Vautrin, is Eugene's blue-blood cousin Madame de Beauséant, queen of Parisian social life, who takes Eugene under her wing. From her and from Vautrin, Eugene learns that challenging Parisian society is tantamount to going to war and that in order to succeed one must divest oneself of all scruples and sentiment. Goriot, on the other hand, "adopts" Eugene when he learns that the latter has become Delphine's lover. Eugene soon comes to the bitter realization that both Delphine and her sister Anastasie care more about themselves than about their selfless father (although his indulgence of their every whim is partly responsible for their behavior). At the novel's end, when Old Goriot lies dying, neither daughter comes to his bedside, and it is Eugene who arranges and pays for Goriot's pauper's funeral. The final pages of the novel show a sadder but wiser Eugene who has completed his Parisian education. After Goriot is buried, the young man stands alone in the Père Lachaise cemetery, looking down at Paris: "Rastignac [. . .] took a few steps to the highest point of the cemetery and looked down at Paris spread out along the winding banks of the Seine where the city lights were just beginning to come on. His eyes enviously sought out the area between the column in the Place Vendôme and the dome of Les Invalides, the city's most elegant section of which he had tried to become a part. Casting down upon this humming beehive a look indicative of his desire to partake of its honey, he defiantly challenged the city: 'It's between the two of us now!'" And how does he begin this next phase of his campaign? He goes to have dinner with Delphine! Paris is indeed a jungle, and a cynical one at that.

DEMOCRACY IN AMERICA

De la démocratie en Amérique (1835/1840)

◆

Charles Alexis Clérel de Tocqueville (1805-1859)

A merican democracy and its exportation to other countries has been a much-discussed topic of late. However, as the book of Ecclesiastes puts it so well, "there is nothing new under the sun," and one of the most astute early analysts of the new form of democracy realized by the American Revolution was Alexis de Tocqueville, a French aristocrat who wrote a highly influential and prescient work on the subject in 1835.

But what led a French aristocrat with ties to the Bourbon monarchy to take such an interest in American democracy? Tocqueville's life provides an answer. After studying law in his hometown Paris, he was appointed to the junior and unpaid position of *juge auditeur* (auditor) at the law court of Versailles, where he met the magistrate Gustave de Beaumont, with whom he became close friends. In 1830, when the last Bourbon king, Charles X, was overthrown and replaced by the July Monarchy of Louis Philippe, all civil servants were required to take an oath of loyalty, which Tocqueville did with some reluctance. When his friend Beaumont became interested in reforming the French penal system, he and Tocqueville decided that this was a good opportunity to absent themselves from France in order to spend nine months in the United States, studying the American penal system. This "study abroad" experience provided Tocqueville with the basic material for his great treatise on American democracy.

Democracy in America has been described as one of the very first sociological studies, for Tocqueville maintains the detachment of a social scientist as he analyzes the American system. On the plus side he believes that democracy could create equilibrium between freedom and equality, and he sees in it a force in which individualism does not exclude a sense of community and a striving for the common good. He deftly analyzes the important role attributed to moneymaking in American society and the widely held belief that hard work and determination enable individuals to prosper and increase their fortunes. The relatively egalitarian nature of American society, he believes, is aided by the fact that the acquisition of land was comparatively easy in North America, and so the creation of a landed aristocracy as it existed in Europe was much less likely. But while Tocqueville admires many aspects of the American model, he also addresses issues of racism, particularly with respect to Native Americans and enslaved Africans. Although a committed abolitionist, he is pessimistic about the possibility of full assimilation of both of these populations into American society. Furthermore, Tocqueville fears that American-style democracy could produce a culture of mediocrity that rejects any person or group considered "elite." Another risk he identifies is that the importance attributed to monetary gain may result in an overly materialistic society, which could become subject to corruption and greed, both of which are damaging to the democratic process.

Tocqueville's masterwork consisted of two parts: the first appeared in 1835, the second in 1840. Thanks to a very favorable review in England by John Stuart Mill, part 1 of his book catapulted Tocqueville into the limelight, winning him the coveted *Légion d'honneur* (Legion of Honor) in 1837 and election to the Académie française in 1841. Tocqueville, in addition to his writing, pursued a political career on his return from America and occupied several important positions in the *département* of la Manche. He traveled to England, producing a *Memoir on Pauperism* (*Mémoire sur le paupérisme*, 1835), then undertook a journey to Algeria, after which he wrote a number of reports that supported Louis-Philippe's colonization project—although Tocqueville stated his preference for the English colonial model that separated the colonized from the colonizers to the French model of assimilation. When the July Monarchy fell in February 1848, he was elected member of the Constituent Assembly of 1848, and was among those to be entrusted with the task of drafting the Constitution of the Second Republic. In spite of his ideas on democracy and the importance of liberty, he did not take the side of the socialists and workers in the June 1848 uprising and supported General Cavaignac's crushing of this insurrection. He did, however, oppose Louis-Napoleon's coup d'état that terminated the short life of the Second Republic in 1851. He continued writing, publishing a book on the French Revolution, *The Old Regime and the French Revolution* (*L'Ancien Régime et la Révolution*), in 1856. Having contracted tuberculosis in 1850, he endured increasingly poor health until he was forced to move in with his brother in Cannes in 1858. He died the following year. While it is impossible to do justice to his great work in a brief overview, it is easy to see how important Tocqueville remains to this day, and how many relevant questions his book raises about the nature and future of American democracy.

THE COUNT OF MONTE CRISTO

Le Comte de Monte-Cristo *(1844)*

◆

Alexandre Dumas (1802–1870)

Dumas's exciting adventure stories are among the best-known and best-loved books of popular literature. Widely read in their day, such novels as *The Three Musketeers* (*Les Trois Mousquetaires,* 1844) and *The Count of Monte Cristo* are in modern times often known only secondhand, through one of the numerous movie or TV adaptations, or perhaps via an abridged version. None of these venues do justice to Dumas's work. In the case of *The Count of Monte Cristo*, with its 1,200 pages and its huge cast of characters, seeing a movie adaptation is a bit like reading a comic book version of a classic novel.

The relatively simple plot line is a sure-fire formula for success. When the novel opens the hero is poised for marriage, success, and happiness. Jealous rivals arrange for his arrest on trumped-up charges; the hero is imprisoned but miraculously escapes and finds great wealth before embarking on a campaign of justified revenge against his enemies. He finally succeeds in rendering a nineteenth-century version of vigilante justice. While there are many books with similar stories, *The Count of Monte Cristo* is several cuts above the rest. First, in purely material terms, this is exciting, edge-of-the-seat reading, with villains punished and the hero prevailing. It's a true page-turner, and the reader's pleasure and fascination are sustained chapter after chapter. Second, there is something quite archetypal about its plot line: Edmond Dantès, its hero, takes on almost mythical status, is a master of disguise, and in many ways the precursor of the modern superhero. Third, it is a coming-of-age novel about the young, naive nineteen-year-old protagonist we meet in the first chapter. Thanks to his imprisonment in the Château d'If, on a small island just off Marseille, Dantès meets another prisoner, Father Faria, a priest who is a prodigious scholar and intellect. Besides revealing to Dantès the location of a fabulous treasure hidden on the small island of Monte Cristo, Faria gives Dantès a broad education in such things as foreign languages, history, and economics, thereby teaching him to navigate the complicated world of French society. This in-depth instruction enables Dantès to pursue his revenge successfully by adopting all sorts of disguises, including the one that gives the novel its name. In addition to reinventing himself as a count, the novel's hero dons the disguises of a priest, an English banker, the philanthropist Lord Wilmore, and Sinbad the Sailor. However, Dantès, whose name evokes both the author and principal character of the *Divine Comedy*, is far from a flat character, a mere action hero. When he involuntarily causes harm to innocent people in the course of his machinations, his confidence fails him and he is filled with self-loathing. After many trials and tribulations he does eventually find happiness with Haydée, a slave girl whom he had purchased and freed, and who falls deeply in love with him, thus bringing his exciting and varied adventures to a very satisfactory happy end.

Born in a small town in Picardy, Alexandre Dumas is sometimes known as Alexandre Dumas père (Senior), to distinguish him from his son Alexandre Dumas fils who was also a noted author. Dumas's family background is interesting. He was of mixed race because his grandfather, having settled in Saint-Domingue, had married (or perhaps not—the sources are divided on this issue) Marie-Cesette, one of the household's slave women (not unlike what transpires in *The Count of Monte Cristo*). His father, a famous general in the imperial armies of Napoleon, passed down his political proclivities: Dumas had Bonapartist and then republican sympathies. Amazingly productive, Dumas began his literary career as a playwright and then turned to historic adventure novels. Writing in collaboration with Auguste Maquet, part research assistant, part ghostwriter, Dumas published his novels first in serialized form in newspapers, a common practice at the time. This was the case for *The Count of Monte Cristo,* which actually takes place in Dumas's own century, unlike his historical novels. In 1847 he purchased an estate, Port-Marly, not far from Paris, where he had built a replica of a Renaissance castle. Unfortunately, two years later, being deeply in debt, he was obliged to sell what he called his "earthly paradise." Faithful to his literary origins as a playwright, he transformed many of his novels into plays, and they were very well received. In 1860 he joined the Italian patriot Garibaldi's victorious campaign in Sicily and Naples. Since the rulers of Naples were of Bourbon origin and since the Bourbon monarchy in France had been instrumental in having Dumas's father poisoned, their overthrow was deeply satisfying to Dumas. The Catholic church placed Dumas's works on the Index of Prohibited Books in 1863, a condemnation which did nothing to curb his popularity. He continued writing and traveling until his death in 1870, leaving a legacy of unforgettable and perennially popular characters.

CARMEN

(1845)

◆

Prosper Mérimée (1803-1870)

O ne of the most famous femmes fatales of all times is Carmen, the lead in Bizet's ever-popular opera. How many opera buffs know that this character, who also inspired the 1940s Broadway musical and subsequent movie *Carmen Jones*, in fact originated in a novella written by Prosper Mérimée? His telling of Carmen's story differs considerably from the later versions most of us know. An archaeologist and inspector of historic monuments, Mérimée was fascinated by the unusual and the exotic, and by the differences between mainstream European society and the culture of its ethnic minorities. Thus Mérimée's narrative is as much a warning about the power of passion and the age-old connection between love and death as it is a sociological study of Gypsy culture.

Born in Paris, Mérimée, the son of a well-known painter, received a cultured middle-class education, but after trying his hand at law he found the study of foreign languages more to his liking. His close friend Stendhal, whom he met in 1822, encouraged him to pursue a literary career. Mérimée first became known with two literary hoaxes, *The Theater of Clara Gazul* (*Le Théâtre de Clara Gazul*, 1825), supposedly a translation of the work of a Spanish actress, and *La Guzla* (1827), a collection of ballads about murder and vampirism, supposedly translated from Illyrian. He then turned to historical fiction, inspired by the current vogue for Walter Scott, but he found his real strength in the novella and short story, genres that could easily be accommodated in the pages of the rapidly expanding periodical press. Many of his stories first saw the light of day in *La Revue de Paris* and *La Revue des deux mondes*. Aside from *Carmen*, his best-known stories are the Corsican revenge tale *Mateo Falcone* (1829), *Tamango* (1829) about a revolt on a slave ship, *The Venus of Ille* (*La Vénus d'Ille*, 1837) that features an apparently murderous statue, and *Colomba* (1840), another Corsican revenge drama. Unlike so many other nineteenth-century writers, Mérimée was not (as far as we know) involved in any romantic liaisons. He did entertain a lifelong correspondence with a young woman, Jenny Dacquin, and enjoyed an enduring friendship with a Spanish noblewoman, the countess of Montijo, who was the mother of the future wife of Napoleon III, the empress Eugénie. Thanks to the latter connection, he was able to frequent the royal court and was even named senator, although he was not overly fond of Napoleon III. He died just a few weeks after the defeat of the French army at Sedan during the Franco-Prussian War.

The narrator of *Carmen*, an archaeologist like Mérimée himself, relates how, on an expedition in Spain, he halts at a mountain spring, where he encounters another traveler. He is surprised to see the stranger carrying a shotgun and notices that one of his own guides is looking fearfully at the man. The archaeologist befriends the stranger, learning that he is a famous bandit with a price on his head, Don José Navarro. When they stop together at an inn, the guide slips away to denounce the bandit in the hope of collecting a reward. The archaeologist warns Don José, who escapes before the arrival of the police. The archaeologist then continues to Cordoba, where he has a chance meeting with a beautiful woman, Carmencita. "One evening, after the sun had set, I was smoking a cigar, leaning on the railing overlooking the river. A woman came up the stairs that led down to the river and sat beside me. In her hair she wore a bouquet of jasmine, the petals of which perfumed the evening in a tantalizing way [. . .] I immediately threw away my cigar [. . .] but she hastened to inform me that she liked the smell of tobacco and indeed smoked cigarettes." Intrigued by her forwardness, her air of mystery, and her beauty, he accompanies her home where she promises to tell his fortune. As she does so, another man bursts into the room. To the archaeologist's astonishment it is none other than Don José. The latter ushers him outside and gives him directions back to his inn. Stopping at Cordoba on his return journey several months later, the archaeologist discovers that Don José is in prison, awaiting execution for murder. The archaeologist visits him, finally persuading him to tell his story. Don José relates how he had fallen victim to Carmen's charm when he was still serving in the army, and how, under the influence of this woman whose name, not coincidentally, means both "song" and "charm," he had turned to a life of crime that led to his current sentence. Mérimée's tale-within-a-tale does not end here. Rather, the author concludes with a short treatise on Gypsies (or Roma), their culture, and the difficulties of pursuing research into their origins and culture. This final section reveals Mérimée as not merely a storyteller recounting a tale of tragic love but also as an anthropologist, giving us a lesson on the character and mores of the enigmatic Gypsies. This erudite and rather impersonal ending lends an ironic distance to the narrative and serves as a foil to the extreme emotions displayed by the principal characters.

THE DEVIL'S POOL

La Mare au diable (1846)

◆

George Sand (Amantine-Aurore-Lucile Dupin)

(1804–1876)

Despite its rather dire title, *The Devil's Pool* is a charming love story with a happy ending. In this simple, pastoral representation of peasant life in the Berry region of France, George Sand wrote about what she knew, for she had spent her childhood there. Moreover, from 1839 until her death in 1876, her principal residence was in the town of Nohant in the Berry. *The Devil's Pool*, a peaceful and indeed wholesome novella, was penned by a woman whose name was associated with scandal in her earlier years. Born to a couple whose marriage crossed class lines (her father, of noble descent, had married a woman of bourgeois background), Sand tried in vain during her youth to be part of both classes. Convent-educated, she soon forsook religion and was married at age sixteen to Baron Casimir Dudevant. The union was not happy. Leaving her husband in order to earn a living for herself and their son, Maurice, Sand went to Paris where she took advantage of her new freedom to indulge in many love affairs, including liaisons with the author Alfred de Musset and the composer Frédéric Chopin. She further shocked her contemporaries by wearing masculine clothing and living a bohemian life. Her novel *Indiana* (1832), having brought her fame and some fortune, launched her career. It was followed by a string of successful works that she produced tirelessly, writing daily—or, more accurately, nightly—from 10 p.m. until 5 a.m. These included the novels *Valentine* (1832), *Lélia* (1833), *Jacques* (1834), and later *Consuelo* (1842). She also authored a substantial autobiography, *The Story of My Life* (*Histoire de ma vie*, 1854). Sand was also a political activist, taking up the cause of women's rights and social reform. During the latter part of her life, she led a more tranquil life on her estate at Nohant, and it was here that she wrote the series of rustic stories that began with *The Devil's Pool*, followed by *Little Fadette* (*La Petite Fadette*, 1848) and *François le Champi* (1848). As lady of the manor she managed to live out the pastoral dream of many aristocrats (including the ill-fated Marie Antoinette), and eventually died in Nohant.

Her story opens with a reference to an engraving by the Renaissance artist Hans Holbein that depicts a man plowing his fields, accompanied by a skeleton representing Death (a memento mori meant to inspire fear in the observer). This leads the narrator to undertake a brief meditation on the role of art in society. But while Holbein's plowman is old, exhausted, clad in tattered clothing, and accompanied by Death, the protagonist of Sand's story is Germain, a strong and vigorous plowman in the Berry accompanied by his son, a handsome seven-year-old. However, the beauty of the countryside is not sufficient to bring Germain happiness, because he mourns his recently deceased wife. Under prodding from his late wife's father who believes that his son-in-law needs to remarry, Germain goes to meet a rich widow from a neighboring village. Eventually it is not the widow that he will marry but rather a young woman, Marie, from his own village who—despite her youth and poverty—proves to be the better match. Marie demonstrates wisdom, resourcefulness, virtue, and keen intelligence. She first endears Germain's son to her, and it does not take Germain long to realize that, despite her youth, Marie would make an ideal wife—although the course of true love is, as is usually the case, fraught with obstacles. The story's title comes from a mysterious place called the Devil's Pool where Germain, his son, and Marie are forced to camp out when they become lost in the forest. The pastoral ambience of the story does not prevent Sand from raising some important social issues. She reveals the social tensions within the peasantry, tensions that mirror the prejudices of the society as a whole. But Marie, first considered "unsuitable" because of her lowly status in the village, is able to prevail because of her qualities, which transcend the disadvantages of her birth. Indeed, although Sand has chosen a male protagonist for this story, it is the female character Marie whom the feminist author gives the most desirable qualities. Sand also subverts the idyllic pastoral tone of much of the story by introducing the theme of sexual harassment when Marie accepts a position as shepherdess in a neighboring village. She quickly realizes that her new master is bent on having her submit to his sexual advances, and she adopts the only course available to her—she flees, although she is poor and in need of the job. While there is a certain romanticizing of the peasants' lifestyle, Sand shows that she is keenly aware of its less desirable aspects and that she is very much on the side of the victims. This apparently quiet tale makes for pleasant reading with its evocation of the delights of simple country living, but its confrontation with the social questions of its day gives it considerable depth and sophistication.

MADAME BOVARY

(1857)

◆

Gustave Flaubert (1821-1880)

If *Tristan and Iseut* inaugurated the West's obsession with literary extramarital affairs, the character who has become in more modern times the poster child for adultery is the titular heroine of Gustave Flaubert's *Madame Bovary*. Allusions to Emma Bovary are legion and appear regularly in the movies and on TV—for example in the recent film *Little Children* and in the popular series *Desperate Housewives*, in both of which women's book clubs read and discuss the novel.

Gustave Flaubert, respected not only by readers but also by the literati (Henry James, for example, referred to him as the "writer's writer"), was born in Rouen. A surgeon's son, he showed a precocious talent for literature, by some accounts as early as his eighth year. After completing high school, he enrolled without much enthusiasm as a law student in Paris while continuing to write. An attack of epilepsy interrupted his studies and inaugurated a long period of illness, forcing him to return home to convalesce in the hamlet of Croisset just outside Rouen, in the summerhouse purchased by his father overlooking the Seine. Flaubert found the setting conducive to work, and it was here that most of his subsequent writing was done. After travels in France, Egypt, and the Middle East, Flaubert began work on *Madame Bovary* in 1851, completing it five years later. His next novel, *Salammbô* (1862), was well received, but he was disappointed by the lack of enthusiasm for *The Sentimental Education* (*L' Éducation sentimentale*, 1869). This disappointment, together with the uncertain political situation that followed the downfall of the Second Empire (1870), serious financial troubles, and the loss of his mother in 1872, as well as the subsequent deaths of several friends, made the last decade of his life difficult. However, he continued writing and produced one of his most enduring successes, *Three Tales* (*Trois contes*), in 1877, and was working on the satirical novel *Bouvard and Pecuchet* when he died in 1880.

Madame Bovary is by far his most popular work, often regarded not only as a masterpiece of French literary realism but also as the greatest novel of world literature. Initially, it was the scandal surrounding it that assured its success, as Flaubert and his publisher were hauled into court for offenses against morality and religion. Flaubert's lawyer prevailed, and the novel has continued to enchant readers ever since.

What is the source of its wide appeal? Does it stem from the ambiguity surrounding the central character, Emma Bovary? Some readers see her as a loose woman, others as the victim of a repressive social order. Or is it Flaubert's style that makes the novel so compelling, a style that has been called "indeterminate" because it "shows" rather than "tells," forcing readers to draw their own conclusions? It was precisely this lack of a narrator who could serve as a moral compass for the reader that so enraged the censors.

Flaubert once described *Madame Bovary* as a work "about nothing," a curious description for a book in which a great deal happens. What he really meant was that he had deliberately selected a trite subject in order to show that even banality could be redeemed by art. Emma Bovary is a convent-educated young woman whose head has been stuffed full of idealistic romantic notions about love, thanks to her passion for reading novels of romance. When her father breaks his leg, they summon Charles Bovary, the local health officer—the town is too small to warrant a fully licensed medical doctor—who successfully sets the leg. Emma invests Charles with all her romantic dreams, naively ignoring the fact that he is boring and of limited intelligence. The fortuitous death of his ill-tempered wife soon frees Charles to ask for Emma's hand. However, married life bears no resemblance to the great romantic love that is presented in literature, and in a desperate attempt to experience passion and ecstasy, Emma engages successively in two extramarital affairs, neither of which brings her happiness. She also falls victim to the wiles of a fabric merchant who tempts her with the latest fashions and extends easy credit to her, driving her deeply into debt. The narrative chronicles her increasingly futile attempts to seek fulfillment and her sad demise. The only character who lives "happily ever after" is the village pharmacist, Homais, the incarnation of self-satisfied bourgeois mediocrity who receives France's highest order, the Legion of Honor.

This cruelly ironic ending has caused some readers to perceive Flaubert as unfeeling. However, if he describes his characters with a coldly objective eye, they are not caricatures, and the reader either identifies with them or feels antipathy for them, sometimes simultaneously. Indeed, whether viewed as a daring feminist or as an immoral narcissist, Emma Bovary has become a literary icon who has acquired almost mythical status.

THE FLOWERS OF EVIL

Les Fleurs du mal (1857)

◆

Charles Baudelaire (1821-1867)

Although probably not popular with florists, the title of Baudelaire's great collection of poetry is one of the most captivating in literature, juxtaposing as it does the negativity of evil with a term associated with love and beauty. One of the world's major poets, Baudelaire was a rebel who expressed his revolt against contemporary bourgeois society through verse considered so scandalous in his day that he was put on trial for "affront to public decency," fined the sum of 300 francs, and ordered to remove six particularly offensive poems from the collection. The provocative title of Baudelaire's collection reveals a new poetic vision in which things and people not normally considered beautiful become the object of his poetic gaze. Indeed, it is up to the poet to extract the beauty—the "flowers"—from ugliness and evil (one of Baudelaire's poems is even devoted to roadkill).

The poems of the collection, although they can be read as individual pieces, describe an intellectual and spiritual journey in which the poet oscillates between his quest for the "ideal" and a kind of melancholy that he calls "spleen," produced by his failed attempts to reach the ideal. The first edition of the *Flowers of Evil* (1857) contained five sections, named "Spleen and Ideal," "The Flowers of Evil," "Revolt," "Wine," and "Death." The 1861 edition suppressed the censored poems and added some important new poems and a section entitled "Parisian Tableaux."

Baudelaire is regarded as the forerunner of the Symbolist movement that reacted both against naturalism and the ideal of "art for art's sake," cultivating instead a symbolic and spiritual vision of the world in which the poet finds a unity that other people miss. One of his most famous poems, "Correspondences," extols this ability to make a connection between visible and invisible worlds on the one hand, and between the senses on the other, to create a universe in which "fragrances, colors, and sounds echo one another." With his special vision, the poet relentlessly seeks for the ideal in love, in art, in travel, in revolt against society and religion. Another well-known poem, "Hair," added to the collection in 1861, is a hymn to sexual desire and eroticism, symbolized by the abundant black locks of one of Baudelaire's mistresses. He describes how the look and the scent of a woman's hair can provide him with an imaginary escape to exotic lands:

> Languorous Asia and burning Africa,
> A whole distant world, far away, almost extinct
> Lives in your depths, an aromatic forest!
> Just as other spirits sail away on waves of music,
> Mine, O my Love, swims, afloat on your perfume.

The euphoria of "Hair" disappears when he describes his moments of melancholy in the poem "Spleen IV":

> When the sky, heavy and low, weighs down like a lid
> On the spirit groaning under the burden of never-ending troubles.

And when the poet has exhausted the possibilities of this life, he embarks on the final journey, bound for death in "The Voyage," undertaken not so much out of necessity as in the hope of finding something new.

Baudelaire had a troubled childhood in Paris, having lost his father at a young age and hating his stepfather, Jacques Aupick. The year 1839 saw him rebelling against the latter's desire that he pursue legal studies; instead he lived the bohemian life in Paris's Latin Quarter, contracting venereal disease from the prostitutes he frequented. Aupick, attempting to straighten his stepson out, forced him to embark on a long sea voyage, but Baudelaire jumped ship at the first port of call, the island of Réunion. Upon his return to Paris, he began writing poetry in which, ironically, the maritime experience figured prominently. But Baudelaire's debut on the literary stage came not from his poems but from his novella *La Fanfarlo* (1847) and from his reviews of art exhibits. He became fascinated by Edgar Allan Poe in 1847 and translated much of Poe's work in the early 1850s. After the publication of the *Flowers of Evil*, Baudelaire turned to what he called *petits poèmes en prose* (little prose poems), which were published posthumously in 1869. His last years were dogged by illness due to his syphilis and other maladies probably brought on by his lifestyle and drug use. He died in a nursing home in Paris in 1867. He was indeed a *poète maudit* (a cursed poet), although the curse was largely of his own making. Perhaps the best résumé of his poetry is a line he himself wrote: "You have given me your mud, and I have turned it into gold." Baudelaire was a true Alchemist of the Word.

SATANISM AND WITCHCRAFT

La Sorcière (1862)

◆

Jules Michelet (1798–1874)

When we think of historians we usually think of scholars who meticulously collect data from documents stored in musty archives and then proceed to organize and analyze their research with impressive objectivity. However, in the last few decades historians and particularly biographers have written best-selling books that have brought history to life with imaginative writing and a decidedly personal vision. To some extent they were foreshadowed by the great nineteenth-century French historian Jules Michelet, whose life work, a monumental *History of France* (*Histoire de France*), took him thirty years to complete and comprised nineteen volumes in its posthumous 1879 edition. Michelet believed that historians should not merely recite or even analyze "facts," but rather that they should look at as many aspects as possible of the period or people they were examining, including areas such as diet, cultural practices, popular attitudes, and the like. He contrasted his interdisciplinary understanding of history with that of others: "Augustin Thierry called history narration; Guizot, analysis; I call it resurrection." Michelet's goal was to make a past era come alive, certainly by using the traditional tools of the historian but also by looking at other relevant disciplines and by using intuition and imagination. His is a very personal interpretation of history, and while his presentation is lively, entertaining, and even epic in scope, it is also far from objective—to the point of being sometimes distorted by his own preconceptions and prejudices. He became very anticlerical, for example, and it shows. However, modern scholars who are as interested in historiography (the writing of history) as well as in history proper have gained a new appreciation of Michelet's work, particularly as they have realized how much even apparently objective historians often use the rhetorical and narrative techniques normally associated with literary texts in their studies. Readers interested in such issues don't need to plow through Michelet's magnum opus, for they can gain access to his thought and method by reading a fascinating shorter work, *Satanism and Witchcraft* (the wordier English title expands upon the simple *La Sorcière*—The Witch—of the original). This study, which resembles prose poetry as much as history, retraces the origins and development of the idea of the witch in Western Europe and incorporates not only the well-known and documented medieval witch hunts, but also examines the person of the witch and sees in her the representative of Woman, downtrodden and persecuted. Thus, *Satanism and Witchcraft* can be read as a history of the condition of women in the Middle Ages. Interestingly, Michelet's views evolved considerably in the course of his career. Whereas earlier he had stigmatized witchcraft as a revival of the pagan orgy, he later became a champion of women and saw in the appalling treatment meted out to witches an example of their repression at the hands of male-dominated institutions. In this work, witchcraft is presented as a revolt against the various fears and oppressions that were rampant during the medieval period, and the witch is seen as a positive figure who—because of her proximity to nature—knew the art of healing and midwifery and, according to Michelet, even helped facilitate the development of science and medicine. "Nature made women witches— this is Woman's nature and temperament. She is born as Fairy [. . .] she is Sybil. Through love, she is a Magician. Through her perceptiveness, her mischievous nature [. . .] she is Witch and casts spells which at the very least allay and stave off evil things."

A printer's son from Paris, Michelet was a brilliant student who became an equally brilliant teacher of history and philosophy, first at the École Normale Supérieure and later at the Collège de France. Very involved in the politics of his era, he did not hesitate to stand up for his principles. For a time he supported Louis-Philippe, then criticized him, and when a coup brought Napoleon III to power in 1851, Michelet's opposition to the new regime resulted in the loss of his post at the Collège de France in 1852. After the death of his first wife, Michelet's marriage to Athénaïs Mialeret (or Mialaret), twenty-eight years his junior, gave him a new burst of creative energy, as she collaborated with him on works devoted to natural history for a more general audience. With the fall of Napoleon III in 1870, Michelet's work was back in favor, although—much to his chagrin—he was not reappointed to his teaching post. He had completed his massive *History of France* in 1867, then started a history of the nineteenth century, but only got as far as the Battle of Waterloo before his death in 1874. A writer of great expressive power whose view of the interdisciplinary nature of history is quite modern in its approach, Michelet's vision still touches us today. We can also admire him as one of the first historians to present a sympathetic and tolerant portrait of the Witch and to decry the superstitions that led to the persecution of women across the ages.

THÉRÈSE RAQUIN

(1867)

◆

Emile Zola (1840-1902)

If Emile Zola were alive today, he could earn a lucrative living as a screenwriter for horror movies. A number of the scenes in his novel *Thérèse Raquin* have a similar impact on readers as, for example, the shower scene from Hitchcock's *Psycho* has on its viewers. However, Zola is much more than a master of gruesome descriptions. He is also a storyteller of immense talent, able to endow the tales he spins and the characters he creates with both a gritty reality and at the same time a mythic, universal quality.

Born in Paris, Zola spent much of his boyhood in Aix-en-Provence, where he became friends with the young Cézanne. After the death of Zola's father, the family moved back to Paris, where, having failed his baccalaureate, he finally managed to get a job with the Hachette publishing house. He wrote a collection of short stories and his first novel in the early 1860s and gained a reputation as a political journalist and as an art critic, particularly for his defense of the painter Edouard Manet. He resigned from Hachette in order to devote himself fully to his career as a writer. The publication of *Thérèse Raquin* marked the beginning of his ascendancy as a novelist and motivated him to present to the publisher La Croix a proposal for a series of novels recounting the fortunes of the Rougon-Macquart, a family dogged by ill fate and genetic flaws. From 1870 until 1893 Zola published twenty volumes in this series, of which *L'Assommoir* (1877), *Nana* (1880), and *Germinal* (1885) are perhaps the best-known. In 1898 Zola became a crusader for another cause. Convinced of the innocence of Alfred Dreyfus, who had been condemned to prison for espionage, Zola published his famous letter, "*J'accuse*," in the newspaper *L'Aurore*, protesting that the evidence against Dreyfus had been fabricated and calling for a retrial. The negative reaction of the authorities drove him into exile in England for a year, and he was only able to return to France after the documents used to incriminate Dreyfus had been proven to be forgeries. Zola did not live long enough to see Dreyfus completely exonerated—this did not happen until 1906—since he died of carbon-monoxide poisoning due to a blocked chimney in his home in 1902. Although his death was pronounced accidental, there remains a strong suspicion of foul play at the hands of his political foes.

Thérèse Raquin, while it is not part of the Rougon-Macquart series, introduces many of the themes of the later work and clearly shows the influence of the theories of the nineteenth-century historian Hippolyte Taine, who believed strongly in physiological and genetic determinism, claiming that human behavior could be explained by studying the combined effects of heredity, environment, and historical moment. Zola sees novels not just as works of literature but as laboratories in which he can analyze the interaction of characters of different temperaments. Although the ostensible theme of *Thérèse Raquin* is adultery, the novel is in fact the study of two different character types, the hysteric-nervous Thérèse and the sanguine-phlegmatic Laurent. Zola eschews the psychological analysis that had been a staple of the traditional novel since *The Princess of Clèves* and engages instead in a psycho-naturalistic study of his characters—human animals rather than human beings, motivated by the most basic drives and instincts. Thérèse, the daughter of a French soldier and a North African woman, is brought back to France by her father after her mother's death and deposited with his sister, who is to raise her alongside her own sickly son, Camille. Thérèse, while outwardly calm and introverted, is inwardly propelled by the primitive animalistic drives that Zola, who is not exempt from racial stereotyping, associates with her African heritage. Laurent, of solid peasant stock, outgoing and jovial, is lazy and interested above all in the satisfaction of his physical desires. When the two meet after Thérèse has, without enthusiasm, married Camille, they are violently attracted to each other, but since their opportunities to satisfy their lust are limited, they determine to solve the problem by doing away with the hapless husband. The longest part of the novel is devoted to the narrative of their crime and its unexpected aftermath. Presented with the inevitability of a Greek tragedy, the novel paints a stark picture of the interaction of two fundamentally incompatible character types who contribute to each other's destruction.

Zola's bleak view of humanity, which, unfortunately, is corroborated daily in our newspapers and on TV, has neither lost its gruesome appeal nor its power to shock.

20,000 LEAGUES UNDER THE SEA

Vingt mille lieues sous les mers (1870)

♦

Jules Verne (1828–1905)

Rocket ships, submarines, life in futuristic twentieth-century Paris: the nineteenth-century author Jules Verne imagined all of these things with an often uncanny accuracy. Although he had no scientific training and was not always the first to evoke certain scientific marvels, he still stuns the reader today with his prescience. In *From the Earth to the Moon* (1865), for example, he tells the story of a spacecraft, shot from a large cannon in Florida, which carries three travelers to the moon in a vehicle whose dimensions are similar to that of the Apollo spacecraft. *20,000 Leagues under the Sea* is less innovative in the sense that it is inspired by Robert Fulton's invention of a working submarine in 1800, although Jules Verne's model is much more sophisticated and modern. Verne, however, chose to honor Fulton's invention by giving his submarine the same name as the original: *Nautilus*. This novel, which combines mystery with its science fiction theme, is a rollicking tale of adventure, featuring an enigmatic hero of almost mythical proportions, the inventor and commander of the submarine, Captain Nemo. The hero's name, Latin for "Nobody," also suggests "omen" when read backwards. *And* it refers to another great traveler, Ulysses, who, when he met the terrifying Cyclops Polyphemus, concealed his identity by telling him his name was "Nobody." Such sophisticated wordplay supports the view of recent scholars that Verne's novels are not the "simple," adolescent reading they were once thought to be. The narrator of *20,000 Leagues under the Sea* is a French marine biologist, Pierre Aronnax, who is invited to join an American expedition to search for a mysterious marine monster that had been sighted several times and had even attacked and damaged a passenger vessel. The U.S. naval ship *Abraham Lincoln* sails from Long Island to the Pacific by way of Cape Horn, finally locating the monster, which rams the American vessel. The shock of the collision projects Aronnax, his assistant Conseil, and a Canadian harpoonist, Ned Land, overboard and lands them on the monster's body, which, to their great surprise, is composed of metal. They are on a man-made craft! Before the mysterious vessel dives, the three are captured by her crew and brought before Captain Nemo, who gives them a guided tour of his marvelous invention, which is able to roam the seas hidden from view, and which is also luxuriously equipped. Nemo, an outcast from civilization, had built his submarine on a desert island, and uses it now for scientific purposes, but also to take revenge on society for its many injustices. (A sequel, *The Mysterious Island* [*L'île mystérieuse*, 1874], gives details of Nemo's past not yet revealed in *20,000 Leagues*, thus leaving the mystery surrounding Nemo intact here.) In order to preserve his secret, Nemo informs his prisoners that they are free to explore the *Nautilus*, but they can never leave it. Subsequently, the submarine visits various undersea locations, some real (under the ice shelf of the Antarctic) and some imaginary (Atlantis), and—among many other adventures—is attacked by a giant squid and by an unknown vessel that the crew manages to sink. Nemo, deeply disturbed by the loss of life he has caused even though he considered his action was justified, allows the *Nautilus* to stray into a maelstrom off the coast of Norway, and during the ensuing pandemonium the three prisoners manage to escape and return to land unharmed. However, we learn nothing of the fate of the *Nautilus* and its crew—this will only be revealed in the sequel.

Born in Nantes, the creator of *20,000 Leagues* and many other science fiction adventures was always fascinated by water and the sea. Like many other authors of his day, Jules Verne began to study law, but his father cut off his financial support when he discovered his son was engaged in writing (at first opera libretti and then travel stories). Verne met both Alexandre Dumas, who became a close friend, and Victor Hugo, and received advice from them on pursuing a literary career. However, the most important contact Verne made was with Pierre-Jules Hetzel, Hugo's publisher, who collaborated with Verne in order to make his novels commercially successful. He proposed, for example, the addition of humor and irony and suggested happier endings for novels that he considered too dark. This partnership was mutually beneficial, and Jules Verne produced fifty-four novels in the series *Voyages extraordinaires* (Extraordinary Journeys), as well as other novels, plays, and short stories. One novel, *Paris in the Twentieth Century*, written in 1863 but not published in his lifetime, was discovered in manuscript form by his grandson in 1989, and was finally published in 1994. Among the most widely translated authors in the world (most surveys place him in the top five), Jules Verne is the father of modern science fiction. His novels have inspired numerous movies over the years, proof that his foresight and imagination have not lost their ability to captivate their audience in a world where many of his predictions have come true.

"The Drunken Boat"/A Season in Hell

"Le bateau ivre"/Une saison en enfer (1871-73)

◆

Jean-Nicolas-Arthur Rimbaud (1854-1891)

A teenage prodigy, Arthur Rimbaud burst upon the Paris literary scene in the 1870s, but his time in the limelight was short-lived, lasting a scant five years. Raised by a strict Catholic mother in Charleville, Rimbaud was at first a model child, regularly winning prizes for his scholastic achievements. His first published poem, "The Orphans' Christmas Presents" ("Les Etrennes des Orphelins"), appeared in *La Revue pour tous* (*The Review for Everyone*) in 1870 and drew the attention of one of Rimbaud's teachers, George Izambard, who became his first mentor. It was at this point that Rimbaud began his revolt against his stifling upbringing, running away to Paris several times that year, while continuing to write poetry. The following year he began a correspondence with the poet Paul Verlaine, who invited him to Paris. Rimbaud accepted the invitation, bringing with him his latest poem, "The Drunken Boat." Rimbaud soon alienated Verlaine's family and friends with his crude language and deliberately provocative behavior. He began to drink absinthe and smoke hashish, becoming the very incarnation of *le poète maudit* (the cursed poet). Verlaine and he began an affair marked by violence and punctuated with ruptures and reconciliations. Rimbaud, who continued writing during this time, had a violent confrontation with his lover in Brussels: Verlaine, in a fit of drunken fury, fired a revolver at the young poet, wounding him in the hand, for which he was arrested and imprisoned. Devastated, Rimbaud finished *A Season in Hell*—the title sums up their stormy relationship. The last time they met was after Verlaine's release from prison. Verlaine had become an ardent Roman Catholic, and the final break occurred when he tried to persuade his young friend to follow his example. After 1875, Rimbaud abandoned poetry to enter the world of commerce, taking a number of positions in Europe and Africa. His last post was in Algeria, from which he was forced to return to France in 1891 because of severe leg pain. His health continued to deteriorate and he died the same year, at the age of thirty-seven.

Rimbaud's poetry is remarkable for its bold use of language and its visionary nature. He conceived the role of the poet as that of priest and prophet of humankind. This was already the credo of the Romantic poets and indeed goes back at least as far as the Renaissance. But Rimbaud pushed the envelope: he believed that the poet must be a kind of clairvoyant (*un voyant*) who has to explore human experience by the derangement of the senses (*le dérèglement de tous les sens*), assisted by alcohol (absinthe in particular) and hashish. This would enable the poet to see beyond normal reality and to penetrate to the depths of human consciousness. Although he was inspired to some extent by Baudelaire, Rimbaud's vision goes further than that of his predecessor and anticipates the credo of the surrealists, for whom he was to become an icon.

In "The Drunken Boat" he uses the image of a boat cast adrift to make its way down a highly symbolic river to the ocean, a voyage in which the boat—the poet—sees a kaleidoscope of visions, some reassuring, some terrifying. The boat/poet has seen:

Glaciers, suns of silver, iridescent waves, skies aflame!
Hideous wrecks at the bottom of brown gulfs
Where giant snakes eaten away by bugs
Fall, twisted tree trunks, with dark perfumes.

The later *Season in Hell* is a collection of prose poems, alternating with some verse, in which the deep conflicts within the poet's soul are played out in a series of oppositions: good and evil, God and the Devil, Heaven and Hell. Rimbaud shows a remarkable mastery of the prose poem, a genre to which Baudelaire had turned after the *Flowers of Evil*, and thanks to "the alchemy of the word" portrays his inner struggles in the most graphic of terms. However, in the final poem, "Adieu," he looks back lucidly at his struggles and expresses doubts about his poetic quest:

I have tried to invent new flowers, new stars, new flesh,
new languages. I thought I could acquire supernatural
powers. Well, it turns out that I must bury my imagination
and my souvenirs.

Nevertheless, there is consolation. If Rimbaud finds the present moment "very severe," he can nevertheless say that "victory is mine," that it is now time to be "absolutely modern" ("il faut être absolument moderne"). After all, he has only spent a season, not eternity, in hell. Thanks to his fearless exploration of self, he is now free to "possess the truth in both soul and body." Carried along on the "waves of poetry," the reader who accompanies Rimbaud on his poetic journey can understand the poet's sense of freedom.

SHORT STORIES

(1880-90)

◆

Guy de Maupassant (1850-1893)

M any who did not grow up in a French culture have heard of Guy de Maupassant because of one of his short stories that appears relentlessly in school anthologies: "The Necklace" ("La Parure") features a woman of limited means who borrows a necklace from a wealthy friend to attend a ball with her husband. She loses the necklace and, without informing her friend, buys an identical one to replace it, spending the best part of her life working to pay off the debt, in vain as it turns out. (If you have read the story, you'll remember the surprising ending; if not, you will enjoy reading it.) This is a great tale, but despite its many qualities it gives us only a limited view of its author's talents and tremendous range. Maupassant penned not only stories recounting the domestic dramas of the Parisian bourgeoisie but also war stories, ghost stories, travel narratives, as well as tales featuring prostitutes, Norman peasants, petty functionaries, madmen, and others. He wrote several well-regarded novels, too, including *Bel-Ami, Pierre et Jean, Mont-Oriol, A Woman's Life (Une vie)*, and *Strong as Death (Fort comme la mort)*, while contributing regular pieces to newspapers. Amazingly, almost all of his literary production occurred in just a ten-year period, from 1880 to 1890. This man was like a writing machine!

Maupassant was born in Normandy, according to most accounts in the Château de Miromesnil, not far from Dieppe, and brought up by his mother in Etretat, after his parents had separated. With the outbreak of the Franco-Prussian War in 1870, Maupassant enlisted, and his experiences provided the material for a number of his short stories, including "Boule de suif" (variously translated as "Butterball" or "Ball of Fat"). After the war Maupassant led the boring life of a civil servant, first in the ministry of the navy, then in the ministry of education, writing for a number of newspapers in his spare time and receiving moral support from Flaubert, a childhood friend of his mother. The year 1880 was a breakthrough year for him: "Boule de suif" was published in *Les Soirées de Médan*, a collection of six short stories that took its name from Zola's country residence at Médan, near Paris. Claiming to represent the Naturalist movement in literature (a cultural movement that aimed to present an objective portrait of reality), the collection included stories by Zola and Huysmans, but it was "Boule de suif" that attracted the most attention. It made Maupassant an overnight celebrity, enabling him to resign from his civil service job and live from his writing. His productivity was astounding, particularly as he also found time to travel (Sicily and North Africa) and to sail his yacht, *Bel-Ami*. Unfortunately, always a lady's man and a frequent client of prostitutes, he had contracted syphilis at a young age, and his symptoms became increasingly serious during this period and completely debilitating after 1890. Declared insane and institutionalized, he attempted suicide in 1892 and died the following year.

Of Maupassant's more than three hundred short stories, only three can briefly be mentioned here: "Boule de suif," his earliest masterpiece, is a satirical portrait of French provincial society at the time of the Franco-Prussian War. It concerns a representative selection of Rouen citizens who are fleeing the Prussian advance in a stagecoach. The attractively plump prostitute Elisabeth Rousset, nicknamed Boule de suif, is snubbed by the more "respectable" travelers—until the coach is slowed by snow and they discover that she alone has brought provisions for the journey. Generously sharing her food with the others, she suddenly finds herself accepted by them. However, when the group stops for the night at Tôtes, a Prussian stronghold, the commander refuses to let the coach and its occupants leave until Rousset sleeps with him. She patriotically refuses, and it is only after her fellow travelers conspire to persuade her to give in that she complies. However, when the journey resumes, the other coach occupants hypocritically treat her with disdain because she has slept with the enemy. (This story is thought to have inspired John Ford's famous movie *Stagecoach*.) In the amusing "Madame Tellier," Maupassant gives another sympathetic portrait of prostitutes, telling how Madame Tellier and the employees of her brothel take a short vacation to attend the First Communion of Madame Tellier's niece. With the brothel closed, mayhem breaks out in the town, while at the ceremony itself the prostitutes weep at the thought of their own lost innocence as they watch the young communicants. In "Le Horla," Maupassant's eeriest fantastic tale, a first-person narrator tells in diary form how his house is invaded by an alien presence, leaving us in doubt as to whether the narrator is mad or not.

Maupassant's short stories provide endless hours of pleasure, yet they are far more complex and sophisticated than they first seem. It is not surprising that they have been translated into many languages and that Maupassant is considered one of the great short story writers of world literature.

AGAINST NATURE

À rebours (1884)

◆

Joris-Karl (Charles-Marie-Georges) Huysmans

(1848–1907)

The last member of an illustrious noble family whose lineage has been sapped by inbreeding, the young but world-weary protagonist of this novel, Des Esseintes, decides to isolate himself from society in a house outside Paris. He is ill, suffering from what had become a fashionable disease in literary and artistic circles in the 1800s—neurosis (*la névrose*), which generates an unusual assortment of physical and psychological symptoms. At first the novel appears to have no real plot line, until we realize that the various episodes are linked by the stages of Des Esseintes's illness, and that his retreat from Parisian society to the countryside is no return to nature. In fact, he does all he can to distance himself from the natural world, cultivating the artificial, the unnatural, the aesthetic, and devoting himself henceforth to the antinatural represented by books and works of art. When he lived in Paris he was already reputed to be an eccentric, wearing "white velvet suits, gold-embroidered waistcoats and, in place of a cravat, a bunch of Parma violets inserted in the opening of his unbuttoned shirt." Significantly, the Parma violets, having no fragrance, already seem to be removed from nature. When setting up house in Fontenay, Des Esseintes has builders install an inner sanctum that resembles a ship's cabin. Exterior light is filtered into this room through a porthole in which there is an aquarium filled with mechanical fish. Unlike the Romantics who preceded him, he is filled with contempt for nature, insisting that man can build replicas of it that are superior to the real thing. He purchases a tortoise and has a jeweler come to his house to incrust the tortoise's shell with various precious stones, a procedure that ends up killing the poor creature. He reads Latin literature, concentrating on authors who wrote during the decline of Rome, since he believes (as many French did after their defeat in the Franco-Prussian War of 1870–71) that France is following the same path as ancient Rome. Like Huysmans himself, Des Esseintes is a blatant misogynist and recounts the disappointments of his past sexual experiences. Being attracted to Miss Urania, an American acrobat with a muscular build who he hopes to be his dominatrix, he is disappointed when he discovers instead a somewhat puritanical and girlish young woman. Another unsatisfactory affair, with a female ventriloquist who recites passages from Flaubert, makes him turn away from women to try a homosexual relationship, but this brings him no joy either. Desiring a change of air, he asks his servants to pack his bags for an extended visit to London, but only gets as far as Paris, then returns to Fontenay the same evening. His illness finally progresses to a point where he summons a doctor, who successfully treats his physical ailments but refuses to continue the treatment unless Des Esseintes abandons his solitary life, moves back to Paris, and engages in social intercourse. Des Esseintes rails against the bourgeois society he will have to face there, but, ironically, acquiesces. The last sentence is a surprising prayer asking God to take pity on the "Christian who doubts and the unbeliever who wants to believe." (Huysmans, a nonbeliever when he wrote the novel, later converted to Catholicism and added a "religious" preface to *Against Nature* in 1903.)

Huysmans, born in Paris to a Dutch father and a French mother, became a civil servant at the ministry of the interior and was called to military service during the Franco-Prussian War. His first literary works seemed to place him squarely in the Naturalist camp, and he collaborated with Maupassant, Zola, and others on the story collection *Les Soirées de Médan* (see also page 113). However, his earliest publication, *The Spice Dish* (*Le Drageoir à épices*), a collection of prose poems published in 1874, already featured some of the artificial elements later found in *Against Nature*, which is sometimes called the Bible of the Decadent movement. Decadence as a cultural movement was dominant in late-nineteenth-century Paris; it focused on satirizing bourgeois mediocrity and on presenting women as an evil force that, together with the mob, opposes the aspirations and creations of the artist. Although initially critical of religion, Huysmans marveled at the magnificent art, music, and literature it inspired. This, together with his hatred of contemporary bourgeois society, led him to the church, particularly as the First Vatican Council (1869–70) had revived a traditional, authoritative form of Catholicism. Huymans's misogyny was translated into a fascination with female martyrdom and the horrible sufferings endured by women saints as they fulfilled the Christian mission in the world.

Against Nature—which some believe to be the unnamed "poisonous" French novel that helped ruin the life of the hero in Oscar Wilde's *The Picture of Dorian Gray*—weaves a morbidly fascinating spell on its readers with its blend of decadence, humor, and unexpected juxtapositions that bears witness to its author's darkly fertile imagination.

Mister Venus

Monsieur Vénus (1884)

◆

Rachilde (Marguerite Eymery) (1860-1953)

In 1884 there appeared on the shelves of bookstores in Belgium a scandalous new novel that was quickly banned by the authorities. It was signed Rachilde, a mysterious pen name that could have been a first name or a family name, and one that could be either masculine or feminine. It turned out to be the pseudonym of Marguerite Eymery, a young French woman who had already published a number of fictional works in newspapers, either anonymously or using this pen name. Eymery, until then a virtually unknown author, was catapulted to success in France because of *Mister Venus*, no doubt aided by the action of the Belgian censors. (Ironically, French authors often published works they feared would be censored in France in other countries such as Belgium and the Netherlands, where censors were usually more liberal.) What made this novel so piquant was that it dealt with the subject of female desire in a radically new and open way. While gender-bending was not unknown previously (we find examples of such practices in de Sade's work, among others), *Mister Venus* places the subject front and center. Its female protagonist, a somewhat imperious young noblewoman by the name of Raoule (its pronunciation is identical to the male name Raoul) de Vénérande, is smitten with a handsome young working-class man, Jacques Silvert, who makes artificial flowers in order to earn money to care for his ailing sister, Marie. This initial situation contains nothing particularly surprising, except perhaps the almost banal desire to traverse class boundaries by the young female aristocrat. However, we quickly learn that Raoule's desire is far from banal, that she wants to play a masculine role in the affair she hopes to have with Jacques and that she intends him to become her mistress. She is good-looking but somewhat mannish, while his handsomeness has a feminine quality—and it is she who takes the initiative in the courtship, even going so far as to dress in masculine costume, while he waits for her in an extremely feminine boudoir. The novel recounts the progressive feminization of Jacques, which takes on a homoerotic character when he attempts to seduce, in his female role, an aristocrat named de Raittolbe, one of Raoule's masculine suitors. The novel explores the power play that is involved in

Raoule's desire to dominate her lover whom she persuades to marry her as her "bride." When the nature of their relationship becomes known in Paris, they find themselves socially isolated and shunned by their former friends and acquaintances, except for de Raittolbe. However, the threesome they become (not quite a ménage à trois in the usual sense) goes awry and ends tragically, leaving the female protagonist to play an even more perverse and macabre role in the final chapter of the novel.

Was this best-known of Eymery's works inspired by the fact that her father, a French career military officer, had told her repeatedly that he was disappointed she was not a boy and that he despised writers and literature? Perhaps it was a belated attempt to seek his favor, since she, like some other *femmes de lettres* (women writers) such as George Sand, often wore masculine clothing. Indeed, Rachilde liked to refer to herself as *un homme de lettres*. During her rather solitary childhood (she grew up in the Dordogne region), her education was neglected, but she did have access to her grandfather's library where she made the acquaintance of works by de Sade, Voltaire, and others. Thanks to *Mister Venus* and later novels like *La Marquise de Sade* (1887) and *Madame Adonis* (1888), she was a noted figure on the Paris literary scene as part of the Decadent movement (see also page 116) that remained popular until World War I. In 1889 she married Alfred Vallette, and founded with him the important literary journal *Mercure de France*. This brought her into contact with other writers including Alfred Jarry, whose biography she wrote in 1929, and with the novelist Colette. Her husband died in 1935, leaving her in an impoverished state, but she continued to write until six years before her death. Her last work was *When I Was Young* (*Quand j'étais jeune*, 1947). While her early novels made quite a splash, her reputation waned together with that of the Decadent movement. But her work has been rediscovered recently by critics and readers interested in gender roles and the power play present in sexual relations. Although there is disagreement as to whether her literary examinations of these subjects are feminist or not (she wrote an essay titled "Why I Am Not a Feminist"), one cannot deny the interest and importance of this female *homme de lettres*. Readers will have to decide for themselves whether Rachilde is a female misogynist—or a feminist who wants to portray women in masculine roles. But however that may be, there is no question that *Mister Venus*, with its study of sexual deviance and its taste for the strange and the macabre, is a pioneering and controversial work.

Tomorrow's Eve

L'Eve future (1886)

◆

Auguste, Comte de Villiers de l'Isle-Adam (1838-1889)

Blending the fantastic with science fiction, *Tomorrow's Eve*, set in Menlo Park, New Jersey, features Thomas Edison as hero. This may seem to be an unusual choice for a French novelist, but in 1877 there had been great excitement in France at the announcement of Edison's invention of the phonograph. This had fanned the positivist enthusiasm of the age, suggesting that science could unlock the secrets of the natural world and could even rival the accomplishments of nature. Villiers, who did not share this view, decided to write about Edison in a work of fiction that would satirize this modern scientific pretension. His novel went through various drafts with different titles, and the complete version did not appear until 1885–86, first serialized in the newspaper *La Vie moderne* and then published as a book with its present title. Edison, at home with his inventions and laboratories, receives the visit of a young friend from England, Lord Ewald. The young man arrives in an anguished state, because he has fallen in love with a singer, Alicia Clary, a woman whose classical, ethereal beauty has won his heart, but who is a vapid philistine, lacking aesthetic judgment and possessed of opinions that are boringly bourgeois. After a Grand Tour of Europe, which awakens no enthusiasm in his companion, Lord Ewald decides to take her to see the famous statue, the Venus de Milo: "One day, as a joke, I took her to the Louvre, telling her, 'My dear Alicia, I do believe I'm going to surprise you.' We walked through various galleries and suddenly I had her standing in front of the famous marble statue. Miss Alicia lifted her veil and then exclaimed in stupefaction: 'My goodness, it's *me*.' But an instant later she added: 'Well yes, but I still have my arms and I look more distinguished.'"

After learning that Lord Ewald is so distraught at loving a woman of such mediocre taste that he is contemplating suicide, Edison reveals to his friend that he has invented a female *Andréide* (the author coins this term, *Andréide*, so that this creation will not be confused with the mechanical dolls of the eighteenth century which were called androids). He proposes, as an experiment, to transform the Andréide into the physical double of Alicia, but to add what her human counterpart lacks, namely judgment, taste, and refinement. If Ewald can transfer his love to the Andréide—named Hadaly—he will be cured of his frustrating passion for Alicia. After some hesitation, Ewald accepts Edison's proposal, which comes with one condition: Ewald must truly believe in this artificial incarnation of Alicia. In order to make sure that the Andréide is physically identical to Alicia, Edison invites Alicia to Menlo Park to verify the likeness. While Edison is working in his laboratory, apparently putting the finishing touches to his invention, Ewald spends an evening with a woman he first believes to be Alicia, but when he listens to her intelligent conversations and the opinions she expresses, he realizes that he has in fact been with speaking with Hadaly. Cured of his love for Alicia but now thoroughly entranced by Hadaly, he packs the Andréide in a coffin, according to Edison's instructions, in order to transport her back to England, where he will be able to resuscitate her. However, disaster strikes: the ship on which they are traveling is shipwrecked, the coffin is lost, and Ewald, one of the few survivors, sends a telegram to Edison, saying that he is inconsolable and bidding him farewell. The melancholy Edison is left to contemplate the night sky with its unchanging stars, as a shudder runs through his body.

Villiers, a descendant of an aristocratic family impoverished by the Revolution, hailed from Brittany but became enamored with the Parisian literary and artistic scene as a young man. Leading a typically bohemian life in the French capital, he was introduced to Baudelaire and at his suggestion began to read Edgar Allan Poe, whose works gave him a taste for the strange and fantastic. Like many of his fellow writers, Villiers began by writing poetry before turning to prose fiction. He was unlucky in love, being spurned by several women, including an English heiress, before setting up house with an illiterate woman, Marie Dantine, who had his child in 1881 and whom he officially married just before his death in 1889. He wrote a number of short stories—inspired by those of Edgar Allan Poe—which were published individually before being collected in *Cruel Tales* (*Contes cruels*, 1883) and *New Cruel Tales* (*Nouveaux contes cruels*, 1888), and also several plays, including *Axël* (published posthumously in 1890). However, he was dogged by poverty and received little monetary reward for his works. *Tomorrow's Eve* is one of his most extraordinary creations. If at times the fictional Edison tends to be somewhat windy in his explanations of how his mechanical woman is constructed, Villiers's novel and its unforgettable character Hadaly raise many ethical and scientific questions concerning cloning and the creation of life that remain unanswered.

THE JOURNAL OF EUGÈNE DELACROIX

Le Journal d'Eugène Delacroix (1893)

♦

Eugène Delacroix (1798–1863)

"I am finally starting the project which I've formulated so many times: to write a journal. What I want to keep in mind is that I am writing it for only myself; this will ensure that I stick to the truth, I hope, and that it will be a means of self-improvement, since what I write down will reveal my inconsistencies to me. I am beginning my project in the best of spirits." So begins the first entry of Eugène Delacroix's journal on September 3, 1822. This is a precious document indeed, since it gives us a sense of the artist's own life and opinions and allows us insights into the mind of one of the greatest French painters, one who bridged the gap between the old masters of baroque and rococo painting and the new ideas about painting that came with romanticism and subsequent artistic movements. The journal is highly personal, full of charming and interesting anecdotes. Delacroix complains of his small stature, tells of his dalliances with certain models who have come to pose for him ("I risked catching the pox from Marie," he wrote on October 27, 1822), and also his embarrassment when he is painting them: "I'm constantly blushing; I just don't have the composure I need. I suffer for the model. I don't spend enough time just observing before beginning to paint."

Recording his love of nature, he observes that listening to the song of a nightingale is like watching the sea—one always wants to see one more wave break before tearing oneself away from the spectacle. One of the defining moments of his life came when he visited Morocco in 1832. The sights and sounds he experienced there were a revelation and added a new element of exoticism to his paintings. His description of a Jewish wedding, which he transposed into one of his paintings, gives us an idea of how an artist conceives a scene: "The guitar case is on the musician's knee; around his belt it's very dark, a red waistcoat, brown ornaments, blue behind the neck [. . .] shirt sleeves rolled up to reveal the biceps; green woodwork on the side; a wart on his neck, small nose." Also revealing are his comments on other paintings as well as on other artistic endeavors. Although he admires Shakespeare, he does not consider him superior to Virgil and Racine, whose styles he prefers. However, he admits that great style on its own does not make a great work of literature and that the most beautiful prose, if used to describe banal things, is ineffective. Fortunately, Virgil and Racine are great stylists who also deal with elevated subjects, thus bringing them—in Delacroix's opinion—close to perfection (which is an interesting point, since for most authors and artists associated with romanticism Shakespeare ruled supreme). Of course Delacroix has much to say about painters, older ones like Veronese and Titian, and more recent ones such as Turner and Reynolds. He generally prefers the classical artists to the more modern ones and speaks with some disparagement of the way the moderns exaggerate the contrasts of light and darkness in the skies they paint. The only regret a reader might have with this endlessly fascinating journal is its discontinuity: after its promising beginnings in 1822, Delacroix set it aside in October 1824, picked it up briefly when he went to Morocco in 1832, and then put it down again until 1847. Once he had resumed his project, however, he continued writing until just a few months before his death in August 1863.

Eugène Delacroix, the greatest proponent of romanticism in French painting, was born in Charenton-Saint-Maurice, close to Paris. His father, Charles-François Delacroix, a lawyer who had played an important role during the Revolution and was subsequently appointed prefect for the *département* of Bouches-du-Rhône and later for the *département* of Gironde, died when Eugène was only seven years old. Rumors persisted that his birth father was not Charles-François but rather the diplomat Maurice Talleyrand—which would explain Delacroix's strong resemblance with this famous man. He began to study painting under Guérin, but the most important influence on him at this stage of his career was Géricault, who gave him a sneak preview of the famous *Raft of the Medusa*, a painting that filled Delacroix with enthusiasm. In 1822, the same year that he began his journal, he presented his painting *Dante and Virgil in the Infernal Regions* (aka *Bark of Dante*) to the Salon in Paris, and—as is so often the case with art that breaks with accepted traditions—it was greeted with scorn by a majority of viewers. However, his *Massacre at Chios* (1824), expressing sympathy for the Greeks in their war of independence, found favor with the public (if not with all the critics), and Delacroix went on to become one of the most important painters of the Romantic period, with paintings like *The Death of Sardanapalus* (1827) and the iconic *Liberty Leading the People* (1830). Although it is of course his paintings that ensure him a place among the Immortals, Delacroix's *Journal* shows him to have considerable literary talent, and affords the reader a privileged look into the life and mind of a great artist.

THE IMMORALIST

L'Immoraliste (1902)

♦

André Gide (1869-1951)

The conflicts that pit flesh against spirit, freedom against responsibility, the senses against the intellect, and conventional morality against homosexuality, cause the tensions with which André Gide, winner of the Nobel Prize in Literature in 1947, struggled throughout his life and which provided the major themes of his writing. He was born in Paris into a strict Protestant family; his father, a university professor, died when André was eleven. Gide would eventually adopt a philosophy of "authenticity" (absolute sincerity) and "availability" or *disponibilité* (living in the moment and being open to every passing sensation). He began his literary career with *The Notebooks of André Walter* (*Les Cahiers d'André Walter*, 1891), the first expression of his inner struggle. In spite of his claim never to have felt physical desire for a woman, he married his cousin Madeleine Rondeaux upon his mother's death in 1895 in the hope that she would provide him with a measure of moral stability. The marriage was never consummated, although Gide later fathered a daughter, Catherine, by another woman. His search for authenticity led him to travel to North Africa several times, and there he discovered his homosexuality and experienced both a sensual and spiritual liberation. He wrote a number of longer works including *The Counterfeiters* (*Les Faux-Monnayeurs*, 1925–26), but one of his favorite genres was what he called a *récit*, a deceptively simple and usually ironic first-person narrative, often in the form of a confession, such as *Strait Is the Gate* (*La Porte étroite*, 1909) and *The Pastoral Symphony* (*La Symphonie pastorale*, 1919). Gide was roundly condemned for his defense of homosexuality in *Corydon* (1924), just as he had been earlier for his anticlericalism in *The Vatican Cellars* (*Les Caves du Vatican*, 1914). He participated in the founding (in 1909) and management of the famous French literary magazine *New French Review* (*La Nouvelle Revue Française*) and was briefly a "fellow traveler" of Russian Communism in the 1930s. When he died in 1951, he was remembered as one of the central figures on the French literary and intellectual scene in the first half of the twentieth century.

In *The Immoralist*, one of Gide's *récits*, an apparently credible and sympathetic narrator, Michel, recounts the story of the last three years of his life. His audience consists of three friends whom he has not seen since his wedding and whom he has asked to visit him in Algeria after his wife's death.

Michel begins his story by recounting the honeymoon trip he and his wife, Marceline, took to Tunisia. There he discovers that he has tuberculosis, and there also—at the same time—his austere, intellectual upbringing yields to the sensual pleasures of this exotic country, as Marceline devotedly nurses him back to health. Upon their return to Paris, where Michel has been appointed to the prestigious Collège de France, he also agrees to take charge of a large family farm in Normandy. On the farm, the hedonistic instincts Michel had discovered within himself in Tunisia come to the fore again, and he participates in the illegal poaching that is taking place on his own property. On one of his visits to Paris he encounters the sinister Ménalque, a true immoralist who accepts his own deviant nature and has no qualms about defying conventional bourgeois morality. Meanwhile, Marceline has become pregnant but suffers a miscarriage that compromises her health and leads her to contract tuberculosis. Michel does not show his wife the same solicitude she had manifested to him, and his proposal that they undertake a journey together to restore her health is in fact motivated by his desire to return to the places where he had discovered the pleasures of the flesh. The third part of the book adopts a frenetic rhythm as they go from Switzerland—where Marceline was in fact starting to improve but which Michel found dull and abhorrent—to Italy and finally to Algeria, where her health deteriorates alarmingly. After a night on the town, Michel returns to the hotel room where he had left his wife alone and finds her on the verge of death. As a sign of her total despair, Marceline, a devout Catholic, has thrown her rosary beads onto the floor. Michel is shamed into staying with her for the last few hours of her unhappy life.

One of the three friends remarks at the end of Michel's story that the very act of listening to it has made the three of them accomplices: because of the way Michel has presented his story they cannot help but sympathize with him, in spite of his often reprehensible behavior. "Michel remained silent for a long time. We also did not speak, prey to a strange uneasiness. Alas, we had the impression that by telling us his story, Michel had made his actions more legitimate." We, as readers, are faced with a similar dilemma, since, in spite of ourselves, we too are seduced by the power of the narrative of Michel, who is the consummate immoralist.

In Search of Lost Time: "Combray"

À la recherche du temps perdu: "Combray" (1913)

♦

Marcel Proust (1871–1922)

One of world literature's greatest novels, Marcel Proust's *In Search of Lost Time* (*À la recherche du temps perdu*), presents a challenge to the reader. It is a seven-volume work, originally published from 1913 to 1927, the last three volumes only appearing after Proust's death. Although it is exquisitely written and a joy to read, it moves at a very leisurely narrative pace and its length may appear daunting to some readers. However, "Combray," the first section in the novel's first volume, *Swann's Way* (*Du côté de chez Swann*), provides a fascinating entryway into the complete work. It has been seen as a kind of overture, introducing readers to the novel's most important themes and characters and initiating them into the subtleties and beauties of Proust's long sentences and leisurely paced narration. Written in the first person and recounted by a narrator whose name is Marcel, "Combray" seems to support the thesis that Proust's monumental work is a thinly veiled autobiography. But even though Proust, like so many authors, writes about what he knows, any personal experiences he incorporates are transformed by the author's imagination and the power of literature, thus transcending the autobiographical.

Born in Paris to a prominent physician and his wife, Marcel Proust was a sickly child, overly attached to his cultivated mother. Asthma dogged him from the age of nine and disrupted his schooling. But he was an avid reader, acquiring through his reading a wealth of knowledge about literature, music, and the fine arts, a knowledge that is everywhere apparent in his writing. Proust's earliest literary endeavor, a collection of short stories, was not particularly successful, and he turned to literary and art criticism, writing a series of essays on the English critic John Ruskin. After the death of his father in 1903 and of his mother in 1905, he withdrew from society, working assiduously on his magnum opus in a room (at No. 102 Boulevard Haussmann in Paris) with triple curtains and walls lined with cork that provided protection from distracting exterior light and noise. He published *Swann's Way* in 1913, but to his great disappointment it attracted little attention at the time. The Great War delayed until 1919 the appearance of the second volume, *Within a Budding Grove* (*À l'ombre des jeunes filles en fleurs*). It won the prestigious Goncourt Prize in 1920 and propelled Proust into the limelight. Before his death from pneumonia in 1922 he had published volumes three and four, *The Guermantes Way* (*Le Côté de Guermantes*) and *Sodom and Gomorrah* (*Sodome et Gomorrhe*); but although he had completed the entire novel prior to his demise, he had not managed to revise the final three volumes, *The Captive* (*La Prisonnière*), *The Fugitive* (*Albertine disparue*), and *Time Regained* (*Le Temps retrouvé*), which were published posthumously thanks to the efforts of his brother, Robert.

"Combray," a fictional name for Illiers, the small, provincial town near Chartres where Proust and his parents would spend summers, opens with the mature narrator Marcel looking back on his childhood and in particular on the bouts of insomnia that he suffered as a child. This section poignantly translates the anguish experienced by children in the face of events that, although insignificant to adults, can assume monumental proportions to the young. Proust excels at showing how apparently trivial occurrences can become a fundamental component of the fabric of human life. Another important subject introduced in "Combray" is that of time. Proust is interested in the way human beings can transcend time when an object, an odor, or a sound evokes complete episodes from our past, so that we have the impression that we exist simultaneously in the present and the past. Perhaps the most famous example of what Proust has called "involuntary memory" is the episode of the madeleine cake. Dipping his madeleine into a cup of tea, the narrator finds his mind flooded with the memory of performing the same action when he was a child. This experience, transforming a dreary afternoon into a moment of pure joy, "made life's problems seem unimportant, life's disasters ultimately harmless, and its brevity simply an illusion." "Combray" also introduces most of the important characters who play a central role later in the novel: the neighbor Swann, whom Marcel's family treats with a certain disdain, not realizing that he moves with ease in much higher social circles than they do; the local piano teacher, Vinteuil, whom nobody in town takes seriously, until after his death it is discovered that he was a great composer; and of course the members of Marcel's own family.

"Combray," a poetic and enchanting view of life in a bygone age, presents us with universal insights into the dramas of childhood, the multilayered nature of time, and the bursts of happiness and insight that can surprise us in the apparently unimportant events of our daily lives.

Alcools / Calligrammes

(1913/1918)

◆

Guillaume Apollinaire

(Wilhelm Apollinaris de Kostrowitzky) (1880-1918)

An art critic before becoming a published poet, Apollinaire launched his career in the heady atmosphere of Paris's early-twentieth-century artistic world, promoting the new directions being explored by his friends Picasso, Derain, Vlaminck, and the Douanier Rousseau (whom he helped "discover"). His life had begun in Rome where he was born to the free-spirited Polish adventuress Angelica de Kostrowitzky, whose love of gambling led her to raise him and his younger brother on the French and Italian rivieras. In 1901, after becoming a tutor in a German family in the Rhineland, he fell in love with the family's English governess, Annie Playden, who did not share his passion and who is evoked in many of his poems, including the well-known "The Song of the Badly Loved" ("La Chanson du mal aimé"). After leaving this position, he traveled around Germany and Austria before returning to Paris where he frequented for a time the Bateau-Lavoir, a center of cubism in Montmartre, and engaged in a torrid affair with the painter Marie Laurencin—an affair also echoed in his poetry, the first collection of which, *Alcools* (meaning, "Alcohols"), appeared in 1913. When the war broke out the following year, Apollinaire, then still an Italian citizen, tried in vain to enlist in the French army. A second attempt was successful, and his war service enabled him to become a French citizen. He continued to write poetry in the trenches, but as a result of a serious head wound he was reassigned to noncombat duty in Paris, where he found time to engage in various literary projects, including composing and producing the avant-garde play *The Breasts of Tiresias* (*Les Mamelles de Tirésias*) in 1917. In 1918 he published his second great poetry collection, *Calligrammes*, shortly before marrying Jacqueline Kolb, the "pretty redhead" ("*la jolie rousse*") who appears in his later poems. Several months later, Apollinaire's life abruptly ended, when he succumbed to the great flu pandemic.

Apollinaire was one of the poets who set the course for the innovations introduced into poetry in the twentieth century. A master of language like all great poets, he experimented both with words and poetic forms. Apollinaire can write a poem that resembles, and yet does not resemble, a ballad from the past, or he can create verse that contains a series of striking visions, replete with unusual and memorable juxtapositions of images. The fragmentary nature of this type of verse seems to reflect the fragmentation of the individual—an important theme of his verse and indeed of much modern poetry. One of Apollinaire's innovations was the complete suspension of punctuation. Stéphane Mallarmé had already used this approach in certain of his poems starting in 1895, but Apollinaire was the first French poet to eliminate punctuation consistently. In his later *Calligrammes* he rejuvenated an old poetic form in which the words on the page create a visual representation of the object described.

One of the most famous examples of his renewal of the ballad-type poem is "Mirabeau Bridge" (in *Alcools*), where the traditional image of water flowing under a bridge refers both to the passage of time and to the passing nature of love itself:

> As the days and weeks pass by
> Neither past time
> Nor our loves return
> Under the Mirabeau Bridge the Seine keeps flowing
> Let the night come and the clock strike
> The days go by I remain

The opening poem of *Alcools*, "Zone," shows the modernist aspect of Apollinaire's poetry with the striking image of the Eiffel Tower shepherding the bridges of Paris:

> All things considered you are tired of this old world
> O Shepherdess Eiffel Tower the flock of bridges is bleating this
>   morning

Apollinaire is fascinated by modern inventions such as the airplane, and he combines religion and aviation in "Zone" in a stunning image:

> It is Christ who soars up to heaven higher than the aviators
> He holds the world's record for altitude

However, his modernism does not ignore the past, and he points out that the aviators of the present and even Christ himself have predecessors like Icarus, Enoch, and Elijah, who are all supposed to have made aerial journeys of one sort or another.

Apollinaire's innovative use of language and his juxtaposition of images drawn from the world of his day with images from the past make reading this prophet of modernity an exhilarating experience.

CHÉRI

(1920)

◆

Sidonie-Gabrielle Colette (1873-1954)

The story of a love affair between a wealthy courtesan in her late forties, Léa, and a young man, the son of another well-off courtesan, might appear at first to be part of the long tradition of French stories of a younger man being initiated into sexual intimacy by an older woman. But Colette, who used her last name only as her pen name, took what had become a conventional theme and gave it a new twist: "Léa! Give it to me, give me your pearl necklace, do you hear me, Léa? Give me your necklace! [. . .] Why won't you give it to me? It looks as good on me as it does on you, even better in fact!"

Who is speaking? None other than the young Fred Peloux, the "Chéri" of the novel's title, a strangely hermaphroditic figure who has many feminine traits yet still possesses a masculine sexuality and handsomeness that attract women. And unlike his literary predecessors who were usually sexually naive when they began their relationships with older women, Chéri is sexually already quite experienced. Neither partner appears particularly happy in this liaison: the young man is usually so unresponsive and indifferent that his older mistress, Léa, often feels she is making love with both a stranger and a foreigner who cannot speak her language. Their affair has been going on for six years when the novel opens, and shortly thereafter Chéri meets a beautiful but rather insipid young woman, Edmée, on a visit to his mother's house, and decides that he will wed her. He confides to Léa that he does not love Edmée but is marrying her for her money. Léa feigns relief at finally untangling herself from her young lover and succeeds in convincing herself that it is good riddance, until one day—while the newlyweds are in Italy on their honeymoon—she goes to meet some older female friends and sees Lili, a woman close to seventy, with an adolescent lover. Finding her completely grotesque, Léa returns home, depressed at what the ravages of age have wrought on these women. However, for the first time she begins to miss Chéri actively. As an antidote to her depression she decides to take a trip south, returning to Paris after several months' absence. Meanwhile, things are not going swimmingly for Chéri and Edmée, and they contemplate divorce. A brief reunion between the two former lovers ends badly when, the next morning, Chéri observes Léa before she has made herself up and realizes how much she has aged. Léa, devastated, enjoins him to return to his young wife. But will he obey her? This short introduction to the novel cannot and indeed should not yield all its secrets—readers will have to find out for themselves.

Colette, who paints the trials of aging with such a fine brush, had already led a tumultuous life by the time she wrote *Chéri*. After an idyllic childhood in Burgundy, she married Henri Gauthier-Villars in 1893, an unscrupulous rake who, under the pseudonym Willy, published a collection of titillating novels that were penned by ghostwriters. He set his wife to work on a new series of novels featuring a young woman named Claudine, encouraging her to add erotic episodes. The *Claudine* novels became very successful. However, tired of being exploited commercially and sexually by her unfaithful husband, Colette divorced him after thirteen years of marriage and began a new career as a music hall dancer and mime. During this time she also became involved in a number of lesbian relationships, which did not prevent her from having an affair with the famous Italian poet Gabriele D'Annunzio. In 1912 she married Henri de Jouvenel, a newspaper editor, and had her only child, Colette Renée, in 1913; but apparently Colette paid little attention to her daughter. After a second divorce, probably precipitated by a scandalous affair she had with her stepson, she wrote a sequel to *Chéri, The Last of Chéri* (*La Fin de Chéri*), that appeared in 1926. She remarried in 1935, and this marriage lasted until her death. In the course of her long and varied life she authored over fifty novels, as well as short stories and other writings. These works include the novels *The Vagabond* (*La Vagabonde*, 1910) and the famous *Gigi* (1944) that inspired the popular movie of the same name, a series of autobiographical reminiscences beginning with *Claudine's House* (*La Maison de Claudine*, 1922), and memoirs of the war years she spent in Paris with her Jewish husband, *Looking Backwards* (*Journal à rebours*, 1941) and *Paris from my Window* (*De ma fenêtre*, 1944). Elected to the prestigious Goncourt Academy in 1945, Colette became its president in 1949, and when she died in Paris in 1954 she was honored with a state funeral. During her lifetime she was one of the most popular novelists in France, thanks to her perceptive depiction of French society and her dissection of its hypocrisies, often seen through the eyes of members of the demimonde. Colette takes us into this world with *Chéri*, a lively, gender-bending novel presented from a feminine perspective.

THÉRÈSE DESQUEYROUX

(1927)

◆

François Mauriac (1885-1970)

We watch a woman apprehensively leaving a courthouse with her lawyer. He calls out to a man waiting outside under a tree, "Case dismissed." The woman is Thérèse Desqueyroux and the man is her father, but we are puzzled at the way he receives the news. No word of congratulation, no embrace; instead he ignores her completely, plunging into a conversation with the lawyer to reassure himself that the verdict will not be overturned. We learn Thérèse's story piecemeal, as she muses over her past and over the events that led up to her trial for attempted murder. Mauriac based his story on a real trial that had occurred some twenty years previously in Bordeaux, in which a woman had attempted to poison her husband by forging his prescriptions. Since her husband refused to testify against her, she was acquitted of the murder charge but jailed for forgery. Mauriac uses many of the details of this case, and creates a highly enigmatic character in Thérèse, who appears to be inhabited by some instinct that pulls her irresistibly toward evil. But her action can also be seen as a gesture of revolt against the stifling bourgeois milieu in which she lives, where the family name and family honor must be protected at all costs. It is not out of pity or love that her husband Bernard refuses to testify against her, but simply so that the family name will not be sullied. When Thérèse had agreed to marry Bernard, she had done it for practical reasons; both her family and his had considerable landholdings in the Bordeaux region, and Thérèse had "the love of property in her blood." She soon finds marriage stultifying and sees an opportunity to murder her husband by increasing the dose of a medication prescribed for him, Fowler's drops, a preparation containing small amounts of arsenic. As Bernard becomes sicker, Thérèse's plot is discovered by the family doctor and the local pharmacist. When these facts are reported to the authorities she is brought to trial but acquitted because Bernard will not testify against her. However, her troubles do not end here since her husband, in accepting her back, makes a virtual prisoner of her, only agreeing to let her live her own life when he is sure that she can do no further harm to the family's name or honor. He helps her move to Paris, fulfilling a dream she has nourished for a long time. Before he departs Paris he accompanies her to a café, where for the first time in their marriage they are on the verge of having a real conversation. But Bernard's lack of sensitivity and stolid self-assurance frustrate any real communication. The meaningful conversation never takes place and he bids Thérèse good-bye, leaving her alone on the café's outdoor terrace to smoke and drink wine, as she contemplates the passing throngs. She reapplies her makeup, and, with a faint smile that suggests the possibility of happiness, leaves the café and moves aimlessly off into the crowd.

Mauriac's fictional character Thérèse fascinated him, and he wrote three more stories featuring Thérèse. He saw in her a tragic figure, a kind of monster but one who might possibly be redeemed. In a short preface to the novel addressed to her he confessed: "I had hoped that your suffering, Thérèse, would have led you to God [. . .] at least on the sidewalk where I leave you, I cherish the hope that you are not alone." Not limited by a narrow, bourgeois view of morality, Mauriac found her intriguing because he saw in her the reflection of his own sinful human nature. As an outspoken Catholic writer, Mauriac was able to feel love for the sinner if not the sin.

Born in Bordeaux, François Mauriac was raised by his mother and grandparents after the death of his father. He began his writing career as a poet but soon turned to novels; The Leper's Kiss (Le Baiser au lépreux, 1922) was his first success. It was followed by Génétrix in 1923, The Desert of Love (Le Désert de l'amour) in 1925, and then Thérèse Desqueyroux. His many subsequent novels included The Vipers' Tangle (Le Nœud de vipères, 1932), The Frontenac Mystery (Le Mystère Frontenac, 1933), and his last novel, Maltaverne, which appeared posthumously in 1972. Although on the political right, he condemned the rise of fascism in Europe and, during the Nazi occupation, was a member of the Resistance. During the Algerian War, Mauriac strongly criticized the use of torture by the French military, and he became a firm supporter of De Gaulle when he was elected president of the Fifth Republic in 1958. Mauriac's literary honors included election to the Académie française in 1933 and the Nobel Prize in Literature in 1952. He died in 1970, having returned to the character of Thérèse several times in his subsequent work. In spite of his obvious sympathy for her, however, he never allowed her to obtain religious redemption. In many ways she can be seen as a modern version of Racine's Phaedra, who is often described in terms of a Jansenist conception of predestination as "a soul to whom Divine Grace was denied."

NADJA

(1928)

◆

André Breton (1896-1966)

S trolling down the Rue La Fayette in Paris one afternoon, the first-person narrator of this novel, whom we will call André because of the novel's semiautobiographical nature, notices a mysterious young woman who is strangely made up and is so thin and frail that she seems to float rather than walk. Experiencing a strange attraction to her, he makes her acquaintance, discovering that she has taken the name Nadja, because "this is the beginning of the word 'hope' in Russian but also because it is only the beginning." Thus commences a strange odyssey in which the two meet regularly in cafés or on the street and stroll aimlessly around Paris. Nadja is a woman on the fringes of madness, living in an imaginary world unfettered by logic or morality. In the eyes of a surrealist like Breton, this mental state provides a direct connection to the unconscious, so important to the adherents of the surrealist movement who wanted to distance themselves from the positivist, rational current prevalent in Western thought since ancient Greece. This current, said Breton in his 1924 *Manifestos of Surrealism*, "seems to me hostile to intellectual and moral advancement. I despise it, for it is a combination of mediocrity, hatred, and dull conceit." Surrealists believed that the usual division established between the "real," material world and the world of the mind, the unconscious, was mistaken. Influenced by Freud but also by the visionary poets of the nineteenth century (like Rimbaud), they were fascinated by dreams, by psychic phenomena, by coincidence, which they saw not as haphazard but as revealing secret connections that cannot be deduced by rational thought. *Nadja* opens with a question that the narrator asks himself: "Who am I?" The narrator's meditation on this question leads him to a French proverb, "Dis-moi qui tu hantes et je te dirai qui tu es" (literally, "Tell me whom you haunt, I'll tell you who you are," i.e., "People are known by the company they keep"). This is particularly appropriate for a surrealist, since the verb "to haunt" in French and English means both "to frequent" and "to haunt." André's fascination with Nadja is therefore part of his search for self-knowledge, which comes not just from the "real" world but also from the realm of the unconscious. André recounts the time spent with Nadja—and their relationship is not physical but based on a more intellectual attraction—until she is committed to an asylum because of her increasingly erratic behavior. The last words of the novel have become famous: "La beauté sera CONVULSIVE ou ne sera pas" ("Beauty will produce a CONVULSIVE reaction in the beholder or it will not be beauty"); this is illustrated in the book by Nadja's particular beauty, which constantly attracts the attention of others. In order to show that the surreal is not distinct from reality but rather a part of it, Breton has interspersed his text with forty illustrations consisting of photos of the areas of Paris the couple frequented, reproductions of artwork, and several of Nadja's own drawings (and these are works of the real "Nadja" who inspired the story), which, not surprisingly, have a surrealist quality. He presents a vivid picture of Paris, with Nadja's surreal presence revealing all manner of hidden connections in the novel's world.

Breton himself came from Normandy and started out as a medical student but soon turned to poetry and art. After flirting with Dadaism, circa 1919 he joined together with other writers and artists such as Louis Aragon, Paul Éluard, Philippe Soupault, and Pierre Reverdy to form a new surrealist group that was interested in the role of the subconscious in both art and life. Fascinated by automatic writing (a literary extension of Freudian free association), by the role of chance and chance encounters, and by paranormal phenomena, they were also committed to promoting freedom in all its forms. The surrealist artists and writers often produced startling images and unusual combinations of objects, comparing their artistic goals to that of the nineteenth-century poet Lautréamont, who famously juxtaposed a sewing machine and an umbrella on an operating table in one of his poems. Breton joined the French Communist Party in 1927 but left it in 1935, after major disagreements over party policies. In 1938, on an official French mission to Mexico, he met Trotsky, and together they wrote a manifesto calling for the "complete freedom of art." During World War II, after the Vichy government banned his writings, he sought asylum in the United States. He returned to Paris after the war and became an outspoken opponent of French colonialism, remaining true to the ideals of surrealism until his death in 1966. A seminal writer whose influence was enormous, Breton left a rich collection of theoretical writings including three surrealist manifestos (1924, 1930, and 1934), poems, as well as a series of prose writings that include *Nadja* and *Mad Love* (*L'Amour fou*, 1937). His exploration of the connectedness of dream and reality, of the conscious and unconscious, make this novel intriguing, compelling, and—indeed—surreal.

LOCK 14

Le Charretier de la Providence *(1931)*

◆

Georges Simenon (1903-1989)

If we were asked to name the best-known fictional detective in the English-speaking world, our immediate answer would be Sherlock Holmes. Likewise, a francophone, when asked for the French equivalent, would immediately designate Inspector Jules Maigret, of the Quai des Orfèvres (the French equivalent of Scotland Yard) in Paris. Maigret is the creation of the intensely prolific Belgian writer Georges Simenon, who was born in Liège but lived successively in various French cities, including Paris (where he had an affair with Josephine Baker). Suspected of collaboration with the Germans during the Second World War (although the facts are far from clear), Simenon moved to Canada and then to the United States, returning to Europe in 1955 with his Canadian wife Denyse and their daughter, finally settling in Lausanne, Switzerland. His personal life was tragic: Denyse, his second wife, was committed to a psychiatric institution in 1964 and never returned home, publishing a biting exposé of their married life in 1978. That same year, their daughter committed suicide. When Simenon died in Lausanne in 1989, he left instructions that his body be cremated and his ashes mixed with those of his daughter and scattered behind his house.

Simenon wrote over two hundred books under his own name, and many others under various pseudonyms. He loved to mingle with high society and was a great self-promoter. Indeed, biographers have difficulty separating truth from fiction, and not all of his boasting is as easy to dismiss as the clearly preposterous claim that he had slept with more than 10,000 women. It is thus interesting that his most famous character, Maigret, is the incarnation of bourgeois respectability, living in a middle-class Parisian neighborhood with his devoted wife, Louise, who loves to spoil him with hearty meals. The only trait Maigret has in common with his creator is their propensity for heavy drinking. The inspector even consumes large quantities of beer, wine, and Calvados during the course of his investigations. Maigret, who also smokes a trademark pipe, solves his cases not by stunning Sherlockian flashes of deduction, but by solid, meticulous police work. But he is also very conscious of the importance of character and milieu, and his "method" consists of identifying as completely as possible with both victim and perpetrator. Simenon excels not only in creating believable and well-drawn characters but also in evoking an authentic sense of place. He brilliantly captures the Paris of the 1930s, 1940s, and 1950s, evoking equally convincingly the lives of average Parisians and those of the wealthy, and developing plots that often set the different classes on a collision course. This talent extends to his representation of French provincial life.

Lock 14, one of the earliest of the Maigret stories, takes place along the canals of northern France in the 1920s. Even today, Europe's excellent fluvial network is an important means for transporting merchandise. This was even more the case at the time *Lock 14* was written, when motor vessels shared the canals with barges drawn by horses plodding along the towpaths, and occasionally with pleasure boats belonging to the idle rich. In his representation of French society, Simenon delights in juxtaposing the working people with well-off bourgeois and aristocrats, and the gap between the classes is easily bridged by Maigret, a farmer's son who was raised on the property of an aristocrat. The novel begins with the discovery of the corpse of a fashionably dressed young woman, hidden under the straw that the *Providence*, one of the older horse-drawn barges, keeps on board as fodder for its animals. Maigret's attention is soon drawn to a smart-looking yacht, the *Southern Cross*, which is sailing up the same stretch of canal. Belonging to an English aristocrat with a weakness for wine and beautiful women, it is transporting a motley group of international society people on a pleasure trip. The body proves to be that of Mary Lampson, the aristocrat's wife, who had disappeared two days previously after an altercation with her fellow passengers. Maigret begins an exhaustive investigation of the two worlds that intersect at the crime scene, the daily grind of the working-class barge people and the superficial and extravagant lives of the society types. Suffice it to say that Maigret's method is effective once more, that the criminal is unmasked, but not without many twists and turns of the plot.

Lock 14 provides today's readers not only with an unusual mystery to unravel, but also with a realistic and fascinating look at a segment of French life that is still attractive, as evidenced by the current popularity of barge vacations in France. These elements are enriched by the author's use of the canal and its traffic as a metaphor for the vagaries of everyday life and for the chance events that can become the instruments of destiny. It is no accident that the name of the barge at the center of the drama is *Providence*.

MAN'S FATE

La Condition humaine (1933)

◆

André Malraux (1901–1976)

While popular opinion stereotypes the typical author as a reserved, bookish person who spends most of her or his time in a study or library, the reverse is more often true, and there are many examples—both past and present—of writers who managed to juggle several careers and played important roles on the political, social, and literary scenes. However, few writers have led a more adventurous and varied life than André Malraux. The son of a Parisian stockbroker who committed suicide in 1930, Malraux became a kind of pre–Indiana Jones figure, exploring the Cambodian jungle for archaeological artifacts with his first wife when he was just twenty-one years old. He ran afoul of the French authorities by removing some bas-reliefs from a temple and was arrested upon his return to France. His contact with Asian culture did profoundly influence him, and he produced a series of novels set in Southeast Asia, including *The Conquerors* (*Les Conquérants*, 1928) and *The Royal Way* (*La Voie Royale*, 1930), both set in Cambodia. For Malraux, art was one of the principal ways in which humankind could give meaning to existence. In his last novel, *The Walnut Trees of Altenburg* (*Les Noyers de l'Altenburg*, 1943), he mused: "The greatest mystery of all is not that we have been cast at random between the profusion of matter and the heavens, it is that [. . .] we are able to draw from within ourselves images that are powerful enough to deny our nothingness." In 1933, he published *Man's Fate*, a novel for which he was awarded the coveted Goncourt Prize. Set in Shanghai, *Man's Fate* tells of a struggle in 1927 between the communists and Chiang Kai-shek's nationalists. Its plot suggests another way in which humankind can give purpose to existence: through action and, above all, political action. Like many left-leaning Americans and Europeans, Malraux took part in the Spanish Civil War against the Nationalists. Enlisting in the French Army at the outbreak of World War II, he was captured by the Germans, managed to escape, and joined the Resistance. After the war, abandoning his leftist politics, he was appointed minister of information and later became France's first minister of culture, a post he occupied until the end of de Gaulle's presidency in 1969. No longer writing novels, he authored a series of works about art that became *The Voices of Silence* (*Les Voix du silence*, 1951), and also wrote a number of autobiographical works including the acclaimed *Antimémoires* (1967). Malraux's personal life was marked by tragedy. During the Second World War, he and his first wife, Clara, divorced. His second wife, Josette, was killed when she slipped while boarding a train, and their two sons died in an automobile accident in 1961. Malraux died in 1976, and in recognition of his literary achievements, his writings on art, and his work to preserve France's cultural heritage his ashes were transferred to the Pantheon in 1996, the greatest tribute France can pay to one of its citizens.

Man's Fate is an exciting, dynamic novel in which the action sequences are interspersed with periods of reflection by its characters on how to confront the riddle of human existence. Because Malraux's existential philosophy had no religious dimension, his protagonists justify their own lives by their political action and their gestures of solidarity toward their fellow human beings. The novel opens with a breathlessly suspenseful scene, portraying an assassin, Tchen, who is about to kill a political opponent asleep in his bed. The almost cinematographic sequence presents the assassination from Tchen's point of view, making the reader privy to his fears when, after silently breaking into the enemy's bedroom, he hesitates before finally stabbing the recumbent body. "Should Tchen lift up the mosquito net or should he strike through it? His stomach was knotted with fear [. . .] but he was fascinated with this mass of white muslin hanging from the ceiling [. . .] from which one foot protruded [. . .] a living thing—human flesh." There are other scenes that stay indelibly imprinted in our minds. In one, a group of communist prisoners who have been betrayed by the Chinese nationalists are awaiting a particularly gruesome form of execution: being thrown into the fired-up boiler of a steam locomotive. One of them, Katov, has a cyanide capsule that he intends to take, exactly as his friend and fellow revolutionary Kyo has just done, rather than submitting to this horror. However, when he hears two other prisoners expressing their intense fear of dying in this brutal fashion, he gives them the cyanide to allow them the easier death he had been reserving for himself, showing his compassion and human solidarity. This selfless gesture is Katov's way of assuming his own destiny and giving meaning to his life and death. *Man's Fate* is a powerful novel, and the various questions it raises will engage readers and perhaps even cause them to reflect on their own life choices.

Nausea

La Nausée (1938)

♦

Jean-Paul Sartre (1905-1980)

Antoine Roquentin has a problem: he is suddenly afflicted by a strange disconnect with reality. We find him, in his thirties, in a fictional town, Bouville (Mudville), located on the northern French coast and clearly modeled on Le Havre. Here, trying his hand at writing a history of an obscure eighteenth-century aristocrat, he is doing research in the town library. It is not just that things seem meaningless—they also seem to have no tangible relationship with Roquentin. This feeling gradually invades his whole existence and fills him with anguish. When, for example, he runs into an acquaintance in the library, he records his reaction: "This morning, at the library, when the Autodidact came over to say hello, it took me ten seconds to recognize him. I saw a strange face, which I scarcely recognized as a face. And then there was his hand, which, when we were shaking hands, was like a big white worm in my own." To this strange feeling of alienation, most often provoked by the objects of everyday life, but sometimes by surrealist visions associated with these objects, he gives the name "nausea." Sartre's first novel, *Nausea* illustrates the early phase of Sartre's existentialism. It takes the form of a diary written by Roquentin, who begins jotting down his thoughts in order to find out what is happening to him. What Roquentin is feeling is what existentialists call absurdity, which means that the world has no significance beyond individual existence and that it is up to each person to create his or her own meaning. Humankind, blessed or perhaps cursed with free will, is responsible for its own destiny. This revelation comes to Roquentin one day when, in the town park, he gazes at the partially exposed root of a chestnut tree and suddenly realizes that it exists totally independently from his own existence. As he puts it, "This moment was an extraordinary one [. . .] I understood Nausea [. . .] To exist is simply to be there." The realization that he is completely contingent, that he is *de trop* (superfluous), and that everything, including he himself, is *gratuit* (gratuitous), paradoxically gives his life new meaning. He decides to abandon his scholarly project, and, inspired by an American jazz tune, he recognizes the value of art that can transcend mere existence and bring happiness. In the closing pages of the book, Roquentin is packing his suitcase in order to move to Paris where he intends to write a novel. Artistic creation will, so he hopes, give meaning to his existence. Although *Nausea* is a philosophical novel, it is extremely readable as one man's intellectual and spiritual odyssey. By confronting his hero with a cast of mediocre characters such as the Autodidact, a man who decides to educate himself at the town library by reading all the volumes of the encyclopedia from A to Z, Sartre criticizes the superficiality and the hypocrisy of the typical bourgeois existence.

Jean-Paul Sartre was the leading light of the existentialist movement. Born in Paris into a bourgeois Protestant family, he was related to Albert Schweitzer. He attended the École Normale Supérieure to become a teacher of philosophy. Interestingly, having failed his final exams initially, he had to retake them the following year at the same time as the woman who was to become his life partner—Simone de Beauvoir. *Nausea* was accepted by the publishing house Gallimard, which persuaded him to change the original title from *Melancholia*. Conscripted into the army in 1939, Sartre was taken prisoner by the Germans in 1940 but managed to get himself released on account of his eye problems. On his return to Paris, he started writing plays, including *The Flies* (*Les Mouches*, 1943) and *No Exit* (*Huis clos*, 1944, perhaps his most famous play), as well as his philosophical magnum opus, *Being and Nothingness* (*L'Etre et le néant*, 1943). After the war, Sartre embraced communism and became France's leading intellectual. Disillusioned by the Soviet invasion of Hungary in 1956, he turned his attention to human rights violations in Algeria. A staunch leftist, he supported the student uprisings of May 1968. His health and eyesight worsened as he grew older, and his long and extraordinary career finally ended on April 15, 1980. If Roquentin sought through art to benefit from a sense of engagement and personal responsibility, these traits also defined the work and life of his creator. The famous line from *No Exit*, "Hell is other people" ("L'enfer, c'est les autres")—which according to Sartre only referred to specific situations and was not a general statement—did not prevent him from working for and with others for the betterment of humankind. His controversial decision to decline the Nobel Prize in Literature, offered to him in 1964, testifies to his fierce independence. Sartre was one of the great writer-philosophers of our time.

THE STRANGER

L'Étranger (1942)

◆

Albert Camus (1913-1960)

Albert Camus once described the basic thesis of his famous novel in the following way: "In our society any man who does not cry at his mother's funeral runs the risk of being condemned to death." This was his way of illustrating a key element of his works—the existence of the absurd, by which he meant the irrational nature of human existence. Camus, born into extreme poverty and raised in the sun-drenched country of Algeria, was a *pied noir*, a descendant of French settlers who had made their home in Algeria after it became a French colony in 1830. A talented young man studying philosophy at the University of Algiers, Camus was athletic and apparently healthy when he suddenly discovered that he had contracted tuberculosis. This illness, which recurred throughout his life, forced him to interrupt his studies. Although he did complete a bachelor's degree later, he was unable to pursue a doctorate as he had originally intended. He saw this illness as a concrete and personal manifestation of the absurd in his own life, and it is a constant theme in his works, which include *The Plague* (*La Peste*, 1947), *The Fall* (*La Chute*, 1956), a number of plays such as *The Misunderstanding* (*Le Malentendu*, 1944) and *Caligula* (1945), as well as short stories and philosophical writings. He moved to Paris in 1942 for further treatment of his disease and worked at the Resistance newspaper *Combat*, of which he became principal editor after the liberation of France.

The Stranger, which some have described as an existential novel (although Camus has refused this label), recounts the story of Meursault, a young *pied noir* whose unexceptional life is centered on sensual pleasures. As the novel begins, Meursault has just received a telegram informing him of his mother's death in a retirement home not far from Algiers. He and his mother had become virtual strangers (one of the many instances of estrangement evoked by the novel's title), and although he dutifully attends the funeral, he neither feels nor manifests any of the usual emotions society associates with such an event. Meursault is no monster, but he refuses to display emotions that he does not feel. The same sincerity holds true for his affair with Marie, a former coworker whom he sees again at the beach just after his mother's death. Although he desires her, he does not love her: "When she laughed, I found her even more desirable. A moment later, she asked me if I loved her. I replied that it didn't really mean anything and that I didn't think so. She looked sad." A series of chance encounters and events leads to the culminating event that changes his life. On a weekend excursion to a nearby beach with some friends, Meursault, after having consumed a great deal of wine—whence the appropriateness of his name, which is also that of a famous white burgundy—and dazzled by the sun, finds himself face to face with an ethnic Algerian (referred to as simply *l'Arabe*—the Arab—in the story) with whom he and his friends had had a prior altercation. The ethnic Algerian draws a knife and as the sun glints on its blade Meursault, in a kind of hallucination, believes he is under attack and shoots the man: "It seemed to me that the sky had split open and was raining fire down upon me. My whole being had become taut and I clasped the revolver with my hand. The trigger released and I touched the polished surface of the grip [. . .] I understood that I had destroyed the peace of the day and the silence of the beach where I had been happy. Then I fired four more bullets into the motionless body on the sand and it was as though I was knocking four times on the door of misfortune."

The second part of the novel deals with Meursault's trial and the way in which the lawyer for the prosecution absurdly invokes the lack of sensitivity he had displayed at his mother's funeral in order to find him guilty of first-degree murder and to sentence him to death. Meursault rejects the solace of religion offered by the prison chaplain, and by consciously accepting his fate, he realizes the "tender indifference of the world" and the possibility of happiness, even in the face of his imminent execution. Coming to appreciate the importance of his fellow human beings, Meursault expresses the hope that there will be many spectators present when he is guillotined, since even "their cries of hate" will remind him that he is not alone. In spite of the absurdity of life, human solidarity—whatever form it takes—is an immeasurably precious part of the human condition.

Camus once said that the most absurd way to die is in a car accident. Just a little over two years after winning the Nobel Prize in Literature (1957), above all for his writings against capital punishment, he and his publisher, Michel Gallimard, were killed in an automobile crash near Villeblevin in the northern part of Burgundy. Camus was forty-six years old.

THE LITTLE PRINCE

Le Petit Prince (1943)

◆

Antoine de Saint-Exupéry (1900-1944)

Aéropostale is still a name to conjure with. It was a company of intrepid young pilots in the early days of commercial aviation that inaugurated a worldwide airmail network. *Aéropostale* was originally founded by Pierre Latécoère, a French aircraft manufacturer. First known as *Lignes aériennes Latécoère,* or simply *la Ligne* (the Line), it became *Aéropostale* in 1927. These were heady and dangerous times for those who took to the air in flimsy planes with rudimentary instrumentation, poor charts, and temperamental motors. In this pre-radar environment, many planes simply disappeared on flights over the Atlantic, the desert, or the jungle. Amelia Earhart's still unsolved disappearance over the Pacific Ocean is only the most famous of many such aviation mysteries.

Antoine de Saint-Exupéry (nicknamed "Saint-Exup"), born to aristocratic parents in Lyon, was one of these daring young pilots. Fascinated by planes and aviators since childhood, he finally learned to fly during his military service. Subsequently, after trying his hand at business, he decided that a career in aviation was his true vocation, and in 1926 joined the Line as a mail pilot on the Toulouse-Dakar run. Stationed at the airfield of Cape Juby on the coast of Northwest Africa, he wrote his first book, *Southern Mail (Courrier Sud,* 1928), recounting the tribulations of the gallant aviators who established a transatlantic link to South America, an enterprise in which he participated alongside his colleague, the famous Jean Mermoz. Other works followed, including *Wind, Sand and Stars (Terre des hommes,* 1939)—a hymn to the solidarity of humankind—and *Flight to Arras (Pilote de guerre,* 1942), about his wartime flying experiences during the Battle of France in 1940.

In 1935 he attempted a flight from Paris to Saigon but crash-landed in the Libyan desert, only saved in extremis by wandering Bedouins. On a transatlantic flight in 1938, his plane crashed in Guatemala, causing him serious injury. In 1940, after the French armistice with Germany, he took refuge in the United States, where he wrote *The Little Prince* (the original manuscript is held by the Morgan Library in New York City). After the Allied invasion of France, he returned home and resumed his combat flights while continuing to write. On July 31, 1944, he took off from Corsica on a reconnaissance mission over France, but his plane disappeared. Various theories about his disappearance have been formulated over the years, but none has been accepted as the final word on the matter. The mystery surrounding his death remains.

Saint-Exupéry was not only an aviator and a writer, he was also a philosopher, and his books chronicle the adventures of early aviation while expounding a philosophy praising the value of love and friendship in an otherwise solitary world. This perhaps naive but touching philosophy is nowhere more simply and eloquently expressed than in *The Little Prince*. Ostensibly a children's book, illustrated by the author himself, it is also a fable for adults that aims to teach them to look at the world through childlike eyes and to recognize that material possessions are unimportant in life. What makes life worthwhile are intangible things like love, hope, and friendship. The story is narrated in the first person by an aviator, who, because of a mechanical problem, has to make a forced landing in the desert, just like Saint-Exupéry had to. While attempting to repair his aircraft, the aviator spies a young boy who seems to have appeared out of nowhere and who asks him to draw a sheep. The narrator attempts to comply, but the young boy is not satisfied with the result until the narrator draws a box with holes in it and proclaims that the sheep is inside. The young boy, referred to as the Little Prince, is delighted because the sheep he imagines in the box is far superior to the aviator's renditions. The aviator learns that the Little Prince has come from a tiny faraway planet on which he had left a cherished rose, stopping on various other planets on his journey to earth and meeting various human species such as the King and the Businessman, all of whom are satirized, their complicated and materialistic characters being contrasted with the Little Prince's own clear-sighted wisdom. We learn that the Little Prince regrets having left his planet and is concerned about the welfare of his rose. When he sees an adder in the desert sand, he allows himself to be bitten so that he will die and can then return to his planet. Looking for the boy's body the next morning, the aviator discovers that it has disappeared, a sign that the Little Prince has been reunited with his rose. Summing up his philosophy, Saint-Exupéry writes: "What is important is invisible to the eye [. . .] What I see before me is just a shell, the essentials are invisible." Love triumphs and proves to be the most important blessing to which humans can aspire. The message may be old, but it is one that is eternally new, particularly when presented as simply and exquisitely as in this wonderful little allegory.

ANTIGONE

(1944)

◆

Jean Anouilh (1910-1987)

Idealism versus realpolitik, youth versus age, collaboration versus resistance, all these conflicts can be seen in Jean Anouilh's play *Antigone*, which he wrote during the Nazi occupation of France. Taking the basic plot of Sophocles's ancient Greek tragedy of the same name, Anouilh—while keeping the original characters—gives the play a much more contemporary flavor. The actors wear modern dress, smoke, and talk about going to bars. The chorus, a staple of traditional Greek tragedy, gives often ironic commentary on what is happening or is going to happen, and of course the actors speak in prose, not verse, as was the case with the original Greek play. Anouilh's basic plot is a family drama, pitting the idealistic and uncompromising young Antigone, daughter of her ill-fated parents, Oedipus and Jocasta, against her uncle Creon, who is now king, having prevailed in the power struggle that had followed Oedipus's departure from Thebes and subsequent death. Both of Antigone's brothers, Eteocles and Polynices, had participated in the struggle on opposite sides and had ended up killing each other in the final battle. To cement his victory, Creon decides to give Eteocles, who had chosen his side, a hero's funeral while Polynices's body is to be left to rot for a month as punishment for treachery against the state. Creon has issued a stern edict warning that anyone trying to bury the body will be sentenced to death. Even though she was not particularly close to her brothers, Antigone is revolted by the fate meted out to Polynices and defies Creon's orders by putting a small quantity of soil on her brother's body by night to give it at least a partial burial. The naive nature of this gesture is underlined by the fact that she uses the sort of small shovel a child uses to dig in the sand at the beach. The soldiers guarding the body catch her in the act and bring her before Creon, who tries to reason with her. He reveals that her brother Polynices was a less than admirable character, but that in any case, the bodies of the two brothers were so mutilated that he is not even sure he chose the right body for public humiliation. He confides in her the daily compromises he must make in order for the ship of state (the metaphor he himself uses) to continue sailing, and in the name of the common good. Antigone is unyielding and threatens to commit the same "crime" if she is released. The inevitable happens, with tragic consequences not only for Antigone but also for her fiancé, Hémon. At the end of the play Creon is left on stage, weary and disillusioned, talking to a young page. "Are you eager to grow up?" he asks the lad. When he receives an affirmative answer, he continues: "You're crazy, my boy. Don't ever grow up."

Although not a true tragic heroine, since she admits at one point that she is not sure why she is sacrificing her life, Antigone nevertheless embodies the spirit of the Resistance and its rebellion against the compromises of the Vichy government. The play was censored when it was first published in 1942, but was finally staged in Paris in 1944, just a few months before the city's liberation.

Jean Anouilh was something of an unlikely man of the theater. Born in Bordeaux, the son of a tailor, he was brought up in near poverty. He spent a short time in Paris studying law, but quickly abandoned his studies in order to write copy for a publicity firm. His contacts with the theater began when he married an actress in 1931 and took the post of secretary to the great actor Louis Jouvet. In 1932, he began writing his first plays, which were not successful. During the German occupation, he did his best to appear neutral and no doubt hoped that the subversive message of *Antigone* would not be obvious, since—technically at least—it is Creon, not Antigone, who prevails. However, the authorities were not fooled. After the war, he had a string of successes, including his play about Joan of Arc called *The Lark* (*L'Alouette*, 1953), which is also about a young woman who refuses to compromise. A highly successful film adaptation of his play *Becket* (1959) starred Richard Burton as the archbishop of Canterbury and Peter O'Toole as King Henry II. Anouilh's plays were so varied in their subjects and approaches that he divided them into categories: black (tragedies and realistic dramas), pink (those based on fantasy), jarring (those with black humor), brilliant, and so on. Although he gained an international reputation, in Paris his star shone less brightly when the theater of the absurd—with its emphasis on nonrealism and its exploitation of the existential notion of absurdity—monopolized the attention of theatergoers in the 1950s. In view of Anouilh's enthusiastic endorsement of Beckett's *Waiting for Godot* (see page 155), this is rather ironic. Nevertheless, his version of the story of Antigone and Creon, one of his finest plays, still provokes lively and meaningful debate: is it better to emulate Creon's practical politics and willingness to compromise, or Antigone's refusal to betray her principles, idealistic though they may be?

THE SECOND SEX

Le Deuxième Sexe (1949)

♦

Simone de Beauvoir (1908-1986)

Often considered one of the most significant books of the twentieth century, and certainly one of the founding texts of the modern feminist movement, *The Second Sex* is a brilliant study of the subservient position of women in society since antiquity. If parts of it seem somewhat dated today, it is only because Beauvoir's analysis and those it spawned have been instrumental in alleviating many of the problems and obstacles confronting women in contemporary Western society. Of course, in certain other societies, little or nothing has changed. Although it is not possible to encapsulate a wide-ranging, 360-page work in one sentence, its best-known phrase concisely expresses its basic thesis: "You are not born woman, you become one" ("On ne naît pas femme: on le devient"). While Beauvoir does not deny the biological differences between the sexes, she points out that the gender role traditionally attributed to women by society is not determined by any biological, psychological, or economic "destiny." Beauvoir lays the blame for the oppression of women squarely at the feet of male-dominated civilizations. "It is civilization as a whole that has created this product halfway between the male and the castrato that is called 'female.'" Gender roles are constructed by society, she says, and that mythical quality, "the eternal feminine," is a pure fabrication, its purpose to keep women in a state of subservience. As Beauvoir points out: "Until age twelve, a girl is as robust as her brothers, she demonstrates the same intellectual qualities, and there is no area in which she is not allowed to compete with them." Of course the same is true of boys: they are not born "men," they become them, the crucial difference being that men are not confined to the subservient, powerless position forced upon women—men can assume infinitely more roles. *The Second Sex* is simultaneously a history of the subjugation of women, a philosophical text that shows that the passive role assigned to women has no logical or physiological basis, and a rallying cry for women to demand equal rights. Beauvoir, influenced by her lifelong companion, Jean-Paul Sartre, and existential philosophy, believes in the power that each of us has to create our own destiny. Women must react aggressively against the passive roles of wife and mother that have been forced upon them, so that when, with increasing age, they are no longer able to produce children, their whole identity will not be called into question. Beauvoir does not place all the blame on men, however. In the final section of her work she criticizes the way most women accept and justify their secondary position because it is socially acceptable and indeed comfortable. Breaking loose from the traditional mold is difficult, and according to Beauvoir the only way to do so is to gain economic independence by working outside the domestic arena. Today, many women in Western societies have accomplished this feat and are no longer "solely" wives and mothers. However, as any working woman can attest, those who wish to undertake both work and motherhood still encounter many more obstacles and problems than men who are both workers and fathers. Although progress has been made, much remains to be achieved, and *The Second Sex* is still relevant to these serious preoccupations.

Simone de Beauvoir was a model for her message. Born in Paris to bourgeois parents, she knew that her father would have preferred to have sons, or at least a son, rather than the two daughters he and his wife had. However, he did encourage Simone to pursue her studies and nourished her love of literature, which he shared. She studied philosophy in Paris and prepared for the rigorous *agrégation* exam. She succeeded brilliantly, coming second only to Jean-Paul Sartre, who was taking the exam for the second time. She and Sartre became lifelong companions, although their relationship was an open one, which allowed them both to engage in other amorous liaisons. They decided not to have children and, curiously, never actually lived together, preferring to maintain their individual freedom, that quality so essential to an existential lifestyle. In addition to philosophical texts, Beauvoir also wrote fiction, and after her first novel, *She Came to Stay* (*L'Invitée*, 1943), was published, she gave up teaching philosophy to become a writer. In 1954 her novel *The Mandarins* (*Les Mandarins*) was awarded the Goncourt Prize. At first tempted by Communism (as was Sartre), she became disillusioned by conditions in the Soviet Union and China, although she remained in many ways a Marxist and took a stand against French atrocities during the war in Algeria. She took to the streets on the side of the students and workers in the May 1968 riots. In 1981, after Sartre's death, she wrote *Adieux: A Farewell to Sartre* (*La Cérémonie des adieux*).

The Second Sex, the most influential among Simone de Beauvoir's many literary and philosophical works, has inspired many of the social and economic advances women have achieved since World War II.

BLACK SHACK ALLEY

La Rue Cases-Nègres (1950)

◆

Joseph Zobel (1915-2006)

The relative prosperity of present-day Martinique, whose capital, Fort-de-France, could almost be a French Mediterranean seaside resort transplanted directly into the volcanic soil of that lush and beautiful island, should not blind us to the fact that it has not always been so and that it has known the grinding poverty that is still the norm on some other Caribbean islands. The autobiographical novel *Black Shack Alley* (sometimes translated as *Sugar Cane Alley*) reminds us movingly and with wistful humor what it was like for a black child to grow up in the Martinique of the 1930s. Since the mother of the protagonist, José, has had to take a job as a live-in domestic in the house of the white owner of the local sugar mill, José is raised by his grandmother, whom he calls m'man Tine (an abbreviation of M'man Amantine), in a little shack on Rue Cases-Nègres. The young boy is left to his own devices during the day when his grandmother has to join other parents who live on the street in backbreaking work in the sugar cane plantations, still a staple crop of the island at that time. Although slavery had been abolished in the previous century, Martinique society was still highly stratified, divided into whites (the powerful, moneyed class), mulattos, and blacks. José lives in poverty, often has little to eat, and only sees his mother occasionally because of her job as a domestic in Fort-de-France. The father is absent and it is the indomitable, pipe-smoking m'man Tine's tough love that is the dominant influence on the young boy's life. José takes a liking to an old man, Médouze, who lives on his street and who becomes a kind of surrogate father for him, telling him of life beyond the narrow confines of the Rue Cases-Nègres and of Médouze's own African heritage in Guinea. José often gets a thrashing from m'man Tine, well deserved because he regularly gets up to mischief with the other children on the street, also left alone during the workweek. One day, for example, they find some eggs that they decide to cook. Not having matches, they send one of their number to a nearby store to procure them, fabricating the story that they are for his mother, who has also asked for some rum (the children think this makes this errand more realistic), to be put on the family's tab. When the child returns to his friends, they drink some of the rum and start playing with matches, almost setting fire to the houses on the street. Fortunately the catastrophe is averted in extremis and all are soundly beaten. However, m'man Tine is not an abusive parent and her discipline's effect is shown when José, able through her sacrifices to attend school, proves to be an outstanding student. He eventually wins a partial scholarship to attend the prestigious high school Lycée Victor Schoelcher in Fort-de-France and leaves his grandmother. His mother is forced to leave her job as a domestic and become a washerwoman, a harder but more lucrative trade, in order to make up the difference between the partial scholarship and the full cost of her son's schooling. José is at first lonely and unhappy as the only black child in the school and by far the poorest, but he eventually makes a few friends and manages to complete his baccalaureate, much to his mother's and grandmother's joy. The novel ends on a melancholy note with m'man Tine's death. José cannot attend the funeral but retains the image of his grandmother's work-worn hands: "Those hands, as familiar as her voice, had passed me dishes of vegetables, had spruced me up with a tenderness that did not however alleviate the roughness of her skin, dressed me [. . .] One of these hands had grasped my own small hand to take me to school: I can still remember how good it felt."

Joseph Zobel's early life closely paralleled José's. After attending the lycée in Fort-de-France, Zobel could not afford to go to France to begin his university studies (Martinique did not yet have a university of its own), and so he took a government position, later becoming a tutor at his old lycée. He began to compose his first stories about life on rural Martinique and was encouraged by the great Martinican poet Aimé Césaire to write his first novel, *Diab-là*. It was published in 1947, the year after Zobel was finally able to travel to France to enroll at the Sorbonne. In Paris he wrote *La Rue Cases-Nègres* and met the distinguished poet Léopold Sédar Senghor, who later became president of Senegal. In 1957, wishing to discover Africa, Zobel, his wife, and their three children went to Senegal, where he taught in several schools before becoming a producer of cultural and educational broadcasts for Radio Senegal. Upon his retirement in 1974, he returned to France and settled in a small town in the south, writing poetry, making pottery, and sculpting, and died there in 2006. He received considerable acclaim for his poetry, his novels, and for his collections of short stories such as *Mas Badara* (1983).

La Rue Cases-Nègres, made into a delightful film in 1983 (its English title is *Sugar Cane Alley*), gives the reader a moving insight into what life was like in Martinique in the early part of the twentieth century.

MEMOIRS OF HADRIAN

Mémoires d'Hadrien (1951)

◆

Marguerite Yourcenar (Marguerite de Crayencour)

(1903-1987)

To most modern readers, the name of the Roman emperor Hadrian (76–138 CE) evokes a long ancient wall that crosses the north of England and was designed to stop, or at least hinder, the incursion of the inhabitants of Scotland, the bellicose Picts, into the Roman province of Britannia. However, Hadrian was much more than a prudent leader and politician. Known as one of the "good" Roman emperors deified after his death, he also excelled as a philosopher, poet, and architect.

Hadrian's life was dramatically retold in the 1950s by a writer who held a unique position in the world of French literature. Marguerite Yourcenar, whose pen name is a near-anagram of her birthname Crayencour, hailed from Bruxelles. Having lost her mother shortly after her birth, Marguerite spent her youth in the company of her globe-trotting father. Her literary career began in the 1920s with several novels, including *Alexis* (1929), that prominently featured the theme of male homosexuality, a theme to which she returned often in subsequent works such as *Le Coup de grâce* (1939). Between 1924 and 1929 she began work on what is still her best-known work, *Memoirs of Hadrian*, although the finished version was not published until 1951. In Paris in 1937 she met the American Grace Frick, who became her lifelong partner and who would translate some of her major works into English. Yourcenar came to the United States in 1938, but went back to Europe the same year, taking up residence on Capri, where she wrote *Le Coup de grâce*. Returning to the United States when the war broke out, she taught at a number of universities, including Sarah Lawrence College in New York, and became an American citizen in 1947. Until Frick's death in 1979, the two women shared a white, clapboard New England cottage called Petite Plaisance on a quiet, treelined street in Northeast Harbor, close to Bar Harbor, Maine. Yourcenar continued to live there until her own death in 1987, after which time it became a museum dedicated to her life and work. Among other accomplishments, Yourcenar had the notable distinction of breaking the gender barrier of the illustrious forty-member Académie française, which had been all male until her election in 1980.

Memoirs of Hadrian takes the form of a long letter written by Hadrian to his chosen successor, Marcus Aurelius. Supposedly composed at the end of his life, when he was suffering from the illness that would kill him, the fictional letter becomes Hadrian's autobiography. The fruit of intensive historical research, Yourcenar's novel presents an appealing portrait of the life and accomplishments of Hadrian, while engaging at the same time in a series of meditations on the human condition, the meaning of life, and the pursuit of happiness. Her portrait of the emperor is an entirely positive one, and resolves in his favor the various questions that hang over certain events of his reign, such as the assassination of four Roman senators when he was named emperor, and his alleged cruelty during the Roman-Jewish War. Hadrian is revealed as a lucid, intelligent, and at times self-deprecating individual whose humanity and concern for others immediately attract the sympathy of his readers. As a result of the spell woven by Yourcenar's mesmerizing narrative, the reader is transported back into the first and second centuries CE, gaining a real sense of what the life of a Roman emperor was like. Since the historical Hadrian was a somewhat restless soul who traveled extensively the length and breadth of his empire during most of his career, we are privy to a panoramic view of conditions throughout this great political entity that dominated Europe, North Africa, and the Mediterranean for so many centuries. Hadrian also recounts his loves, particularly for the handsome young Antinoüs who tragically drowned in the Nile during Hadrian's visit to Egypt in 130 CE. So convincing is Yourcenar's re-creation of Hadrian and his world that we have to keep reminding ourselves that we are reading a fictional reconstruction and not a historical text or the translation of an actual autobiography of the emperor. However, the closing words of the text are a paraphrase of one of Hadrian's own Latin poems, and they give poignant closure to "his" meditation on life and impending death: "O little Soul, fleeting and tender, companion and guest of my body, you are now about to descend to that pale, dank place where no games are played. Before we leave this life, let us look one last time upon these familiar shores that we most probably will never see again [. . .] Let us do our best to enter the realm of death with our eyes wide open."

BLACK SKIN WHITE MASKS

Peau noire masques blancs (1952)

◆

Frantz Fanon (1925-1961)

O ne of the founding texts of anticolonial literature, *Black Skin White Masks* examines colonialism and racism above all from a psychological point of view. Its author, often considered a revolutionary because of his later book *The Wretched of the Earth* (*Les Damnés de la terre*, 1961), and on account of his activist role in Algeria's *Front de Libération Nationale,* or FLN (National Liberation Front), was born on Martinique into a mixed-race family. Fanon attended Martinique's famous Lycée Schoelcher, where one of his teachers was the great poet Aimé Césaire (see also page 150), whose literary works were to exercise a considerable influence on him. During World War II, when Martinique supported Vichy France and was blockaded by the Allies, he escaped to join the Free French forces and served in Algeria and France, receiving the *Croix de Guerre* (War Cross) when he was wounded in 1944. After the war he returned to Martinique, worked for the political campaign of Aimé Césaire, and completed high school, thereby qualifying for university studies in France. He studied medicine and psychiatry at the University of Lyon and wrote *Black Skin White Masks* two years after completing his degree, drawing on material from his doctoral thesis.

He begins with an appeal for reason and understanding: "Why did I write this book? Nobody asked me to. Certainly not those for whom it is intended [. . .] Forward to a new humanism . . . An understanding of mankind . . . Of our brothers of color [. . .] To understand and to love . . ." Despite its plea for love and understanding, this is certainly *not* an upbeat book about universal brotherhood. Fanon sees men of color (and as feminists have pointed out, this book is centered above all on males) as victims of colonialism, not only or even primarily because they have been economically exploited, but because they have been made to feel inferior by their white masters. The latter have established a kind of Manichean division between Black and White, and have made Black to be associated with evil, with primitiveness, with ugliness, while they have given White associations with virtue, civilization, and beauty. Fanon, the psychiatrist, sees both blacks and whites as victims of a kind of double narcissism: "*le Blanc*" (the white man) is locked up in his whiteness, while "*le Noir*" (the black man) is a prisoner of his blackness. The first and perhaps most important obstacle the black man has to overcome is that of language. By imposing French on the colonized and enslaved who have been brought to Martinique, the colonizers are imposing their culture and their norms. In one sense, knowing French here is an enormous advantage, and yet it transforms the speaker into what he is *not*. And the francophone Martinican tends to despise the Creole language and to speak it only to servants. A black speaker of French is by virtue of his speech transformed into someone who is almost white, but not quite. And it is this "not quite" that creates the cleavage in the soul of the black man: he aspires to be white but because of the way in which the color of his skin has been devalued, he is doomed to fail. Fanon compares the plight of the black Martinican who comes to France to that of the Jew. Whereas Jews are feared because of their supposed economic power, black men are feared and marginalized because of their alleged sexual prowess, which Fanon exposes as a myth created to continue the oppression of black men. However, after pointing out the many ways in which the French colonizers have oppressed the native peoples, Fanon, in his conclusion, returns to the more conciliatory tone of the introduction: "Superiority? Inferiority? Why not simply try and reach out to the Other, to feel the Other, to reveal myself as Other?"

After completing this book, Fanon went to work in a psychiatric hospital in Algeria, where he used a form of therapy that took into account the cultural backgrounds of his patients, an important innovation at the time. When the Algerians began their revolt against French colonialism in 1954, he left his practice and became an active member of the FLN. He was expelled from Algeria (which was under French rule until 1962) but continued to work from Tunisia for Algeria's liberation from France. In 1960 Fanon was diagnosed with leukemia. He first went to the Soviet Union for treatment, and on his return to Tunisia wrote *The Wretched of the Earth*, a truly revolutionary text that proclaims that only violence can free those oppressed by colonialism from their psychological traumatisms. He went to the United States for follow-up treatment for his cancer, but succumbed to the disease in Bethesda, Maryland, in 1961. His *Black Skin White Masks* continues to be a seminal text in the struggle of oppressed people and ethnic minorities throughout the world.

Waiting for Godot

En attendant Godot (1953)

◆

Samuel Beckett (1906–1989)

Paris in the 1950s had a vibrant cultural and artistic scene, and traditional theater was flourishing. On January 3, 1953, in a small theater on the Left Bank, an avant-garde play in two acts by a little-known writer of Irish descent burst onto the Parisian stage and helped change the theatrical landscape quite radically. *Waiting for Godot*, often falsely described as a play about nothing, seemed an aberration, and although the initial reviews were generally favorable, the reaction of the public was at first often hostile. However, none other than the highly successful playwright Jean Anouilh proclaimed this to be the most significant play to appear on the Paris stage since the 1920s, and this and other endorsements ensured it a first run of some four hundred performances. Often regarded as the emblematic play of the theater of the absurd (a loose term referring to a wide range of plays that represent the struggles of modern men and women in an irrational universe), Beckett's play was not produced in a vacuum. Three years earlier, Eugène Ionesco had generated considerable interest with his play *The Bald Soprano* (*La Cantatrice chauve*), which also represents the absurdity of the human condition. But it is *Godot* that has come to exemplify this theatrical style in the minds of the theatergoing public.

Waiting for Godot is a stark play indeed, classical in the simplicity of its decor (consisting of a single tree), in the small number of characters (only four, with a brief walk-on part for a fifth), and in the amount of time it depicts (two days). All of these characteristics are reminiscent of the strict rules governing seventeenth-century French classical drama. However, the play is most unclassical in its mixture of tones and genres: it moves without transition from farce to vaudeville, then on to slapstick, before veering off into the tragic. Although the plot is virtually nonexistent, these sudden changes rivet the audience's attention and help, in part, to explain its long-lasting attraction. When the curtain is raised (although there is often no curtain, just an empty stage adorned with its minimalist tree), we see two men, usually dressed as tramps or clowns. One of them, Estragon, has foot problems, the other, Vladimir, an oversized and overactive prostate. They are waiting for someone named Godot, which to the English reader suggests God, although Beckett claimed that the name first came to him from the French word *godasse*, a slang word for shoes, relevant here because shoes cause Estragon pain throughout the play. They talk, they joke, they eat, and then a second couple appears: a master, Pozzo, leading his slave, Lucky, on a leash. After this strange couple exits, a young boy comes on stage briefly at the end of the act and informs them that Godot won't be coming today, but tomorrow instead. Estragon and Pozzo briefly discuss the possibility of hanging themselves from the tree, but in the end they stay put, continuing to wait.

Act 2 repeats much of what has transpired in act 1, but with some important variations—the tree now has leaves, indicating the passage of time, and Pozzo is now blind. However, the last words of the play repeat verbatim the end of the first act, summing up its essence as Vladimir says to Estragon: "So, shall we go?" and Estragon responds, "Let's go"— but they stay riveted to the spot still waiting for Godot.

What does it all mean? Are we seeing an existential drama representing humankind's vain quest for a divine being? Is it an investigation of the absurd? The interpretations are legion, and each spectator must make up her or his own mind.

Beckett is one of those rare authors who, like Vladimir Nabokov, have achieved literary renown for their work in two languages. Born in Ireland, he majored in French and Italian at Trinity College, Dublin, becoming an English instructor in Paris in 1928. During this first stay in Paris, he and fellow Irishman James Joyce became friends, and Beckett became a research assistant to Joyce as he worked on what would become *Finnegans Wake*. In 1930, Beckett left France for several years, but he returned in 1936, now making Paris his permanent home. It was in Paris that he met Suzanne Deschevaux-Dumesnil (also spelled Déchevaux Dumesnil), the woman who became his partner and, in 1961, his wife. After the German invasion, the couple joined the Resistance. When the war ended, Beckett, who had already written poetry and novels in English, now composed two novels in French before turning to the theater with *En attendant Godot*. There followed a long series of plays such as *Krapp's Last Tape* (*La Dernière Bande*, 1958) and *Happy Days* (*Oh les beaux jours*, 1963), as well as novels in both French and English, including *Molloy* (1951) and *Malone Dies* (*Malone meurt*, 1951). For his remarkable literary achievement he received the Nobel Prize in Literature in 1969. Beckett's long career came to an end in December 1989 when, succumbing to emphysema, he confronted the ultimate absurdity: death.

THE DARK CHILD

L'Enfant noir (1953)

◆

Camara Laye (1928-1980)

This coming-of-age novel recounts with tenderness and nostalgia the childhood and adolescence of a Guinean man, Fatoman, whose story is largely the autobiography of its author, Camara Laye. A somewhat idealized representation of the protagonist's upbringing in the small Guinean town of Kouroussa, the novel is written in the first person and in a style characterized by its intentional poetic simplicity. Like Laye, Fatoman is the son of a blacksmith who works with various types of metals, including gold, and is known for being the best in his region. The story begins when the young protagonist, seeing a snake near his father's workshop, fearlessly proceeds to play with it. Rescued in the nick of time, he is admonished to avoid snakes in the future. However, when sometime later he sees a small black snake approach his father's workplace and wants to kill it, he is warned by his mother that the black snake is the totem animal of blacksmiths. He watches as his father caresses the snake without coming to harm. This is only the first of many customs and beliefs shared by the townspeople. It turns out that the totem animal of his mother, to whom the book is dedicated, is the crocodile, which means his mother can go to the river to fetch water at times when others dare not for fear of a crocodile attack. The adult who is recounting these tales admits that they appear mythical but affirms that he has seen his mother do such things with his own eyes. The child's visit to his uncle's farm and his participation in the harvest is a joyous occasion, the hard work involved being rewarded at the end of the day with a carefree feeling of accomplishment: "We returned home tired, but tired and happy. The genies had constantly helped us; none of us had been bitten by the snakes we had dislodged during our tramping around the fields [. . .] We sang and sang some more! Oh, how happy we were in those days!" Other rituals are recounted, including the circumcision ceremony and the fears of the boys about to undergo this painful experience. Since this is literally a rite of passage, soon after his circumcision Fatoman leaves his home to travel to Conakry, the capital, where he will live with an uncle and aunt in order to continue his schooling. It is during his second year there that he meets a young woman, Marie, with whom he has a chaste friendship, although his aunts tease the couple, asking when they intend to marry. (In real life Laye married Marie, but at a time well beyond the narrative scope of this novel.) After graduating with honors from the school in Conakry, he receives the offer of a scholarship to study in France, a proposal his mother wants him to reject. However, thanks to his father's support, he is able to convince her that he must go. Although overcome with sadness, she no longer opposes his departure. Marie, too, is unhappy that he is leaving. "'Will you be back?' she asks him, her face bathed in tears. 'I'll come back for sure!' [. . .] He settles into his seat for the long flight to Paris, doing his best to conceal his own tears."

The Dark Child was highly praised as an idyllic portrait of a child's growing up to be a man in Africa. But its publication also provoked discomfort on the part of critics of colonialism, who reproached Laye for failing to represent the indignities and injustices suffered under colonial rule. His novel was written after he had arrived in Paris, where he continued his education and took several jobs in order to support himself while he completed a degree in engineering. Marie Lorifo joined him in Paris and they got married, but returned to Guinea in 1956. Camara Laye, after holding a series of government posts in Guinea, decided to take his family into exile in Senegal in 1965 because of his opposition to the politics of the newly independent Guinean regime—an opposition expressed in his 1966 novel *Dramouss*. After his wife was arrested and imprisoned upon her return to Guinea in 1970 to visit her sick father, Laye had to raise their seven children on his own. During Marie's incarceration, Laye took a second wife and had two more children by her. When Marie was released from prison in 1977, she asked for a divorce, like many modern women rejecting the polygamy of her husband. From 1965 on, Laye struggled sporadically with the kidney disease that would finally kill him in Dakar in 1980.

Despite being criticized for being too indulgent to French colonialism, Laye's *The Dark Child* and his subsequent novels like *The Radiance of the King* (*Le Regard du roi*, 1954) were among the first novels by African writers to receive broad recognition in France and elsewhere. *The Dark Child* still charms today's reader with its lyrical evocation of the childhood of its protagonist and the story of his coming of age.

MYTHOLOGIES

(1957)

◆

Roland Barthes (1915-1980)

Just reading the title of this book we would normally expect some kind of treatise on, or introduction to, the various mythological systems in the world (Greek, Roman, Nordic, Hindu, Mayan, etc.), particularly as comparative mythology has become a perennial topic of interest in our modern, multicultural world. However, this would be to ignore the brilliant but at times quirky mind of its author, Roland Barthes, who was during his lifetime one of France's most prominent intellectuals. Whereas mythology usually refers to a series of stories through which a particular civilization addresses fundamental questions such as the creation of the world, the presence of evil, and the nature of love, Barthes's mythologies are resolutely modern and refer to the hidden presuppositions that underlie today's cultural phenomena. For him the term is an approximate equivalent to ideology. Barthes was a semiotician, someone concerned with the linguistic and cultural signs that are used to give meaning to the world around us. But while it is true that Barthes wrote a great deal about literature and literary texts, *Mythologies* was one of the first attempts by an academic to examine popular culture, long deemed a subject unworthy of university-trained critics who were supposed to use their intellects to dissect the manifestations of "high culture." *Mythologies* is a collection of short pieces (fifty-four in the original French version, although some of the English translations contain only twenty-eight), written between 1954 and 1956 for *Les Lettres nouvelles*, a magazine of leftist persuasion. Each of them is a meditation on an aspect of modern popular culture, and Barthes takes care to allow readers to draw their own conclusions before weighing in with his own. In "Myth Today," the long theoretical essay that concludes his study, he explains his use of the term "myth" and discusses the way in which it functions in contemporary society.

Each piece presents a lucid, often witty analysis that is very accessible but challenges the reader to look beneath the surface of popular wisdom and perceived "truth." For example, in "Wine and Milk" ("Le vin et le lait") he looks at the importance French society accords to wine, remarking that the French nation considers this beverage to be an essential part of its heritage, "as important as its 360 types of cheese and its culture." He calls it a "totem-drink," one that binds all classes of French society together, the worker and the intellectual alike. Anyone rejecting this totem does so at his or her peril, as was proved by the outcry that accompanied the photo of onetime French president René Coty with a bottle of beer. Barthes similarly analyzes the French "totem-meal," *steak frites* (steak with French fries), but also investigates sporting events like the Tour de France, which he sees as the modern equivalent of the epic; magazines like *Elle*, which cater to the dreams of the young working-class or lower-middle-class woman; the automobile, which Barthes considers to be the modern equivalent of the Gothic cathedral; and political questions, such as racism. In "Grammaire africaine" ("African Grammar") he points out how the vocabulary used by journalists writing about African affairs is usually demeaning and reinforces the perceived cultural superiority of France and the French. Barthes concludes that his contemporary society is dominated by an ideology that reinforces the stereotypes and prejudices of the petite bourgeoisie.

A fascinating and somewhat protean personality, Barthes was born in Cherbourg, the son of a naval officer killed in World War I when Barthes was only a year old. He moved to Paris with his mother when he was nine and later attended the Sorbonne in the years just prior to the outbreak of World War II. His poor health—he suffered from tuberculosis—interrupted his studies, but also kept him out of the army. Barthes held a number of teaching posts in France, Egypt, and Romania, and began writing for various newspapers. His first book, *Writing Degree Zero* (*Le degré zéro de l'écriture*), a study of modern literature influenced by Sartre, appeared in 1953, to be followed by *Mythologies*. Although he began his academic career as a structuralist, he altered his critical approach under the growing influence of scholars like Derrida and Lacan. Ever fascinated by language and meaning, Barthes was named to the chair of literary semiology at the prestigious Collège de France in 1976. His career came to an abrupt end in 1980 when he was hit by a van while crossing a Paris street. Gravely injured, he succumbed a month later, on March 25, leaving an intellectual legacy of immense variety, but never having founded a "school" or gathered a devoted band of disciples. Although some of the pieces in *Mythologies* may be either too dated or too culturally specific for all but the most ardent of Francophiles, the wit, acuity, and pertinence of most of them still appeal to inquisitive readers today in search of food for thought.

JEALOUSY

La Jalousie (1957)

◆

Alain Robbe-Grillet (1922-2008)

The 1950s marked the arrival of a new breed of novelists onto the French literary scene. These young Turks were practitioners of what they called *le nouveau roman* ("the new novel"), which broke with many of the conventions of both the traditional nineteenth-century realist novel (Balzac, Stendhal, Zola, etc.) and the political engagement Sartre had preached. In their revolutionary zeal, they wanted to abolish traditional notions of plot and character in order to create a type of realism that would correspond more closely to the way in which the modern era perceives the world.

Alain Robbe-Grillet, born in Brest, was one of the most fascinating and talented representatives of this group, which never became a literary movement as such and whose practitioners often disagreed among themselves. Robbe-Grillet was trained as an agricultural engineer, a rather unusual background for a man of letters. He became one of the chief theorists of the *nouveau roman* in his 1963 essay "For a New Novel" ("Pour un nouveau roman") in which he exhorts writers to see the world with unfettered eyes (*avec des yeux libres*). However, this text was written after his novels like *The Erasers* (*Les Gommes*, 1953), *The Voyeur* (*Le Voyeur*, 1955), and *Jealousy* had already put his theories into practice. His later works dealt with themes of violence, eroticism, and sadism, while his *Repetition* (*La Reprise*, 2001) marked a return to the techniques found in novels like *The Erasers*. Also passionately interested in cinema, he wrote the screenplay for Alain Resnais's *nouvelle vague* (New Wave) movie *Last Year at Marienbad* (*L'Année dernière à Marienbad*, 1961), before directing his own first movie, *The Immortal One* (*L'Immortelle*), in 1963, followed by others such as *Playing with Fire* (*Le Jeu avec le feu*, 1975). Robbe-Grillet was elected to the Académie française in 2004. He died of cardiac problems in Caen in 2008.

Jealousy (*La Jalousie*) is perhaps his most intriguing novel, because its characters are seen only from the exterior, through the eyes of a single narrator who reveals nothing about himself (or *her*self?) to the reader, except an obsessive desire to observe intensely the behavior of the two other principal characters in the novel, a woman simply known as A… and a neighbor, Franck. Even the chronology remains mysterious, because there is no clearly distinguishable plot line, but rather a number of individual scenes, which are repeated with variations several times during the novel and scrambled like the pieces of a jigsaw puzzle. While this type of narration is familiar to a reader today who has seen movies like *Mulholland Drive* and *Memento*, it was quite unexpected and disconcerting to readers of the 1950s.

The ambiguities present in the novel are encapsulated in the French title, which means both jealousy and the type of Venetian blind we call a jalousie, the louvers of which conceal either all or part of what is viewed through them, depending on the angle at which they are set. This ambiguity becomes a metaphor for the elusive nature of "reality," which is always, at least partially, hidden or distorted according to the angle from which it is observed. The narrator's eye becomes our camera, focused on the novel's sparse action, at first seeming to give us a totally objective picture just as a photographic lens is supposed to do. However, we soon notice the almost voyeuristic nature of the narrator's observation, and suspect that behind the apparent objectivity, there is strong emotion at work. Thanks to the novel's title, we assume that the narrator is consumed with jealousy because he (she?) suspects A… and Franck of having an affair. The narrator observes with an obsessive intensity every movement Franck makes: "He seizes his glass from the table, empties it in a single gulp, as though he doesn't need to move a muscle to swallow its contents. He replaces the glass on the table [. . .] and resumes eating. His large appetite is all the more noticeable thanks to the gestures that accompany his eating: his right hand seizes in turn the knife, the fork, and the bread." Normal, everyday gestures are magnified to become threatening. In a strange way, the precision of detail provided by the narrator assumes a kind of surrealist quality, which is at once disturbing and fascinating. Since there are no "givens," no instructions either explicit or implicit as to the interpretation of this text, we are called upon to play an active role in our attempt to answer a series of questions the story poses. What is its precise chronology? Is A… an adulteress or not? Why does a squashed centipede haunt the narrator's imagination, and why is so much time spent describing objects, often at the expense of descriptions of people? Readers who enjoy solving puzzles or who simply like a good mystery spun by an author who, not coincidentally, began his writing career with the "new" detective novel *The Erasers*, will enjoy playing along, provided that they accept that the only solutions at which they can arrive are provisional, never definitive. But that is half the fun of this enthralling novel.

MODERATO CANTABILE

(1958)

◆

Marguerite Duras (Marguerite Donnadieu) (1914-1996)

An apartment overlooking the harbor of a port city somewhere in France, the sun low on the horizon bathing the waterfront in a reddish glow, a bored and somewhat neurotic socialite accompanying her young son to his weekly piano lesson—such are the apparently banal elements of this novel's opening chapter. It is a repetition of what has transpired on many previous Fridays, but this particular Friday is going to be different. Breaking the monotony of the piano lesson, a shrill cry, followed by the sound of voices, intrudes through the open window. The piano lesson is momentarily interrupted but resumes as the boy finally plays his piece, an Anton Diabelli sonata, in accordance with the directions *moderato cantabile*, in stark contrast to what is happening below. When mother and son leave the apartment building, she moves to the front of a crowd where she sees the body of a dead woman, blood trickling from her mouth, and the murderer, who keeps saying "My Love, My Love" to the dead body and kissing the bloody lips before being taken into police custody. As the mother and her son make their way from the working class neighborhood near the port to their luxurious mansion, the mother repeats the piano teacher's lesson as though nothing untoward had happened: "Remember next time that *moderato* means 'moderately,' and *cantabile* 'like a song.'"

Born in Vietnam to French parents, Marguerite Donnadieu had a difficult childhood. She was only four years old when her father died, and the family experienced great financial hardship after her mother had unwisely purchased a working farm. She left Vietnam when she was eighteen to attend university in Paris, and there she met the writer Robert Antelme (whom she married in 1939) and his close friend, the writer Dionys Mascolo. Antelme was deported to a concentration camp in Germany in 1944 but survived. During the Nazi occupation, Duras's attitude towards the Germans and their supporters was ambiguous, but she did end up joining the French Resistance. She began writing her first novels in the early 1940s, taking the name Duras after the French village where her father had owned property. (Perhaps not by coincidence, it was also the name of the successful novelist Claire de

Duras who had written *Ourika* in 1824.) Duras's first works, *Les Impudents* (1942) and *La Vie tranquille* (1944), were fairly conventional in style and plot. It was only with *Moderato cantabile* that she broke new ground with a sparser style and an innovative narrative technique, associated with *le nouveau roman* ("the new novel," see also page 161), that requires an active, vigilant reader. She also began writing screenplays, most famously for the 1959 film *Hiroshima mon amour*, directed by Alain Resnais. In 1984, she was the recipient of the Goncourt Prize for her semiautobiographical *The Lover* (*L'Amant*), also made into a successful film. During the course of her career she wrote over forty works, although her personal life was a troubled one, due to her struggle with alcoholism. She died of throat cancer in 1996.

The theme of alcohol is already prominent in *Moderato cantabile*: Anne Desbaresdes, the mother of the nameless boy of the first chapter, is haunted by the crime she has witnessed and returns each day to the café outside which the murder took place, ordering copious amounts of wine. It is at the café that she meets a man, Chauvin, who was also present at the event. Progressively identifying themselves with the murderer and his lover, Anne and Chauvin begin a strange kind of love affair, verbal rather than physical, so that they create their own reality through the medium of language. Their passion reaches a paroxysm when Anne arrives home late one evening for a chic dinner party organized by her husband. The chapter that describes the meal as a stultifying ritual of bourgeois culture is a masterpiece in itself: "On a silver platter, representing the accumulated wealth of three generations, the salmon makes its entrance [. . .] A man, dressed in black, wearing white gloves, carries it in as though it were royalty, and presents it to each guest, who looks at it in respectful silence." Anne, already tipsy from her previous meeting with Chauvin, becomes increasingly drunk until—under the disapproving gaze of her husband—she finally escapes the guests and takes refuge upstairs, where she regurgitates what little she had eaten of the dinner—a symbolic gesture of revolt against her crushingly boring life. Throughout this unforgettable scene, a voyeuristic Chauvin roams through the garden outside the house, gazing through the window at the events taking place inside. The last chapter shows Anne back at the café the next day, this time without her son, who had accompanied her on all previous visits. The unexpected and highly symbolic events that take place during this final meeting between her and Chauvin have intrigued readers for decades, as has the devastating portrait of a bored and rich married woman longing for escape from her humdrum existence.

ASTERIX

Astérix (1959-present)

♦

René Goscinny (1926-1977)

and Albert Uderzo (born 1927)

The French have a love affair with comic books, which they call *bande dessinée* (comic strip) or simply *BD*, and certain comic book characters have become part of the national psyche. Among the most beloved are Tintin, the boy detective created by the Belgian writer Hergé (the pen name for Georges Rémi) in 1929, and the laconic American cowboy Lucky Luke, a creation of the illustrator Morris (Maurice de Bevere) and the scriptwriter (*scénariste*) René Goscinny. But by far the most popular is Astérix, the brainchild of the illustrator Albert Uderzo and, once more, René Goscinny as the scriptwriter (Goscinny is often considered the creator of the *scénariste* profession for French comic books). Their highly successful collaboration came to an end in 1977 with the death of Goscinny from a heart attack, but Uderzo has continued to produce subsequent *Astérix* adventures on his own.

There are many reasons for the great appeal the *Astérix* comic books hold for the French, but perhaps the principal attraction is the combination of brilliant comedy and well-researched history, as the series humorously taps into the great founding myth of the French nation: the epic struggle between Gauls and the invading Romans in the first century BCE. However, the plucky little Astérix and the adventures and struggles of his Gallic friends against oppression (always with a happy ending) have fired the imagination of countless readers throughout the world, making *Astérix* a universal bestseller with translations into dozens of languages.

Although today we associate the Celts mostly with Ireland, Scotland, and Wales, they were originally a Central European group of tribes who conquered much of Europe, beginning in the second millennium BCE. Those who invaded and settled the land we now know as France were called Gauls. The Gauls were divided into rival tribes, and only when the Romans began their own progressive conquest of Europe did the Gauls band together against their common enemy. The Romans were led by Julius Caesar while the leader of the Gaul resistance was Vercingetorix, who organized a fierce and initially effective resistance against the Roman legions. He was finally defeated by Caesar in 52 BCE at Alésia in Central France. To this day French schoolchildren learn about "our ancestors, the Gauls" (*"nos ancêtres les Gaulois"*), even though the genetic links between this Celtic people and the inhabitants of modern, multicultural France are often extremely slight or even nonexistent. But the fiercely independent Gauls, with their courageous resistance against an enemy of superior resources, are seen by many French as representative of the "French character." Ironically, after their defeat at the hands of Caesar, the Gauls adapted well to Roman civilization, and the Gallo-Roman period gave France a sophisticated culture, evidenced to this day by its many surviving structures, from bridges and aqueducts to villas and amphitheaters.

Astérix, a short, courageous Gallic warrior, lives in a village in Brittany. Thanks to a potion prepared by the village druid Panoramix, he becomes empowered with superhuman strength when necessary. The names of the characters are puns using the typical suffix of Gallic names, "-ix": Astérix evokes asterisk, the name of his best friend Obélix (an obese, good-natured "sculptor" of menhirs who fell into a cauldron of druid potion as a child and thus has perennial superstrength) is a twist on obelisk, Panoramix suggests panoramic, etc. Indeed, puns are at the heart of much of the verbal humor of the series (the French love punning). Most of the *Astérix* books deal with the continuing struggle against the Romans, who are portrayed as oafish dunderheads who are no match for the resourceful and nimble Gauls. The stories contain a mixture of historical fact and popular legend, with nods to contemporary issues such as the problems of regionalism (Brittany) versus centralism (Paris), the dangers of globalization, or the search for oil in the Middle East (*Asterix and the Black Gold/L'Odyssée d'Astérix*). Volumes such as *Asterix the Gaul* (*Astérix le Gaulois,* the very first volume) and *Asterix the Gladiator* (*Astérix gladiateur*) obviously deal with the Roman invasion, while *Asterix and the Falling Sky* (*Astérix: le ciel lui tombe sur la tête*), for example, features visitors from outer space. The indomitable Gauls can also be seen as symbolic of the French Resistance during World War II, a subliminal association that only adds to their appeal for contemporary French who are finally coming to terms with France's ambiguous role during that war. Astérix and his friends are so popular that several *Astérix* films have been made, and even an *Astérix* theme park exists since 1989 north of Paris, with a life-size replica of the Gallic village that is their home in the comic book series. These amusing and often self-critical comic characters provide an interesting window into what we might call the contemporary French psyche.

RHINOCEROS

Rhinocéros (1960)

◆

Eugène Ionesco (1909–1994)

When the inhabitants of Hameln (Hamelin), Germany, found their town overrun by rats, they had the Pied Piper to help them rid the town of rodents—with tragic results, however. But what happens when a small town in the French provinces is invaded by big, lumbering pachyderms with large horns on their snouts? Ionesco's play develops a possible scenario that is at first humorous but ultimately chilling, since it is a meditation on what could happen if the word "rhinoceros" referred not simply to the animal itself, but above all to a political stance. Although this play has certain realistic elements, it soon becomes obvious that it is not in the realist genre. A rather banal normalcy prevails when the curtain rises, as two of the principal characters arrive at a typical French café on the town square on a lazy summer Sunday. One of them, Jean, a dapper and precise fellow, berates the other, his somewhat bedraggled and untidy friend Bérenger, for arriving late to their meeting, even though both men have appeared on stage simultaneously. The condescending Jean also reproaches Bérenger for being overly fond of the bottle, and he evinces little sympathy when Bérenger complains about the boredom of small-town living. Their conversation is suddenly interrupted by the pounding of hooves, and, to the amazement of all, a rhinoceros gallops through the streets. This event provokes a lively but rather pointless discussion, although, strangely, nobody seems alarmed—even when a rhinoceros tramples by in the opposite direction and kills a cat, to the chagrin not only of its owner but also of the beautiful Daisy (on whom Bérenger dotes). There ensues a heated discussion, not about the danger rhinoceroses represent, but about whether the cat-killing rhinoceros is a second beast or the original one, and whether it is an Asian or African rhinoceros. In the second act, we see Daisy attempting to convince her fellow workers that there is a rhinoceros in town, a story corroborated by others, including a Madame Bœuf who is convinced that the rhinoceros is in fact her husband, who has inexplicably mutated. Little by little, the disease of "rhinoceritis" spreads, as the inhabitants of the town are transformed into horned pachyderms. In the third and final act, only Daisy and Bérenger still remain human, but eventually even Daisy succumbs in order to join her fellow-citizen rhinoceroses. As the curtain falls, Bérenger shouts at the crowd: "I will defend myself against you all. I'm the last human being left and I'll continue to be so until the end. I will not surrender."

This drama of the absurd is not so absurd. It is in fact a powerful allegory of the way totalitarian attitudes can take hold of a population. In the first instance, Ionesco was reacting to the rise of a totalitarian regime in his native Rumania in the 1950s, but in fact the allegory applies as well to the spread of Nazi ideology in France, and indeed to any form of totalitarianism. Unfortunately, the continuing relevance of the play's message—how political sickness can overcome a people when it is seen as "normal," inevitable, or even seductive, and that the only cure is resistance—is constantly being confirmed by political events around the world.

Eugène Ionesco, born in Rumania to a French mother and a Rumanian father, was raised in Paris until the age of thirteen. After leaving Paris as a teenager, he studied in Rumania where he became a French teacher, returning to Paris in 1938. He started writing plays relatively late in life; his first was *The Bald Soprano* (*La Cantatrice chauve*, 1950), an amusing parody of the standard French farce of the time that plays fast and loose with any logical development of the plot, the psychology of the characters, and the use of language. Other comedies in the same vein were *The Lesson* (*La Leçon*, 1951), in which a gung-ho student wants to do a "Total Doctorate," and *The Chairs* (*Les Chaises*, 1952). Ionesco characterized them as "anti-plays," representing with a zany humor an absurd world full of latent menace. The Bérenger character who is at the center of *Rhinoceros* first appeared in *The Killer* (*Tueur sans gages*, 1959), and later in *Exit the King* (*Le Roi se meurt*, 1962) and *A Stroll in the Air* (*Le Piéton de l'air*, 1963). Along with Samuel Beckett, Ionesco was the dramatist most closely associated with the theater of the absurd. For his plays and other writings, including some theoretical essays on the theater, he was elected to the Académie française in 1970. One of the most important French playwrights of the twentieth century, Eugène Ionesco died in Paris in 1994.

Fifty years after it was first performed, *Rhinoceros* remains one of his most successful and most readable plays, and Bérenger's final words need to be shouted whenever any form of totalitarianism raises its rhinoceros-like head.

TRAP FOR CINDERELLA

Piège pour Cendrillon (1963)

◆

Sébastien Japrisot (Jean-Baptiste Rossi) (1931-2003)

Some people will do anything for money—not only kill but even undergo self-mutilation. Besides agreeing to help murder her cousin by setting her house on fire, one of the protagonists of this novel is prepared to hold a burning piece of clothing up to her own face—in order to inflict burns serious enough to make her features unrecognizable and to prevent the police from obtaining prints from her fire-damaged fingers. The two protagonists are the rich young heiress Mi (short for Michèle) and her poor cousin Do (Dominique, or Domenica), who were separated after spending part of their childhood together. When they meet up again in their twenties, Michèle is leading the aimless life of the idle rich, devoted to random pleasure but in need of a friend. Do, now a lowly bank employee yet attracted to the high life, fills this need, but she is often treated very shabbily by her spoiled cousin. A third member of the household, Mi's housekeeper Jeanne, also the butt of Mi's thoughtless and rude behavior, plots revenge. Her plan is for Do, after drugging Mi, to set fire to her house. The fire, which will appear to be the result of a gas leak, will burn Mi's body beyond recognition, while Do will survive—but no one will recognize her because of the burns she has sustained. Do will pretend to be Mi and will thus gain access to Mi's fortune, rewarding Jeanne handsomely for her accomplice role. However, even the best-formulated plans don't always work out. After giving Mi a dose of sleeping pills, Do starts the fire. Once the house is ablaze, a young woman runs from it, collapses, and is rushed to a hospital, where she is treated for her severe burns and undergoes restorative plastic surgery. When Jeanne comes to visit the young woman in her hospital room, she discovers that the patient is suffering from total amnesia because of the traumatic fire. Jeanne assumes the plan has worked and that she faces Do—but when the bandages are removed, the patient's features no longer resemble either Do or Mi, and Jeanne begins to have doubts. Could the burn patient be Mi, who somehow foiled the plot and killed Do in self-defense? The novel centers on the mutilated young woman's attempts to rediscover her own identity. However, as she questions various people from her past, she cannot be certain who is telling the truth and who is lying. Is she living a fairy tale, as the novel's title suggests? If so, both she and the reader must be on their guard for traps. The jacket copy of the novel's French edition sums up the enigma that both the protagonist herself and the reader must confront: "My name is Michèle Isola. I'm twenty. The story I tell is one of murder. I am the investigator, I am the witness, I am the victim, I am the killer, I'm all four together, but who am I?"

Sébastien Japrisot, born in Marseille, was the anagram of Jean-Baptiste Rossi. While still in high school, he began writing a novel, *Bad Starters* (*Les Mal Partis*), about the passionate love between a male high school student and a nun. When he went to Paris to continue his studies at the Sorbonne, he completed this manuscript and, at age nineteen, managed to persuade the publisher Robert Laffont, also originally from Marseille, to take a chance on it. The novel, only moderately successful in France, became a bestseller in the United States. Although Japrisot had only had English in high school, the fact that he had a wife and family to support led him to try his hand at translating a number of American novels, including *The Catcher in the Rye*—successfully, as it turned out. Japrisot then joined an advertising agency, but found this work insufficiently creative. He took a leave of absence and began working on several short subject films. When, in 1962, he found himself short of money again, he let himself be persuaded to write a mystery novel, and ended up presenting his publisher with two manuscripts, each of which had taken him just one week to complete: *The Sleeping Car Murders* (*Compartiment Tueurs*), published in 1962, and *Trap for Cinderella*, which won the 1963 French Prize for Detective Fiction. Both novels were subsequently made into successful films. He then wrote a number of film scripts, including *Rider on the Rain* (*Passager de la pluie*), and ten years later began composing novels again. In 1991 he published the highly regarded *A Very Long Engagement* (*Un long dimanche de fiançailles*), a novel that was adapted to the screen the year after his death.

Japrisot adds a new dimension to the mystery novel in *Trap for Cinderella*, in which the novel's title, in addition to its obvious associations, refers to a fictional brand of men's cologne that appears in the novel and provides a clue to resolving the central puzzle. Readers who enjoy detective fiction will find this enigmatic page-turner thoroughly intriguing, but must be on their guard since it sets as many traps for them as for its characters.

FRIDAY

Vendredi ou les Limbes du Pacifique (1967)

◆

Michel Tournier (born 1924)

What would it be like to be marooned on a desert island, left entirely to our own resources in a hostile environment? How would we cope with solitude, despair, isolation? This fantasy has haunted the Western imagination at least since 1719, when Daniel Defoe wrote his famous *Robinson Crusoe*, based on the real-life adventure of Alexander Selkirk. The story line has reappeared in numerous novels, comic books, and movies ever since. Perhaps the most provocative modern version of the Robinson Crusoe story is Michel Tournier's *Friday*, in which Man Friday, not Robinson, is the pivotal character.

Tournier, born in Paris, came to literature rather late, having first aspired to become a professor of philosophy but then failed his *agrégation* examination in philosophy, at the time the only path available to pursue a teaching career in France. However, were it not for this grave disappointment, he may never have become one of the most important French writers of the modern era. *Friday*, his first novel, received the French Academy Prize for the Year's Best Novel when it appeared in 1967. It was followed by *The Ogre* (*Le Roi des aulnes*), which won the Goncourt Prize in 1970, and by a series of well-received novels including *Gemini* (*Les Météores*, 1975), *Golden Droplet* (*La Goutte d'or*, 1985), and *Eléazar* (1996). Tournier is also known for his short stories, including some destined for children, such as "Grouse" ("The Bird") in 1978.

Friday begins with a brief prelude recounting the night when the *Virginia*, Crusoe's vessel, was shipwrecked on an uncharted island during a violent storm. We then see the only survivor, Robinson, face down on the beach. After he groggily gets to his feet, he begins to explore his new environment, replete with wild goats, deer, and abundant tropical fruit. In order to "tame" his new domain, Robinson becomes almost the caricature of the typical European colonizer, even though he actually has nobody to colonize. He names the island Speranza, which means Hope. He then writes a charter for the island, builds a house, and begins to cultivate the land, naming himself governor. However, his desire for order and "civilization" is in conflict with more instinctual drives: he is drawn to the soil of Speranza, which becomes so sexually charged in his mind that he spreads his semen across the landscape, literally making love to the island—which is not only feminized and sexualized, but also becomes a maternal symbol: Robinson undertakes a symbolic return to the womb by exploring a series of caves and tunnels leading to the island's center.

His solitary life changes dramatically when he notices smoke coming from the beach one day: a group of natives from another island have come to Speranza to sacrifice a prisoner. The victim succeeds in breaking away, running toward the hiding place from which Robinson is observing the ritual. In a dramatic but almost comic moment, Robinson debates whether he should shoot the runaway or his pursuers. Deciding it would be more prudent to fell the runaway, he fires but kills one of the pursuers instead, causing the others to beat a hasty retreat. The escapee is pathetically grateful and Robinson decides to turn him into his servant, naming him Friday. Robinson's attempts to impose European civilization on the newcomer meet with limited success, however. The turning point comes one day when, without permission, Friday "borrows" Robinson's pipe. When he hears his master coming, Friday throws the pipe into the depths of the cave to conceal his theft. The cave contains Robinson's supply of gunpowder, and the result is a massive explosion that destroys Robinson's dwelling and possessions. Suddenly, the roles are reversed: Friday teaches Robinson how to live in accordance with nature rather than trying to impose human order on it. Robinson's spirit is gradually freed from its European hang-ups, and when an English ship finally discovers Speranza, Robinson is disgusted by the behavior of the crew and by their harsh treatment of the cabin boy. He decides to remain on the island, but to his horror discovers the next morning that Friday has departed on the English ship. His despair is short-lived, however, because the cabin boy—tired of the brutality he had to endure—has deserted the ship. Robinson is comforted by the thought that he will have a new companion in his old age and will be able to pass on the lessons of un-civilization, continuing the carefree, idyllic existence he has experienced since Friday set off the explosion in the cave.

KAMOURASKA

(1970)

◆

Anne Hébert (1916-2000)

Anne Hébert's prize-winning novel *Kamouraska* is based on a famous and brutal murder which was perpetrated in the nineteenth century in Kamouraska, nowadays considered one of Québec's prettiest villages, some 250 miles northeast of Montréal on the St. Lawrence River. This novel is also the first of a series by Anne Hébert that relates violent events from Québec's past, the best-known of which are *Children of the Black Sabbath* (*Les Enfants du Sabbat,* 1975) and *In the Shadow of the Wind* (*Les Fous de Bassan,* 1982). Anne Hébert was not only a much-praised novelist but also a highly regarded poet and playwright. A Québecoise, she was born in Sainte-Catherine-de-Fossambault, near Québec City. Encouraged by her father, a government official who was also a part-time literary critic, she began composing poetry while still a teenager. After working with Radio Canada and the Canadian National Film Board, she moved to Paris in the 1950s. She frequently visited home, and returned to Canada permanently in 1998 when she learned she had bone cancer. It is here that she died in 2000.

Kamouraska is her re-creation of the historic events that led to the murder in 1839 of Achille Taché by Dr. George Holmes, lover of Taché's wife Eléonore d'Estimauville. In the novel the squire of the village of Kamouraska is called Antoine Tassy, a brutal, drunken aristocrat who abuses his young wife Elisabeth d'Aulnières and makes her life a misery. The story is told in a series of flashbacks through the eyes of Elisabeth, who has conspired with her lover—George Nelson, an American doctor and school chum of her husband—to get rid of Tassy. They make a first clumsy attempt by bribing a young servant girl to travel north in order to seduce and poison Tassy in Kamouraska, where he lives alone now since Elisabeth has fled to Montréal to escape his abuse. A notable womanizer, Tassy succumbs to the young woman's charms but not to the poison she puts into his brandy, which only makes him violently ill. The lovers then decide that it is Nelson who must perform the deed and so he sets out in the dead of winter, driving his sleigh for many miles across the frozen countryside. This time the attempt is successful, but Tassy proves no easy prey and the murder turns into a bloodbath. Hébert paints a series of hallucinating images of the doctor, after he has committed the murder, driving his black sleigh back south across the snow-covered landscape like a madman, his clothes and the bridle of his horses covered in frozen blood from the slaughter. An innkeeper at whose establishment he stops for a night recalls the sleigh: "There were drops of blood hanging like icicles from the sleigh. I scratched at them with my finger. I was frightened [. . .] He accompanied me into the shed to wash his sleigh. I saw with my lantern that there was a lot of blood on the floor of the sleigh. It was all over the seats as well. He poured hot water onto the front and sides of the sleigh [. . .] but as it was cold, the water quickly froze. He told me to wait until tomorrow to clean up the sleigh." Instead of uniting the lovers, the murder of Antoine Tassy drives a wedge between them, and after one grotesque night spent with Elisabeth, Nelson flees across the border to the United States, from where all attempts at extradition prove fruitless. Elisabeth hears nothing more from him, is arrested as an accomplice to the murder, but is released for lack of evidence. After leaving prison, she accepts a proposal of marriage from the mediocre Jérôme Rolland, a notary, not because she loves him but in the expectation that the marriage will restore some semblance of respectability to her life. This union does not bring happiness, since Rolland treats her with indifference and even disdain.

The story of Elisabeth's love affair with Nelson and the murder of Tassy is framed by scenes at Rolland's deathbed. During the long night that she dutifully spends at her dying husband's side, Elisabeth recalls one by one the horrendous events of her past, which the book presents in almost cinematographic fashion. Beneath the façade of the dutiful wife, Elisabeth's emotional turmoil and inner revolt are exposed. The novel's style, simultaneously elliptical and graphic, appeals directly to the reader's own sensibility. We feel both Elisabeth's suffering while at the same time we are shocked by the act in which she is complicit. As Elisabeth watches over her dying husband she bursts into tears, because this night of vigil has awakened in her soul the feelings of horror and remorse for the crime in which she participated. Ironically, it is the dying Jérôme Rolland who is at peace. Having received the last rites, he tells Elisabeth about his joy and tranquillity. It is she who is afraid and who grasps her husband's hand "as though it were a slender thread connecting her to life but one which could break at any moment." Her tears are not being shed for her husband, but for herself and for the living death she has had to endure since the murder of Antoine Tassy.

MY LIFE AND MY FILMS

Ma Vie et mes films (1974)

◆

Jean Renoir (1894-1979)

Renoir is practically a household name in the United States. Anyone who has visited a major American museum has seen some of the paintings by the great impressionist Auguste Renoir, who lived from 1841 to 1919. A number of them show a boy with curly blond hair, one of Auguste's sons, Jean—who became almost as famous as his father in his own medium, the movies. This delightful retrospective of his own life and works was written by the movie director just five years before his death in Beverly Hills. While it is an autobiographical text, it is not a conventional autobiography; it does not present a chronological account of Jean Renoir's life but rather a series of highlights, seasoned with anecdotes and reflections on the cinematographic art and on life in general. Recounted with a self-deprecatory humor, these anecdotes are enlightening, profound, and intensely human. Renoir tells of the strong influence his famous father exerted on him, and of his boundless admiration for him. Auguste wanted his son to become a ceramic artist, and indeed Jean persevered on this path long enough to have produced some museum-quality pieces of pottery. In a chapter devoted to Dr. Barnes, founder of the famous Barnes Foundation in suburban Philadelphia (which also holds a large number of Auguste's paintings), Jean describes some of Barnes's unconventional views, attributing them not to eccentricity but to the doctor's passion for art, which Renoir likens to a religion. He writes: "I like Doctor Barnes and I have a compelling reason for doing so: he was the only person in the world to collect my pottery."

Renoir, who was born in Paris, tells us how he was at first attracted to the cinema as a spectator, going almost daily to see movies. His first wife, Catherine Hessling, one of his father's models, shared his passion, and they both went on to participate in the early days of cinema in France: she as an actress, in films that he directed. At first his films were not a commercial success. In his narrative, Renoir divides his life—"in bourgeois fashion," as he says—into two distinct phases: the first was when he had to pay to have his films produced, and the second when he was paid to make them. During the first phase, he tells that, much to his chagrin, he had to sell some of the paintings left to him by his father to finance his cinematographic enterprises. During World War I, Renoir served at the front until he received a leg wound that gave him a permanent limp. Yet in typical fashion, he was able to see this event in a positive light: "Paradoxically," he writes, "I consider my infirmity to be an advantage: a lame person sees life from a different angle from that of someone who doesn't limp." His condition didn't stop him from doing flight training and getting a pilot's license, although, ironically, what almost scuttled this project was not his infirmity but his excessive weight. But after putting himself on a draconian diet, he was able to become a reconnaissance pilot, and he tells some rather hair-raising stories about his adventures during the war. One of Renoir's most famous films is his *The Great Illusion* (*La Grande Illusion*, 1937), in which he directed the great German actor and director Erich von Stroheim, whose films had greatly influenced him. During the production, he tells how he and von Stroheim had a dispute about the best way to play a particular scene. Renoir was so distraught at having to disagree with the man who was his idol that he burst into tears. Stroheim also began to weep and they embraced each other, Renoir bathing his own jacket with tears, Stroheim doing likewise on the German army uniform he was wearing for the scene. One of the reasons Renoir was such a successful director was his understanding of, and sympathy for, actresses and actors. He describes his role as director as being like that of a midwife: "I have to enable actors to give birth to the children they are carrying inside them and of whom they are unaware." Renoir was a prolific filmmaker, producing over forty films including *Boudu Saved from Drowning* (*Boudu sauvé des eaux*, 1932), *Madame Bovary* (1933), *French Cancan* (1954), and *Lunch on the Grass* (*Déjeuner sur l'herbe*, 1959).

Renoir's life was not easy. One of his greatest movies, *The Rules of the Game* (*La Règle du jeu*), was greeted with scorn when it first played in Paris in 1939. The original film was destroyed in a bombing raid by Allied aircraft, and only in 1950 two French admirers of Renoir managed, with his help, to restore it in its entirety; this time it was greeted with acclaim, provoking the director to comment, "My films seem to take twenty-five years to become successes." In 1940 he went to Hollywood where he worked for a number of studios, although he had difficulty reconciling his artistic vision with the commercial aspects of American moviemaking. He also wrote a number of books, including a biography of his father in 1962. *My Life and My Films* gives us an intimate and touching portrait of a great, multitalented man who recounts his story with wit, modesty, and great humanity.

W, OR THE MEMORY OF CHILDHOOD

W ou le Souvenir d'enfance (1975)

◆

Georges Perec (1936–1982)

Georges Perec was a member of the French literary group OuLiPo (*Ouvroir de Littérature Potentielle*, i.e., Workshop of Potential Literature) that was organized in 1960 by François Le Lionnais and Raymond Queneau and included Italo Calvino, Harry Mathews, and Jacques Roubaud, among others. The group believed that good literature is produced when authors impose rigid restraints upon themselves, and Perec put this central tenet of OuLiPo into practice in many of his works. A virtuoso example is the novel *A Void* (*La Disparition*, 1969), in which the disappearance in the title refers both to the mystery recounted in the plot and to the fact that the letter "e" has also disappeared—both the original French 300-page work and its English translation use no words containing an "e." *W, or The Memory of Childhood* is also innovative in that it juxtaposes two separate stories, a fictional one that begins like an adventure novel, and a second, more fragmentary story that is an attempt to recover the narrator's childhood through the exercise of memory and the examination of old family photographs. This second text is at least semiautobiographical, as the first-person narrator calls himself Georges Perec and refers to events and to people in the author's past. The two texts are distinguished not only by their apparently different subjects but also by the typeface used, the fictional narrative being set in italics, while the autobiographical section is in roman. The narrator of the first story (also a first-person narrative) is introduced as Gaspard Winckler, a name he took when he was given a false identity during World War II. Having always assumed that this identity was invented, he is surprised one day to receive a mysterious letter, summoning him to a meeting with a stranger who informs him that Gaspard Winckler had in fact existed. Winckler, insists the stranger, had gone missing after the shipwreck of a yacht on which he and his family had been traveling in South America's Tierra del Fuego region, and the bodies of everyone except Gaspard had been recovered. The stranger asks the narrator to undertake a mission to try and ascertain what happened to the real Gaspard Winckler. The second strand of the novel gives some standard biographical information about Perec's childhood, but it begins by evoking the difficulty of recuperating child-hood memories and the unreliability of such memories: "I don't have any childhood memories. Until age twelve, my story can be told in a couple of lines." As Georges looks at old photos in an attempt to fill in the gaps of his memories, he undercuts the reliability of his narrative by adding footnotes that question the statements he makes in the accompanying text. One could say that this story, too, is about a disappearance, the disappearance of many of the details of Perec's childhood among other things. And disappearance figures into the structure of the overall novel itself, since it is divided into two parts, separated by a page that is blank except for three dots in parenthesis, implying an important gap between both parts. Indeed, in the second part of the novel a dramatic shift takes place: the autobiographical narrative becomes much more precise and linear, while the adventure story assumes the form of an apparently objective description of an imaginary island called W, near Tierra del Fuego. Although W at first seems to be a kind of utopia for sportsmen, its rigid, cruel, and irrational regime soon reveals it to be a nightmarish dystopia. It is only at the end of the novel that the reader realizes that the novel's symbolic and political dimensions evoke both the concen-tration camps of World War II and subsequent manifestations of the fascist state, in particular Pinochet's Chile.

Born in Paris, Perec was the son of Polish Jews who had immigrated to France. As he tells us in this novel he lost his father, who was killed at the front in the early days of World War II, when Georges was four years old, and his mother disappeared during her deportation to Auschwitz when he was six. After spending the war in various lodgings, he was adopted by his aunt and her husband in 1945. He abandoned his uni-versity studies in order to turn to writing, but, to make ends meet, found employment from 1961 until 1978 as a librarian in a neuro-physiological research laboratory. He won the Renaudot Prize in 1965 for *Things: A Story of the Sixties* (*Les Choses*), went on to write *A Void* (*La Disparition*, 1969) and *W, or The Memory of Childhood*, but it was *Life: A User's Manual* (*La Vie mode d'emploi*) which won him the Medicis Prize in 1978. Its success enabled him to leave his job and make his living as a writer. He then began to travel and went as far as Australia, where the University of Queensland had invited him in 1981. A heavy smoker, he was diagnosed with lung cancer on his return to Paris, and it was there that he died of the disease in 1982. Perec's remarkably innova-tive literary legacy makes him one of the most fascinating French writ-ers of the twentieth century.

MISSING PERSON

Rue des boutiques obscures (1978)

◆

Patrick Modiano (born 1945)

When we speak of identity theft, we usually mean the use of someone else's name and personal information for criminal purposes. However, there is another type of identity theft that is even more tragic: the loss of one's identity due to physical or mental illness. While these days we tend to focus on the lost memory caused by Alzheimer's disease, it is amnesia that drives the plot of Modiano's novel *Missing Person*. Its narrator recounts, in the first person, his quest to discover who he was prior to the onset of the malady that has robbed him of his past.

Patrick Modiano, born in the suburbs of Paris, published his first novel at the age of twenty-three. His early works deal with the contentious subject of the French Resistance and the problem of collaboration during the German occupation of France in World War II, a subject which is also central to the film script he and Louis Malle coauthored in 1974, *Lacombe Lucien*. Modiano won the prestigious Goncourt Prize for *Missing Person* in 1978. He has to date written over twenty novels, including *Ring Roads* (*Les Boulevards de ceinture*, 1972), *Trace of Malice* (*Quartier perdu*, 1984), *Honeymoon* (*Voyages de noces*, 1990), and *Out of the Dark* (*Du plus loin de l'oubli*, 1996). His most recent novel, *Dans le café de la jeunesse perdue* (which means, "in the café of lost youth"), was published in France in 2007.

Missing Person belongs to the type of detective novel in which a private investigator is hired to find someone who has disappeared in mysterious circumstances—but with an original twist: here the protagonist, employed as a private investigator, undertakes a search for himself, or at least the person he was before amnesia struck. As the novel begins, the owner of the detective agency, Baron Hutte, is on the point of leaving for Nice, where he will retire. Some eight years earlier, when the narrator had approached Hutte about elucidating his forgotten past, the baron had taken pity on him and had engaged him as an assistant in his agency. He had also procured the necessary papers to create a new identity for the narrator as Guy Roland. Now, because Hutte knows Roland is still eager to discover his true identity, he places at his disposal the resources of the agency, including a set of phone directories and social registers covering the past fifty years. Roland pursues a number of inconclusive leads that cause him to believe he is first one person, then another. After much dogged research, he manages to reconstruct what appears to be a central event in his past, which concerns a relationship he might have had with a certain Denise Coudreuse and her subsequent disappearance in the French Alps. Their separation apparently occurred during a snowstorm when Denise and her partner (Roland?) were attempting to escape from Nazi-occupied France into Switzerland. After the war, when he returns one summer to what he believes is the site of this escape in the hope of triggering other memories, nothing seems familiar: "I looked through the window [of the taxi] and tried to recognize the road along which we were driving, but with no snow, it didn't look at all like the road we had taken then. 'I don't recognize the landscape,' I said to the driver. 'You've already been here?' 'Yes, a very long time ago . . . when it was snowing . . .' 'It's not the same without snow.'" Still in the dark, Roland decides to follow another lead and embarks for French Polynesia in search of a certain Freddie Howard de Luz, one of the identities Roland had at one time thought might be his true self. But this journey proves fruitless as well. By the end of the novel Roland has only one remaining possibility, an address in Rome: 2, Street of the Dark Shops (2, rue des boutiques obscures, i.e., the novel's French title), and he is heading there as the story closes. Will this provide the clue to his identity? Or will this be yet another dead-end? Trying to reconstruct the past is akin to participating in some kind of shadow play, and the fragile nature of our own identity is highlighted by the ambiguities and uncertainties that abound in *Missing Person*.

At the heart of this fascinating and, at times, puzzling novel lies the question, What constitutes our uniqueness as individuals? How important is it to maintain a connection with the past, since Roland appears to function perfectly well without it? Is the person we were twenty years ago the same person we are today? Or is the most reasonable course of action the advice Hutte gives the narrator in chapter 1: "From now on, my dear Guy Roland, stop looking behind you and concentrate on the present and the future." The fragments of our past that float in and out of our conscious memories can be obscure, and the real nature of our identity often remains shrouded in mystery.

So Long a Letter

Une si longue lettre (1979)

◆

Mariama Bâ (1929–1981)

In Dakar, Senegal, in 1979, a short novel was published to much critical acclaim, written by Mariama Bâ, a primary school teacher from a prominent Dakar family. Titled *So Long a Letter*, it recounts the moving story of Ramatoulaye, a member of a small but growing group of Senegalese women who—by embarking upon careers as teachers— challenged the subordinate and subservient role traditionally attributed to women in their society. The story, a first-person narrative, begins at a critical point in Ramatoulaye's life: her husband, Modou Fall, has just died suddenly, victim of a massive heart attack. In almost cinematic style, the author powerfully conveys the feelings of shock and sadness experienced by the heroine. "Hailed a taxi! Fast! Faster! Throat dry. A big lump in my chest. Fast! Faster! The hospital at last with its smells [. . .] A long corridor which seems endless. Finally, at the end, a room. In the room, a bed. On this bed, Modou's body is lying, cut off from the world of the living by the white sheet that covers him." However, we soon learn that the couple had been separated for five years, after twenty-five years of marriage and twelve children, because Modou, without consulting Ramatoulaye, had taken a second wife— who was not only the same age as his eldest daughter but who was even one of the daughter's close friends. The whole family felt betrayed. Modou had spent lavish sums on his new bride, Binetou, and had lit- erally abandoned his family to live with this co-wife in a seaside villa. In the days following his untimely death, Ramatoulaye learns that her husband has left her and their children nothing but the house they occupy in the center of Dakar. The novel takes the form of a long let- ter, addressed by Ramatoulaye to one of her closest childhood friends, Aïssatou, whose husband had also taken a second wife. But Aïssatou had done what she, Ramatoulaye, had not been able to do: divorce her husband. Aïssatou had gone to university, become an interpreter, and worked at the Senegalese embassy in Washington. The novel chronicles Ramatoulaye's shock at her husband's betrayal, but also her devotion to her late husband in spite of everything. She does not lack for suit- ors after his death, but she refuses them, wishing to remain faithful to her husband and—since her suitors are married—because she does not want to inflict on their wives the pain she herself experienced when Modou took his second wife: "I'm not an object to be handed on from one man to another. For me, marriage is an act of faith and love, a complete giving of oneself to the person whom you have chosen and who has chosen you." Indeed, after recounting the trials of raising a dozen children, three of whom take up smoking, much to their mother's horror, and one of whom becomes pregnant out of wedlock, Ramatoulaye finishes her letter with an affirmation of the importance of a more assertive role for women in Senegalese society: "My heart is filled with joy each time a woman emerges from the shadows, but I also know how they have had to struggle against social constraints and the male ego." However, she also affirms that "the union of man and woman is inevitable and necessary" and that a "successful family is produced by harmony within the married couple." Life may be hard, relationships difficult, but happiness is attainable if men and women are willing to work together in its pursuit.

Many of the events recounted in this moving book reflect the circumstances of Mariama Bâ's own life. Born into a wealthy family in Dakar in 1929, she lost her mother while she was still young and was raised by her grandparents in the Islamic tradition. Like her heroine, Ramatoulaye, Bâ trained to be a primary school teacher, married a politician, and had a large family with nine children. Unlike her character Ramatoulaye, she divorced her husband and subsequently raised her children alone. She worked as an elementary school teacher until ill health forced her to resign. In 1979, she began writing fiction, earning recognition when *Une si longue lettre* won the first Noma Award for Publishing in Africa at the Frankfurt Book Fair in 1980. She had just completed her second novel, *Scarlet Song* (*Le Chant écarlate*), when she succumbed to terminal cancer in 1981. Her writings give voice to the hopes and aspirations of a new generation of Senegalese and countless other African women whose independence and success are won with difficulty because of the barriers of gender and culture. *So Long a Letter* remains Mariama Bâ's powerful testament and testimony for today's readers in Senegal, other African countries, and around the world.

THE PROSPECTOR

Le Chercheur d'or (1985)

◆

Jean-Marie Gustave Le Clézio (born 1940)

When Jean-Marie Gustave Le Clézio was awarded the Nobel Prize in Literature in 2008, it was the crowning achievement of a literary career that spans over four decades and secures Le Clézio a place among the great modern writers of world literature. While his reputation as a major literary figure was established in France many years ago, the Nobel Prize should ensure that internationally, too, he will now receive the recognition he so richly deserves.

Le Clézio's first major work, *The Interrogation* (*Le Procès verbal*, 1963), presented, at least superficially, similarities with the *nouveau roman* ("the new novel"). He soon abandoned the avant-garde narrative technique that characterized this early work, and his style became more accessible and lyrical in works such as *Désert* in 1980 (published in English as *Desert* in 2009). Le Clézio has much to recommend him to a wider audience. His interest in multiculturalism, in particular, makes his work timely. His own experiences—a childhood spent partly in Africa, his study of Mayan culture and myths, his four years with the Emberas Indians in Panama, his family connection with Mauritius—have given him an awareness of the beauty and fragility of different cultures as well as of the natural environment.

The Prospector, a novel which recounts a thirty-year span in the life of its narrator, Alexis, is both the story of a fruitless treasure hunt in the islands that comprise the Republic of Mauritius and a lyrical evocation of the lush beauty of the islands and the Indian Ocean that surrounds them. The story begins in 1892 on a remote inlet on the west coast of the island of Mauritius itself, where Alexis and his sister, Laure (eight and nine years old, respectively), lead an idyllic existence in a paradisiacal setting. This childhood happiness is not destined to last, since their impractical father goes bankrupt and their abode is ravaged by a cyclone that forces them to relocate on the more developed eastern side of the island. After his father's death, Alexis discovers among his father's papers documents that purport to show the location of buried pirate gold on Rodrigues Island. In 1910, Alexis leaves his office job to set sail for Rodrigues on the schooner *Zeta*. Already fascinated by the sea, whose

◆ *183* ◆

charms he had discovered as a child, he is once again entranced as he recounts his awakening on the first day of the voyage: "I open my eyes and see the ocean. It is not like the emerald green sea that, as a child, I saw in the lagoons [. . .] It is the sea like I have never seen it before, free, wild, whose blue is so deep that it gives you vertigo, the sea that lifts the ship's hull, slowly, wave after foam-flecked wave, as it sparkles in the light." He finally arrives on Rodrigues where he is befriended by a native young woman, Ouma, who becomes his chaste but erotic companion and guide to the natural wonders of the island. His unsuccessful search for treasure is interrupted by the First World War, when he enlists in the English army to fight in France. After the armistice, he returns to Rodrigues to continue his search not only for the treasure, but now for Ouma as well. Finding neither, he returns to rejoin his sister and dying mother, Mam, on Mauritius. After Mam's death, he unexpectedly encounters Ouma, who now works in the sugar plantations of Mauritius. They are reunited and spend a happy few months together before they separate again. At the end of the novel Alexis decides to destroy the documents concerning the pirate's treasure, because he has come to realize that not the actual gold he was seeking is really important but metaphorical gold—the joy of living, and the beauty of the sea and the sky. From a hill overlooking the inlet where he had spent his happy childhood, he dreams of a long voyage on a ship he will call the *Argo*, with Ouma as his companion.

Le Clézio was born in Nice, the son of two cousins who married, Raoul and Simone Le Clézio. The family had close ties with Mauritius, to which their Breton ancestors had immigrated in the eighteenth century, acquiring British citizenship when the island, originally in French hands, became an English possession in 1814. While still a child, Le Clézio fell in love with the sea after a long voyage with his mother to spend a year with his father, who was then working as a doctor in Nigeria. After pursuing his studies in Nice, the United Kingdom, Aix-en-Provence, and Perpignan, Le Clézio taught at universities in Mexico, Thailand, and the United States. With his second wife, Jemia, a Moroccan (his first marriage ended in divorce), he now divides his time between Nice, Mauritius, and New Mexico. In announcing his Nobel Prize, the president of the Swedish Academy spoke of Le Clézio as the "author of new departures, poetic adventure and sensual ecstasy," a description that applies equally well to the odyssey of his protagonist, Alexis, in *The Prospector*.

THE SAND CHILD

L'Enfant de sable (1985)

◆

Tahar Ben Jelloun (born 1944)

Tahar Ben Jelloun was born in the great city of Fez in Morocco. As a child he received a typical bilingual education in French and Arabic, but when his parents moved to Tangier, he attended only French schools, going on to study philosophy at the university in Rabat. Sent to a disciplinary camp for having participated in student demonstrations in 1966, he began to write poetry. Upon his release he became a schoolteacher but immigrated to France, where he completed a doctorate in psychology while continuing to write and to work for newspapers, including *Le Monde*. It was the poetic novel *The Sand Child* that brought him international renown in 1985. Not only is it a literary text of great power, it also provides real insights into the culture and civilization of Morocco. Two years later, he published a sequel, *The Sacred Night* (*La Nuit sacrée*), which won him the prestigious Goncourt Prize. Ben Jelloun has written many other works, including the novel *This Blinding Absence of Light* (*Cette aveuglante absence de lumière*, 2000) and the very popular essay *Racism Explained to My Daughter* (*Le Racisme expliqué à ma fille*, 1998).

In the opening chapter of *The Sand Child* we are introduced to the protagonist, who leads a hermit-like existence in his family's dwelling in an unnamed Moroccan city. Who is this enigmatic person, and why has he isolated himself even from the other members of his family? This is the mystery that the novel sets out to solve. As befits the important role that oral culture plays in African societies, the man's story is recounted by a professional storyteller, plying his trade on the city's main public square. He claims to have been given a notebook in which the story of the mystery man is recorded, and announces that he will tell the story divided into seven parts, one for each day of the week, beginning with Thursday, the day of the protagonist's birth. It is at this juncture that the central problem of the novel (which is based on real events) is introduced: The protagonist's parents have been unable to produce a male heir. The father is distraught, because upon his death the majority of his inheritance will not be distributed to his own daughters but to his brothers. No amount of consultation with a parade of healers and witches is able to stem the inexorable procession of seven female offspring. When his wife becomes pregnant for the eighth time, the man decides that, come what may, this child will be a boy. The baby is in fact another girl, but with the complicity of the midwife and thanks to a series of subterfuges that conceal the baby's gender from everyone except her parents and the midwife, she is declared to be male and will be raised as such. So begins the upbringing of "Ahmed," the name bestowed upon the child by the narrator, who recounts that Ahmed, upon learning the truth, at first wants to continue the charade because of the privileged status she enjoys as a male in Moroccan society. Ahmed even contracts an unconsummated marriage with an epileptic cousin, who dies young. But eventually the demands of the body cannot be suppressed, and the desire to have children produces a schizophrenia of sorts in Ahmed, leading to self-imposed isolation and the beginning of a sexual "transformation" into a female named Zahra. At this juncture the storyteller disappears, chased from the great public square where government forces are banishing the traditional acrobats, snake charmers, fortune-tellers, and storytellers in order to construct an urban renewal project. But thanks to the power of storytelling, three of the storyteller's most avid listeners meet and decide to tell their own versions of the conclusion of Ahmed-Zahra's story (there is even a rumor that the original storyteller has died). Henceforward, we encounter a plurality of narrators, so that we no longer know what is "true" and what comes from the imagination of any one of these storytellers. As more and more narrators are introduced the novel takes on a surreal quality, until finally the original storyteller returns, the rumor of his death having been false. He now explains how he procured the story in the first place: a woman had approached him, handing him a notebook and saying that of all the storytellers in the square, he was the one best able to tell the story "of her uncle, who was in fact her aunt." He read and reread the notebook until he was totally possessed by the tale. When he was forced to leave the public square, he took the book with him until one night, as he was leafing through it, the moonlight effaced all the writing except for a few syllables. This proved to be a deliverance from the hold the story had been exerting on him. Finally, the storyteller invites any listener interested in learning the rest of the story to "ask the moon when it is full," and he leaves behind the notebook, together with pen and ink, for anyone wishing to complete the story—which has taken on a life of its own, independent of whether it is fact or fiction.

CROSSING THE MANGROVE

Traversée de la Mangrove (1989)

◆

Maryse Condé (born 1937)

Who was Francis Sancher? Quite literally an international man of mystery, he is found dead at the beginning of this novel. If it appears at first that the enigma surrounding him involves the question whether he was murdered or died of natural causes, the reader quickly discovers that it is the personality and character of Sancher that constitute the real conundrum. It is a tour de force on the part of Condé that she makes the whole novel revolve around a dead man. The inquiry (or one could almost say "inquest," except that this implies a formal, judicial hearing) into Sancher's real identity takes place within the framework of his memorial wake conducted by the villagers of Rivière au Sel, an imaginary village situated in the backcountry of the island of Guadeloupe. Each of the villagers has had dealings of one sort or another with this man who appeared from nowhere to take up residence there. The house he rented is somewhat removed from the main village, and its location at the edge of the forest symbolizes the marginal status of its occupant. The participants in the wake tell their individual stories. Each story is assigned its own chapter, and each one relates the life of a villager as well as his or her relationship with Sancher. The picture that emerges is a contradictory one indeed. For some of the villagers he is an object of hatred and scorn; for others he is the incarnation of kindness. The family of the wild-spirited Mira, who, of her own volition, had come to live with him and became pregnant with his child, sees in Sancher a seducer, or worse still, a rapist. On the other hand he had befriended Sonny, a mentally challenged boy who was teased and ostracized by the other children in the village. As we read the narratives of Rivière au Sel (which means Salt River, suggesting the bitterness of the lives led by those who have ended up here), we are able to piece together some sort of picture, however incomplete, of Sancher. At the same time we are introduced to the history of Guadeloupe itself, a history that could describe almost any of the Caribbean islands that have been subject to colonization and slavery. We discover that Sancher had come to Rivière au Sel to find himself and retrace his origins, origins that go back to the first *découvreurs* (discoverers) of the island. Born in

Colombia, he subsequently traveled to Europe, America, Africa, and Cuba. He was a troubled soul, mentally tortured by the sights of death and suffering he had seen during his career as a military doctor in the war-ravaged countries where he had practiced medicine. He had confessed to one of the novel's characters, Lucien Evariste, that although he was not born in Rivière au Sel, he had found papers that prove that "everything began here." Part of his quest consisted in attempting to find the location of the plantation house his family had built in the region. He described his French ancestor, François-Désiré, as "the first member of this sinister lineage [. . .] who after committing his first crime, crossed the ocean and transplanted his rotten heritage in these islands." Readers must sift through and evaluate the various scraps of information that surface in the course of the villagers' stories. But the difficulty of this task is made apparent when the narrative of Vilma, another of Sancher's lovers, informs us that he was in the process of writing a book with the title *Crossing the Mangrove*—and readers are left wondering what exactly is truth and what is fiction in the things he revealed about himself. Vilma's reaction is telling: "You don't cross the mangrove. You end up getting impaled on its roots, before being sucked down and smothered in its brackish mud."

Maryse Condé is a native Guadeloupean, and this poetic novel was the first work of hers set in her birthplace. After studying in France at both the high school and university levels, she held a number of teaching positions in various African countries before coming to the United States, where she teaches at Columbia University. Condé has written over twenty books, including the award-winning historical novel *Segu* (*Ségou*, 1987) that takes place in the Bambara kingdom in West Africa, and *I, Tituba, Black Witch of Salem* (1986) about the Salem witch trials. She is past president of the Committee for the Remembrance of Slavery (*Comité pour la mémoire de l'esclavage*), established in France in 2004 in response to the Taubira Law that was passed in the French parliament in 2001 and declared slavery a crime against humanity. Although *Crossing the Mangrove* does not deal directly with slavery, which was abolished long before the book's action takes place, the long-term effects of slavery are still palpable in the novel, which gives us a remarkable insight into the problems, tensions, prejudices, and customs of modern-day Guadeloupe. But it equally captures the poetry and mystery of the island's luxuriant landscape and the character of its vibrant society.

SIMPLE PASSION

Passion simple (1991)

◆

Annie Ernaux (born 1940)

Annie Ernaux's novel *Simple Passion* is a frank, apparently autobiographical account of an affair the narrator had with a married businessman from an undisclosed European country who was temporarily assigned to Paris. However, the novel is not the chronological story of this liaison, but rather a meditation on the state of passion itself. Told from the woman's point of view, it charts precisely and movingly the joys, the disappointments, the anxious waiting which characterize most affairs of the heart and which give this particular story its universal quality.

The novel begins with the narrator's confession that she has recently watched her first X-rated movie. She marvels that the sex act, so often censored, suppressed, or evoked by euphemism in times past, has become almost banal today. However, she acknowledges that the first time one observes sexual intercourse is stupefying, and she states her belief that writing should strive to produce in the reader the same stupor, anguish, and suspension of moral judgment. Such is the preamble to the story she is about to relate. For the duration of her liaison, she is so totally consumed by her passion that everything else—her daily life, her work—is conducted on autopilot. She notes that her principal activity is in fact waiting: waiting for her lover to call, waiting for him to arrive, waiting for their next *rendez-vous*. Everything else seems trivial and unimportant. She gives us few details about him, and he is designated by a single letter: A. He is foreign, from somewhere in Eastern Europe; he speaks reasonable but imperfect French, which makes her wonder at what level they are actually communicating when they talk; he is well-off and married. This last fact complicates the relationship, since she cannot call him or write to him at home, for fear that his wife will discover their liaison (this is before there were cell phones). She is totally dependent on him for the continuation of their affair, and she must play second fiddle to both his family and professional life. Their moments together are sporadic, often fleeting but correspondingly intense. A.'s excessive drinking adds an extra element of danger to the affair, for example when he drives too fast while under the influence. "He drank too much [. . .] This frightened me because of the possibility of having an accident on the highway, but it didn't repulse me." Likewise, when he arrives at her apartment, he often has difficulty walking in a straight line and he sometimes burps when he kisses her. The strength of her passion can be measured by the fact that these normally repugnant details do not repulse her but make her feel a greater oneness with him. But what of A.'s feelings? We only witness them from the few details he reveals about himself to her (and therefore to us). She is never sure if the affair is anything but purely sexual for him; her life is attuned only to his desire—or lack thereof—discernible from his physical state when he is with her. No question, this *is* a book that does not hesitate to call a spade a spade, very much like the X-rated movie referred to in the opening paragraph.

Annie Ernaux, one of the most popular French novelists of the modern period, was born to a working-class family in the provinces during one of the darkest periods of French history: World War II. She studied at the University of Rouen and became a high school teacher. Many of her novels, like *A Frozen Woman* (*La Femme gelée*, 1981) and *A Woman's Story* (*Une Femme*, 1989), contain strong feminist themes, although more recent works, such as *Les Années* (meaning, "the years," 2008), have a stronger social and historical orientation than her earlier ones. *Simple Passion* can be read as a "feminist" novel in the sense that its narrator is at liberty to live out her passion and to write freely and openly about it (while in previous eras any expression of female desire was roundly criticized). Yet at the same time, paradoxically, it presents an almost traditional view of a woman's role in a passionate affair: it is she who is consumed by her desire; it is she who must sacrifice for the convenience of her lover; it is he who ultimately calls all the shots. One could sum up this very remarkable novel with the old French expression, "Plus ça change, plus c'est la même chose"—the more things change, the more they stay the same.

BAROQUE AT DAWN

Baroque d'aube (1995)

◆

Nicole Brossard (born 1943)

Baroque at Dawn opens with a graphic portrait of a woman, Cybil Noland, having sex in a hotel room with another woman whom she had encountered just a few hours previously. Although the room number is given (43, the author's birth year), the city is only identified as a North American city that is "armed to the teeth." With this erotically charged beginning, Brossard introduces us to one of the major themes of her poetic and unconventional novel: the relationship between sexual desire and literary creation. For decades, literary critics, zeroing in on this connection, have delighted in revealing the links between "sexuality" and "textuality" in various writers. Brossard explores these associations in her novel from a feminine and feminist point of view. However, although the "sexuality" depicted in the text is lesbian in orientation, *Baroque at Dawn* is not a "lesbian novel"—it has a universality which makes it an exploration of the process of creation. In fact, this opening sequence, as we discover later, is part of an unfinished story (or could it be a finished one?) written by Cybil Noland, who is one of the principal characters in the rest of the book. The novel recounts an expedition aboard the *Symbol,* a research vessel with an all-male crew that is involved in deep-sea ocean exploration off the coast of South America. Cybil has been asked to write a book about the expedition in collaboration with two other women, the oceanographer Occident DesRives and the photographer Irène Mages. All their names are highly symbolic: Cybil's first name evokes the female prophets of antiquity, the Sibyls, while her family name, "No Land," suggests she is from nowhere and everywhere. Occident DesRives, the oceanographer's name, implies a link with Western civilization, but it is a tenuous one, since her name indicates she is on the coast (*rive* means coast, or bank), not in the interior. She may also be adrift, since DesRives phonetically evokes *à la dérive.* Irène's first name suggests peace, since it comes from a Greek word with that meaning, and Mages suggests the magical and prophetic powers that are part of her talent as a photographer. There is no doubt that this voyage of discovery is a symbolic one, exploring, among other things, the role of women in patriarchal Western society, the creative process, and the progression from life to death: Occident dies toward the end of the journey. One of Cybil's constant concerns, a preoccupation that can lead to writer's block, is what she calls "double time": an expression that has many meanings in the novel but evokes the often uneasy association between the time that is presented in the fictional work and time experienced by its writer, as well as the tension between present and future. Cybil is after all a Sibyl who looks toward the future in life and art. She manages to overcome this powerful deterrent to creation thanks to another character in the book, a novelist by the name of—Nicole Brossard! This is Nicole's advice, given in English: "so tape the creative energy around your waist like a safety belt and forget about fear." The novel closes with a series of short reflections by a female novelist of uncertain identity—Cybil Noland? Nicole Brossard, the character? Nicole Brossard, the author?—on the collaboration between her and her female translator, a relation which results in physical union and intellectual communion as the two work together in Montréal. We are left with a series of questions on what this collaboration will bring in the future and on the role of the physical body in the creative process. The tone is optimistic, because novelist and translator feel "tremendously free to plunge into the future" when they return to their hotel after a night at the casino, as the dawning day "spreads its rosy hue over the sky." This is the "Baroque dawn" of the novel's title.

Nicole Brossard, born in Montréal in 1943, is a poet, playwright, and novelist. In her early twenties she was already part of the cultural life of Québec, collaborating in the founding of the review *La Barre du jour*, an avant-garde literary magazine whose goal was to promote different ways of both reading and producing literary texts. She subsequently helped found other literary and cultural journals, while pursuing her own writing career and exploring new ways of writing. Since her first work, a poem that appeared in 1965, she has published over thirty books, including *Mauve Desert* (*Le Désert mauve*, 1987) and *Fences in Breathing* (*La Capture du sombre*, 2007), and has won two prestigious Canadian awards for her work. *Baroque at Dawn* is a strong example of her experimentation with traditional literary forms, and its elliptical narrative style and poetic language quickly cast a spell over the reader, encouraging her or him to reflect upon the creative process and the important insights women bring to the artistic and literary world.

FEAR AND TREMBLING

Stupeur et tremblements (1999)

◆

Amélie Nothomb (born 1967)

The success of Sofia Coppola's film *Lost in Translation* (2003) has made us keenly aware of both the linguistic and cultural abysses that can separate one culture and society from another. *Fear and Trembling* addresses the same problems, as it highlights the difficulties even a Westerner well-versed in Japanese language and culture can encounter in the corporate world of twentieth-century Japan.

Amélie Nothomb, something of an enfant terrible on France's literary scene, has become a French media star. Of Belgian nationality, she was born in Kobe, Japan, where her father, a Belgian diplomat, was stationed at the time. Thanks to their father's different postings, Amélie and her sister lived successively in Japan, China, Burma, and New York City. When she was of college age she attended university in Brussels, and it was there, ironically, that she felt like an expatriate. She returned to Japan after completing her studies, and attempted in vain to enter the Japanese business world, finally returning to Europe where she now divides her time between Brussels and Paris. Her first published novel was *Hygiène de l'assassin* (meaning, "the hygiene of the assassin") in 1992. Although she had been writing since the age of seventeen (she confesses to having numerous unpublished manuscripts in the proverbial bottom drawer), it was this novel that launched her literary career when she was only twenty-five years old. Since then, she has regularly published about a novel a year, chosen from the several manuscripts she composes annually. Her novels include *Loving Sabotage* (*Le Sabotage amoureux*, 1993), *Antichrista* (*Antéchrista*, 2003), *Tokyo Fiancée* (*Ni d'Ève, ni d'Adam*, 2007), and *Le Fait du prince* (meaning, "One does not question authority"), published in France in 2008.

In *Fear and Trembling*, a French bestseller that won the Académie française's Grand Prize for the Year's Best Novel, the author recounts the experiences of her semiautobiographical heroine at a large firm in Japan, painting an acerbically humorous picture of the difficulties faced by Westerners when they try to integrate into Japanese culture. The first-person narrator, Amélie, who has the dual disadvantage of being a Westerner *and* a woman, recounts her progress (or lack thereof) in the fictional company Yumimoto. Although she speaks fluent Japanese, she commits a series of faux pas, as she is assigned office tasks at which she either fails or performs too well. For example, when asked to serve coffee at an all-male business meeting, she does so with the grace of a geisha and the fluency of a native speaker of Japanese. When she is later summoned by a male superior, she expects praise for her performance but receives a tongue-lashing instead: "You made our colleagues feel very uncomfortable because you addressed them in fluent Japanese [. . .] How could they feel at ease in the presence of a white woman who speaks their language?" Faced with these unexpected obstacles, she finds solace in the friendship of her immediate superior, Ms. Fubuki Mori, one of only four female executives in the huge company. However, when Amélie agrees to collaborate with a male executive to produce a report on a Belgian agricultural product, the friendship sours, since Ms. Mori believes Amélie is working for a fast-track promotion instead of putting in her time, as Ms. Mori had been forced to do. She therefore orders Amélie to undertake a series of mind-numbing tasks that the Westerner is unable to complete successfully. Amélie's attempt to repair the friendship with sympathy when Ms. Mori herself receives a dressing-down from a superior is an utter failure, leading her to be assigned ever more humiliating tasks. The irony with which Amélie describes her downward spiral into the most demeaning job of all softens when, after leaving the company, she publishes her novel and receives a congratulatory note from Ms. Mori. By writing her note in Japanese, Ms. Mori has paid Amélie the ultimate compliment.

Although the novel appears to suggest that the gap between East and West is unbridgeable, Ms. Mori's note and the sympathy Amélie receives from a few of her colleagues at Yumimoto do suggest that, with time and great mutual effort, an understanding between Western and Japanese cultures may be achieved. The book is both a salutary lesson about the importance of exercising cultural sensitivity in our dealings with other countries and peoples and an affirmation of the value of humor, which can make the daily dramas and tragedies of cross-cultural interaction more bearable.

MONSIEUR IBRAHIM AND THE FLOWERS OF THE KORAN

Monsieur Ibrahim et les fleurs du Coran (2001)

◆

Eric-Emmanuel Schmitt (born 1960)

"What you give away, Momo, is yours forever; what you keep, you lose forever." This simple but profound advice encapsulates the charm and wisdom of this novella that has been called a modern fable because it relays a moral message, just like the fables of Aesop or La Fontaine. Seeking to promote tolerance and understanding, *Monsieur Ibrahim* recounts the improbable friendship, in Paris, of a Jewish boy named Moses and an aging Muslim shopkeeper whose small convenience store in a Jewish neighborhood is just a few doors from the apartment where the boy lives. Moses goes regularly to the store and the shopkeeper, Monsieur Ibrahim, gives him the nickname Momo, because Moses seems a little too grand for the boy. Monsieur Ibrahim is the "local Arab," although he carefully explains that he is not Arab, but simply Muslim (he is in fact from Turkey). "Arab," explains Monsieur Ibrahim, referring to the small convenience stores typically run by members of ethnic minorities in Paris, means simply "Open from 8 a.m. to midnight, including Sundays." Momo's home situation is difficult. Living with his father, a Holocaust survivor whose wife left him when Momo was young, he has to cook and grocery shop. But his father does not trust him and leaves him only enough money each day to buy that day's provisions. To punish him, Momo begins to steal from his father, and at the same time starts shoplifting from Ibrahim's store, justifying his action by telling himself: "After all, he's just an Arab." Discovering one day that Monsieur Ibrahim knows of his thefts but is still willing to be a friend, the boy is chastened. When his father loses his job and abandons his son to look for work in Marseille, Momo tries to pretend nothing is amiss, but the perceptive shopkeeper realizes what has happened and takes Momo under his wing, becoming like a second, and much more loving, father to him. When Momo receives the horrific news that his father has committed suicide, Monsieur Ibrahim goes to Marseille in the boy's stead to save Momo from the awful task of having to identify his father's body. Monsieur Ibrahim, who is a Sufi, later takes Momo on an overland car trip to his home in Anatolia, and on the way imparts many life lessons to his "adopted" son, taking him to watch whirling dervishes and teaching him to dance like them. Like the staid Englishman in *Zorba the Greek*, Momo learns to dance and discovers that dancing can banish worry and anguish and restore joy. He also learns, as the two of them visit various churches and mosques on their journey, that the world's religions have a common source of wisdom, and Momo reflects: "Being around Monsieur Ibrahim has taught me that Jews, Muslims, and even Christians had a lot in common before they started fighting each other." The reader will find many other pearls of wisdom in this charming story and will be surprised by its twists and turns. Having started its life as a play, *Monsieur Ibrahim and the Flowers of the Koran* was also made into a touching movie in 2003, starring Omar Sharif as Monsieur Ibrahim.

Born in a suburb of Lyon, Eric-Emmanuel Schmitt attended the École Normale Supérieure in Paris, like a number of authors in modern-day France. There he completed a doctorate in philosophy and went on to teach in Cherbourg and Chambéry. Despite the fact that he was raised without religion by atheist parents, he became first an agnostic, then a Christian, and intensely interested in other religions and in reconciliation between the various world faiths. Religion is a major theme in many of his works, and *Monsieur Ibrahim* is one of a quartet of novellas called the Cycle of the Invisible that deal with different religions (the other novellas address Tibetan Buddhism, Christianity, and Judaism). His literary career began on the stage, and his play *The Visitor* (*Le Visiteur*), which recounts a meeting between Freud and someone who is quite possibly God, won the Molière Prize for best play of 1993. Among his other plays are *Enigma Variations* (*Variations énigmatiques*, 1996) and *Between Worlds* (*Hôtel des deux mondes*, 1999). He has also written a number of novels, including *Oscar and the Lady in Pink* (*Oscar et la dame rose*, 2002), and his works have been translated into many languages and have become popular the world over. If at times *Monsieur Ibrahim and the Flowers of the Koran* has a tendency to gloss over important differences and conflicts, it is a feel-good tale brimming with basic humanity, and its universal message of tolerance, forgiveness, and understanding will resonate with readers for many years to come.

KIFFE KIFFE TOMORROW

Kiffe, kiffe demain (2004)

◆

Faïza Guène (born 1985)

O h, to achieve literary fame at the age of nineteen! Such was the good fortune of Faïza Guène when her first novel, *Kiffe, kiffe demain,* appeared. The daughter of first-generation immigrants from Algeria, she was born and raised in Bobigny, a suburb of Paris. The French word for suburb, *la banlieue,* referring to the localities that ring the City of Light, has a connotation quite opposite that of America's often affluent suburbs. Some towns in the nearby *banlieue* are quite poor, with high unemployment, badly maintained public high-rise housing, and persistent clashes between young people and the police. Violence, crime, and drug peddling are frequent. This is the milieu that Guène describes in *Kiffe Kiffe Tomorrow.* But while she does not downplay its grimmer aspects, her fifteen-year-old protagonist, Doria, also demonstrates the resilience of its inhabitants as she gives an account of a year in her life. Born of Moroccan parents, Doria recounts the clash of tradition and modernity with a sassy sense of humor, expressed in the picturesque slang of suburban youth. Doria has been abandoned by her father, who has left her illiterate mother, Yasmina, in order to return to Morocco to find a wife who can give him a son, a feat Doria's mother was unable to accomplish: "Dad wanted a son. Because only a son can bring him pride and honor and carry on his name, and for all sorts of other stupid reasons [. . .] Let's just say that I wasn't what he wanted, and unlike what happens when you buy something at a store, he couldn't exchange the merchandise." Because her teachers find her introverted, Doria has to see a psychologist on a regular basis, and her reactions suggest that France's envied national health service is not always what it's cracked up to be: "Madame Burlaud is old, she's ugly, and she smells of anti-lice medication [. . .] Today she pulled a collection of strange pictures out of her drawer, large blots which looked like dried vomit. When I told her what they made me think of, she stared at me with her bulging eyes, moving her head up and down like those little dogs people place in the rear window of their automobiles." Doria's mother ekes out a living as a cleaning woman for a cheap motel chain, but when the rest of the staff goes on strike—strikes being an archetypal French pastime—she leaves her job. Thanks to a social worker, however, this decision proves to be fortunate, for she is placed in a program where, besides learning to read and write, she receives training to help her obtain a better job. The French welfare state is not all bad after all. Meanwhile, Doria earns extra money by babysitting; becomes infatuated with Hamoudi, a man at least ten years her senior; and is devastated when he starts to court the mother of the child in her care. We also learn of the dramas of other people in the neighborhood: Samra, the girl who lives upstairs, is kept a virtual prisoner by her father and brother but finally escapes and runs off to marry someone her family disapproves of; Youssef, the son of "Aunt" Zohra, a friend of her mother, has to do time for drug dealing and stealing automobiles. Doria's life slowly improves. Although she still has to wear unstylish clothes that her mother buys at second-hand clothing shops, she is able to learn a trade when she is accepted into hairdressing school, and her disappointment over Hamoudi is assuaged when a guy of her own age, Nabil, whom she originally considered a nerd, turns out to be an acceptable boyfriend. This novel of diary-like vignettes of life in the Parisian *banlieue* ends on an optimistic note: instead of thinking that one day is just like another (*kif-kif demain* in French), Doria now believes that life is something to be loved. The *kiffe kiffe* of the novel's title, from the slang word *kiffer* (to love), transforms *kif-kif* into something positive: "Love tomorrow."

Although she shared some of Doria's traits and was also brought up in the Paris suburbs, Faïza Guène's family remained intact, and both of her parents supported Faïza's education. She began to participate in events at a local cultural center when she was just thirteen, and the following year had produced a short film. Thanks to the encouragement and support she received from the cultural center's director, Faïza Guène began writing this novel when she was seventeen and received a book contract to complete it. *Kiffe Kiffe Tomorrow*, a bestseller in France, also became popular across Europe. Guène's self-deprecatory style and acerbic humor capture both the trials of the passage to adulthood and the particular problems of a first-generation immigrant girl (in a single-parent household), struggling against poverty and cultural stereotypes in a country that is home yet remains foreign.

THE POSSIBILITY OF AN ISLAND

La Possibilité d'une île (2005)

◆

Michel Houellebecq (born 1958)

For the French, Michel Houellebecq is a literary phenomenon: whether they like him or dislike him (and he certainly has his detractors) they cannot ignore him, and his works provoke many a lively discussion both in France and abroad. His novel *The Possibility of an Island* is part science fiction, part philosophical, but narrated in a style full of sardonic humor and sexually explicit language that is engaging—despite, or perhaps *because* of its ability to provoke both outrage and controversy. The basic theme of the novel is human cloning and the material immortality that this scientific technique can bring to humans. Perhaps partially inspired by events surrounding a French sect, the Raëlians, which made headlines in 2002 by claiming to have cloned a human being, Houellebecq recounts in the first person the life of the principal character, identified simply as Daniel 1, a successful comedian who becomes both famous and rich through his brand of in-your-face sexist, racist, and intolerant humor. Daniel 1's account is periodically interrupted by the interpolations of some of his later clones, in particular Daniel 24 and Daniel 25, who are reading the narrative of Daniel 1, their "ancestor," several millennia later and who have witnessed the progressive destruction of the human race caused by the devastating effects of pollution and global warming. Daniel 1's principal nonprofessional interest is sex, and he describes in graphic detail his relationship with his wife, Isabelle, of whom he tires when the couple reaches middle age, and his subsequent liaison with Esther, a twenty-five-year-old Spanish blonde, who at first fulfills his sexual fantasies but then moves on to pursue a career in the movies. Because of his celebrity status (he reports having earned over 45 million euros for his comedy routines), Daniel 1 is invited to visit the headquarters of a new religious sect, the Elohims, situated on the Canary Islands. Its founder, the Prophet, expounds a gospel of sexual freedom, although he appears to be the only one permitted to practice what he preaches, surrounding himself with a bevy of beautiful, sexually available young women. He promises his followers immortality through the cloning process when they reach the end of their own lives, by activating their DNA to "resurrect" them in their clones. The sect flourishes and becomes a major religion, and when an apocalyptic series of natural disasters strikes, its cloned members, identified as neohumans, are the only ones able to survive and flourish, whereas the regular humans either die or are reduced to a state of violent primitivism. The French love their dogs, and *naturellement* Daniel is accompanied by his faithful Fox, who is also cloned to be the companion of future Daniels. In the final part of the novel, when Daniel 25 decides to leave the safety of his compound in France in order to journey across a blighted Europe back to the Canaries, he is accompanied by the last clone of Fox, whose death is one of the saddest events in the novel. After pausing for several hours to rest, Daniel 25 suddenly notices that Fox is missing: "I searched the bushes that surrounded the lake for more than three hours, calling out from time to time at regular intervals, surrounded by a silence that increased my anguish as it began to get darker. Just as night fell, I found his corpse, pierced by an arrow. In a supremely cruel act, the savages had cut off his ears." The entire description of Daniel 25's hallucinatory trek across an apocalyptic landscape, scarred by global warming and peopled with savage noncloned human beings, is deeply disturbing.

Michel Houellebecq was born on the island of Réunion in the South Indian Ocean. Neglected by his parents whom he describes as leading a quasi-hippie life, he was sent to France to live with his grandmother. Trained as an agronomist, he began writing poetry, studied filmmaking, became a computer specialist, and began writing novels. His first literary success was *Whatever* (*Extension du domaine de la lutte*) in 1994, followed by *Elementary Particles* (*Les Particules élémentaires*) in 1998, which was an international success. His 2001 novel *Platform* (*Plateforme*), which sharply criticized Islam, was responsible for his being accused of inciting racial hatred in France, a charge of which he was acquitted by a panel of judges who saw his criticism as a legitimate exercise in free speech. Houellebecq does not shy away from expressing controversial and unpopular opinions—indeed he seems to enjoy the role of provocateur—and thus *The Possibility of an Island* will leave few readers indifferent, because it raises many important questions about contemporary society and its attitudes, and will continue to promote debate and discussion. After all, has that not always been one of the primary roles of literature?

AFTERWORD: AND FIFTY MORE

◆ ◆ ◆

Needless to say, there are many, many more than just one hundred great books written in French. Here are fifty additional great books that I hope will interest today's readers, and of course even these fifty additional titles by no means exhaust all the possibilities—hundreds of other titles could be included just as well. Thus the same principles that governed my choice of the featured one hundred great books have been used here. Since I could only present one work by each of the authors in the main text of this book, this Afterword contains other important works by some of these same authors, as well as works by authors *not* included among the one hundred entries. For the purpose of consistency, the following suggestions are in chronological order.

The Middle Ages: Chrétien de Troyes wrote a number of twelfth-century chivalric romances, and readers who like *Yvain, or the Knight of the Lion* should also look at its companion book, *Erec and Enide* (*Erec et Enide*). For a somewhat different treatment of courtly themes, readers would also enjoy Chrétien's *Lancelot, or the Knight of the Cart* (*Lancelot ou le Chevalier de la charette*), or his unfinished mystical work, *Perceval, or the Story of the Grail* (*Perceval ou le Conte du Graal*). All are fascinating and important texts belonging to the cycle of poems concerning King Arthur and the Knights of the Round Table. Those who wish to see the humorous side of the later Middle Ages will enjoy one of several collections of salty tales (*fabliaux*), such as *Fabliaux: Ribald Tales from the Old French*.

The sixteenth century (*French Renaissance*): François Rabelais wrote a prequel about Pantagruel's father, *Gargantua* (1534), as well as sequels to his *Pantagruel*: *The Third Book* (*Le Tiers Livre*, 1546) and *The Fourth Book* (*Le Quart Livre*, 1552) of Pantagruel's adventures deal respectively with the nature of truth and authority and the quest for an answer to the question posed by Pantagruel's companion Panurge—whether or not he should marry—a quest pursued in comic imitation of Homer's *Odyssey*. John Calvin's *Institutes of the Christian Religion* (*Institution de la religion chrétienne*; its first edition in French is from 1541) is of interest to any reader curious to know more about the theological matters at the heart of the religious battles of the sixteenth century. This was the first theological treatise destined for lay readers, and it remains accessible for readers today (a number of selected readings from the complete work are also available). *The Entire Memoirs of Marguerite de Valois* (*Mémoires de Marguerite de Valois*, first published only in 1628) gives a fascinating portrait of court life and intrigue in the latter part of the sixteenth century.

The seventeenth century (*French classicism*): The playwrights Pierre Corneille, Molière, and Jean Racine each wrote a number of plays, and some of them—alas not all—are available in English. Corneille's comedy *The Comic Illusion* (*L'Illusion comique*, 1635) deals playfully with various levels of illusion, including the illusion of the theater itself. His classical tragedy *Cinna* (1641) describes a plot against the Roman emperor Augustus and its surprising ending. Molière continues to charm audiences with his *Tartuffe* (1664), a comic study of religious hypocrisy that almost finishes badly, and *The Miser* (*L'Avare*, 1668), about a miser's love of money and his vain attempts to stop his daughter's marriage. Racine's tragedy *Andromache* (*Andromaque*, 1667), set in ancient Greece, features a love triangle. Although it ends in death and destruction, the title character is allowed to survive and triumph. Another of Racine's plays, *Bérénice* (1669), is a powerful analysis of an impossible love between the emperor Titus and Bérénice. For a seventeenth-century journey into space, Cyrano de Bergerac's novel *Other Worlds: The Comical History of the States and the Empires of the Moon and the Sun* (*Histoire comique des Etat et Empire de la Lune et du Soleil*, 1657) is a real trip, while Jean de La Bruyère's *Characters* (*Les Caractères*, 1688) provides pithy aphorisms à la La Rochefoucauld and amusing portraits of society in the 1600s.

The eighteenth century (*the Enlightenment*): Pierre Marivaux is an excellent comic dramatist, and his *The Game of Love and Chance* (*Le Jeu de l'amour et du hasard*, 1730) is fun to read. (Unfortunately, Marivaux's novels are currently not readily available in English translations.) Voltaire can be explored further in his *Philosophical Letters* (*Lettres philosophiques*, 1733–34)—which are his reflections on English cultural, political, and religious life that implied a strong criticism of France—or in any of his philosophical tales and short stories, such as *Micromégas* (1752). Jean-Jacques Rousseau's best-selling novel, *Julie, or the New Heloise* (*Julie ou la Nouvelle Héloïse*, 1761), would be an obvious choice for readers who like sentimental novels. His *Confessions* (published posthumously from 1782 to 1789) is a masterpiece of autobiography, while

Emile (1762), his treatise on education, and his famous *Social Contract* (*Du contrat social,* also 1762) are excellent and highly readable examples of his philosophical positions. Denis Diderot's *Jacques the Fatalist and His Master* (*Jacques le Fataliste et son maître,* published posthumously in 1796) is a sprawling, fascinating picaresque comic novel and perfect for those who like a dose of philosophy with their fiction. Marquis de Sade's novel *Juliette* (*Histoire de Juliette ou les Prospérités du vice,* 1797), about Justine's sister, shows how Juliette is able to make her fortune by following the path of vice rather than virtue.

The nineteenth century. This period is particularly rich in great texts. Balzac's *The Wild Ass's Skin* (*La Peau de chagrin,* 1831) and *Eugénie Grandet* (1833) give the reader a sense of the panorama of French society the novelist depicted in his *Human Comedy.* Among additional works by the eminently readable Alexandre Dumas, *The Three Musketeers* (*Les Trois Mousquetaires,* 1844) is perfect for anybody who likes swashbuckling adventure in a historical setting. Any admirer of Victor Hugo will also want to read *Les Misérables* (1862)—on which the record-breaking musical is based—as well as *The Toilers of the Sea* (*Les Travailleurs de la mer,* 1866). Alphonse Daudet's *Letters from My Windmill* (*Lettres de mon moulin,* 1869), a collection of short stories set in Provence, is certainly noteworthy. For Flaubert lovers, his novel *The Sentimental Education* (*L'Éducation sentimentale,* 1869), recounting the love life of a young provincial student who makes his way to Paris, will be a joy, just like his *Three Tales* (*Trois contes,* 1877). Emile Zola wrote a number of substantial novels that deal with important subjects, such as *L'Assommoir* (1877), about the ravages of alcoholism and the misery of the working class; *Nana* (1880), about a courtesan whose rise and fall symbolize the glitter and corruption of the Second Empire; and *Germinal* (1885), which describes the appalling conditions in the mines of northern France. In addition to his short stories, Guy de Maupassant is also a novelist of note, and his *Bel-Ami* (1885), about a social climber in Paris, is one of his best novels. The highly influential poet Stéphane Mallarmé wrote between 1865 and the end of the century; selections from his poetry can be found in various editions. One of the founders of modern sociology, Émile Durkheim published his groundbreaking study *Suicide* (*Le Suicide*) in 1897.

The twentieth century. The recent past offers many delights. André Gide's great novel *The Counterfeiters* (*Les Faux-Monnayeurs,* 1925–26) is a story of self-delusion set in Paris in the early part of the 1900s. The surrealist poet Paul Éluard's *Capital of Pain* (*Capitale de la douleur*) also appeared in 1926. Albert Camus wrote the compelling novel *The Plague* (*La Peste*, 1947), in some sense an allegory of the occupation of France during World War II. Charles de Gaulle's memoirs of the Second World War, *The Complete War Memoirs of Charles de Gaulle* (*Mémoires de guerre*, published in three volumes, 1954–59) are a powerful read. In 1955, Claude Lévi-Strauss's ethnographic study *Tristes tropiques* appeared (the English translation keeps the French title, meaning "sad tropics"), the work for which he is most famous. Jean Genet was a subversive writer whose plays often provoked a scandalized reaction. *The Balcony* (*Le Balcon*, 1956), about the clients of a brothel who, when a revolution threatens, are called upon to play important roles in their society (such as judges, clerics, and the like), is one of his most popular plays. The great Martinican writer Aimé Césaire's *A Tempest* (*Une tempête*, 1969) is a magnificent rewriting of Shakespeare's famous play. The intensely prolific social critic and philosopher Michel Foucault wrote a fascinating study of incarceration, *Discipline and Punish: The Birth of the Prison* (*Surveiller et punir: naissance de la prison*, 1975). Film buffs should not miss François Truffaut's book *The Films in My Life* (*Les films de ma vie*, 1975), in which the director talks about the influence of American, British, and German filmmakers on his own films. One of France's prominent recent thinkers, Pierre Bourdieu—a sociologist who examined the power structure of societies and the role that cultural, educational, and other institutions play in upholding it—published *Distinction: A Social Critique of the Judgement of Taste* (*La Distinction*) in 1979. And rounding out the fifty, there is Muriel Barbery's *The Elegance of the Hedgehog* (*L'élégance du hérisson*, 2006), a novel about a Parisian intellectual in disguise—Renée, the unfashionable fifty-five-year-old concierge of an apartment building on the Left Bank whose tenants pay no attention to her as they pass her loge everyday. Renée is an autodidact who has a secret, rich intellectual life that she only shares with Paloma, a highly intelligent girl who lives in the same building. Renée, the unlikely heroine, all spines on the outside but elegant on the inside, is in fact the incarnation of what many French dream of becoming: a true intellectual who despises bourgeois convention and pretension and is only interested in the life of the mind.

It is my sincere wish that the works discussed in the main text of this book, together with these additional suggestions, will introduce or reintroduce today's readers to the vast and fascinating panorama that is French literature, a literature that has held sway over the hearts and minds not only of native French readers, but of readers from around the world, for centuries. Thomas Jefferson's famous observation, "Every man has two countries, his own and France," bears witness to the great influence the culture of France has had throughout the ages. While the visual arts and music have of course played a very important role, it is perhaps above all through its written texts that France has exercised such a strong impact on world culture and thought. Readers who use this book as a key to gain access to some of the great literary treasures written in French—and as an invitation to read or reread these treasures—will find themselves immeasurably enriched.

BOOK NOTES

◆ ◆ ◆

20,000 Leagues under the Sea (*Vingt mille lieues sous les mers*. Paris: Gallimard, 2005): Jules Verne's tale of undersea adventures is available in many English editions, including Philip S. Allen's translation (Dover Thrift edition, 2006).

Adolphe (*Adolphe*. Paris: Livre de Poche, 1988): Benjamin Constant's short novel is available in an English translation by Margaret Mauldon from Oxford University Press (2001).

Against Nature (*A Rebours*. Paris: Folio classique, 1977): Joris-Karl Huysmans's novel has been translated by Margaret Mauldon (Oxford University Press, 1998).

Alcools/Calligrammes (*Œuvres poétiques d'Apollinaire*. Paris: Pléiade, 1956): Guillaume Apollinaire's poems are available in several translations, including Donald Revell's (Wesleyan University Press, 1995).

Antigone (*Antigone*. Paris: Table ronde, 1979): Jean Anouilh's famous play has been translated by Barbara Bray in the Methuen School Classics series (2001).

Asterix (the French *Astérix* comic books are published by Hachette): Many of René Goscinny's and Albert Uderzo's *Asterix* stories are published in English by Orion.

Aucassin and Nicolette (*Aucassin et Nicolette*. Paris: Poche, 1999): A translation by Francis William Bourdillon of this anonymous work is available from Dodo Press (2008).

Baroque at Dawn (*Baroque d'aube*. Montréal: L'Hexagone, 1995): Patricia Claxton's translation of Nicole Brossard's novel is published by McClelland and Stewart (1997).

Black Shack Alley (*La Rue Cases-Nègres*. Paris: Présence africaine, 1984): Joseph Zobel's portrait of a childhood on Martinique has been translated by Keith Q. Warner and published by Lynne Rienner (1980).

Black Skin White Masks (*Peau noire masques blancs*. Paris: Seuil, 1952): Frantz Fanon's classic is available from Grove Press (2008), in a translation by Richard Philcox.

The Book of the City of Ladies (*La Cité des dames*. Paris: Stock, 1986): A translation by Rosalind Brown-Grant of Christine de Pizan's proto-feminist treatise is published by Penguin (1999).

Candide (*Candide*, in *Romans et contes de Voltaire*. Paris: Garnier-Flammarion, 1966): Voltaire's famous tale has been translated into English many times; a recent edition is by Henry Morley and Lauren Walsh (Barnes and Noble, 2003).

Carmen (*Carmen*. Paris: J. Tallandier, 1967): Nicholas Jotcham's translation of what is arguably Prosper Mérimée's best-known story is available from Oxford University Press (2008).

Chéri (*Chéri*. Paris: Livre de poche, 2000): Colette's *Chéri* is published together with *The Last of Chéri* in Roger Senhouse's translation (Farrar, Straus and Giroux, 2001).

The Cid (*Le Cid*. Paris: Gallimard, 1953): Corneille's famous play is published together with his *The Liar* by Mariner Books (2009), in Richard Wilbur's translation.

The Count of Monte Cristo (*Le Comte de Monte-Cristo*. Paris: Gallimard, 1981): Robin Buss's translation of the Alexandre Dumas classic is published by Penguin (2003).

Crossing the Mangrove (*Traversée de la Mangrove*. Paris: Mercure de France, 1989): Richard Philcox's translation of Maryse Condé's novel is available from Anchor (1995).

Dangerous Liaisons (*Les Liaisons dangereuses*. Paris: Garnier, 1959): Penguin Classics has published a new translation of Choderlos de Laclos's work, by Helen Constantine (2007).

The Dark Child (*L'Enfant noir*. Paris: Plon, 1976): Camara Laye's novel of growing up in Guinea was translated by Ernest Jones (Farrar, Straus and Giroux, 1954).

Democracy in America (*De la démocratie en Amérique*. Paris: Vrin, 1990): De Tocqueville's still pertinent analysis of American politics and society is available from Penguin in Gerald Bevan's translation (2003).

The Devil's Pool (*La Mare au Diable*. Grenoble: Glénal, 1998): One edition of George Sand's bucolic tale is published in *The Devil's Pool and Other Stories*, translated by E. H. and A. M. Blackmore and Francine Giguère (SUNY Press, 2004).

Discourse on Method (*Discours de la méthode*. Paris: Fayard, 1986): Barnes and Noble's edition of René Descartes's seminal treatise is translated by John Veitch (2004).

Don't Trifle with Love (On ne badine pas avec l'amour. Paris: Gallimard, 1994): Alfred de Musset's play is available in a collection of his dramatic works translated by Peter Meyer and titled *Alfred de Musset: Seven Plays* (2006). This edition by Oberon Books will give the reader the opportunity of exploring other examples of Musset's theater.

"The Drunken Boat"/*A Season in Hell (Poésies, Une saison en enfer, Illuminations.* Paris: Folio Classique, 1965): Selections from Rimbaud's poetry have been translated by Martin Sorrel and are available from Oxford University Press (2001). Rimbaud's complete works and selected letters have been published by University of Chicago Press as *Rimbaud: Complete Works, Selected Letters* (2005), with Wallace Fowlie's translations.

The Essays (Les Essais. Paris: P. U. F., 1965): Michel de Montaigne's masterpiece is available in several editions, including Donald Frame's translation in *The Complete Works* from Everyman's Library (2003) and M. A. Screech's version titled *The Complete Essays,* published by Penguin Classics (1993).

Fables (Fables. Paris: Gallimard, 1991): Elizur Wright has translated La Fontaine's charming work (Dodo Press, 2007).

The Farce of Master Pathelin (La Farce de maistre Pierre Pathelin. Paris: Champion, 1967): This anonymous comedy is available in Richard Holbrook's translation from Kessinger Publishing (2007).

Fear and Trembling (Stupeur et tremblements. Paris: Albin Michel, 1999): Amélie Nothomb's sly portrayal of corporate life in Japan seen from a woman's point of view has been translated by Adriana Hunter (St. Martin's Press, 2002).

The Flowers of Evil (Les Fleurs du mal. Paris: Imprimerie nationale, 1978): Charles Baudelaire's poetry collection is contained in Barnes and Noble's *Flowers of Evil and Other Writings,* in translations by F. P. Sturm, Joseph Shipley, and W. J. Robertson (2008).

Friday (Vendredi ou les limbes du Pacifique. Paris: Gallimard, 1967): Norman Denny's translation of Michel Tournier's rewriting of *Robinson Crusoe* is published by Johns Hopkins University Press (1997).

The Heptameron (L'Heptaméron. Geneva: Droz, 1999): Marguerite de Navarre's French version of the *Decameron* was translated by Paul Chilton (Penguin Classics, 1984).

History of a Voyage to the Land of Brazil (Histoire d'un voyage faict en la terre du Brésil. Geneva: Droz, 1975): Jane Whatley has translated Jean de Léry's account of his journey to Brazil (University of California Press, 1993).

The Hunchback of Notre-Dame (*Notre-Dame de Paris*. Paris: Garnier-Flammarion, 1967): Signet Classics published Walter J. Cobb's translation of Victor Hugo's famous novel in 2001.

The Immoralist (*L'Immoraliste*. Paris: Mercure de France, 1963): Vintage published Richard Howard's translation of André Gide's text in 1996.

In Search of Lost Time: "Combray" ("Combray," in *Du côté de chez Swann*. Paris: Gallimard, 1987): This is the first section of volume 1, *Swann's Way* (*Du côté de chez Swann*), of Marcel's Proust's seven-volume novel, *À la recherche du temps perdu*. The translation by Scott Moncrieff and Terence Kilmartin is published by Vintage (1982). After finishing the delightful overture to Proust's great work, readers can then continue at their own leisure.

An Introduction to the Devout Life (*Introduction à la vie dévote*, in *Œuvres de Saint François de Sales*. Paris: Gallimard, 1967): François de Sales's spiritual classic is available in English from Vintage (2002) and other publishers.

Jealousy (*La Jalousie*. Paris: Editions de minuit, 1957): Alain Robbe-Grillet's *nouveau roman* comes with another of his novels, *In the Labyrinth*, both translated by Richard Howard (Grove Press, 1994).

The Journal of Eugène Delacroix (*Le Journal d'Eugène Delacroix*. Paris: Plon, 1981): Reading Delacroix's reflections is possible thanks to Lucy Norton's translation from Phaidon, which was first published in 1951.

Justine (*Justine ou les Malheurs de la vertu*. Paris: Gallimard, 1994): Marquis de Sade's work is available in the translation of Austryn Wainhouse in *Justine, Philosophy in the Bedroom, and Other Writings*, Grove Press (1994).

Kamouraska (*Kamouraska*. Paris: Seuil, 1970): Anne Hébert's novel is available in Norman Shapiro's translation from Fitzhenry and Whiteside (1994).

Kiffe Kiffe Tomorrow (*Kiffe, kiffe demain*. Paris: Hachette, 2006): Faïza Guène's debut novel is available in Sarah Adam's translation from Harvest Books (2006).

Lais of Marie de France (*Lais de Marie de France*. Paris: Champion, 1966): Marie de France's poems appear in Keith Busby's translation from Penguin Classics (1999).

Letters of a Peruvian Woman (*Lettres d'une Péruvienne*. New York: Modern Language Association of America, 1993): David Kornacker's translation of Françoise de Graffigny's novel is available from the Modern Language Association of America (1993).

The Letters of Madame de Sévigné (*Les Lettres de Madame de Sévigné*. Paris: Flammarion, 2003): Marquise de Sévigné's portrait of aristocratic life in the seventeenth century can be appreciated in the translation by Leonard Tancock, *Madame de Sévigné: Selected Letters* (Penguin Classics, 1982).

The Little Prince (*Le Petit Prince*, in *Œuvres complètes de Saint Exupéry*. Paris: Gallimard, 1994): This classic children's story, but also destined for adults, by Antoine de Saint-Exupéry has been translated by Richard Howard (Mariner Books, 2000).

Lock 14 (*Le Charretier de la Providence*, in *Simenon, Œuvre romanesque*. Paris: Omnibus, 2002): France's most famous detective, Inspector Maigret, is the principal character in this classic mystery by Georges Simenon, translated by Robert Baldick and available from Penguin (2006).

Lyric Poetry of the French Renaissance (Clément Marot, *Œuvres complètes*. Paris: Poche, 2007–9; Joachim Du Bellay, *Les Regrets*, Paris: Gallimard, 1967; Pierre de Ronsard, *Les Amours*, Paris: Gallimard, 1974): Translations by Norman Shapiro of selected works are featured in *Lyrics of the French Renaissance: Marot, Du Bellay, Ronsard* from Yale University Press (2002).

Madame Bovary (*Madame Bovary*. Paris: Garnier, 1971): There are many translations of Gustave Flaubert's iconic novel, including E. M. Aveling's (Barnes and Noble, 2005) and Francis Steegmuller's (Knopf, 1993).

Man a Machine (*L'Homme machine*, in *Œuvres philosophiques de La Mettrie*. Paris: Coda, 2004): Julien Offray de La Mettrie's materialist treatise is available in a translation by Richard A. Watson and Maya Rybalka (Hackett Publishing Company, 1994).

Manon Lescaut (*Manon Lescaut*. Paris: Imprimerie nationale, 1980): Abbé Prévost's novel of seduction and betrayal is available in a Penguin Classics edition (1992) featuring Leonard Tancock's translation.

Man's Fate (*La Condition humaine*. Paris: Gallimard, 1946): André Malraux's novel can be read in Haakon M. Chevalier's translation (Vintage, 1990).

The Marriage of Figaro (*Le Mariage de Figaro*. Oxford: Voltaire Foundation, 2002): Oxford University Press has combined three plays by Pierre-Augustin Caron de Beaumarchais in *The Figaro Trilogy: The Barber of Seville, The Marriage of Figaro, The Guilty Mother*, in translations by David Coward (2008).

Maxims (*Maximes*. Paris: Imprimerie nationale, 1998): John Heard's translation of François de La Rochefoucauld's *Maxims* is available in a Dover Publications edition (2006).

Memoirs of Hadrian (*Mémoires d'Hadrien*. Paris: Gallimard, 1977): Grace Frick, Marguerite Yourcenar's partner, translated this evocation of the emperor Hadrian that is available from Farrar, Straus and Giroux (2005).

The Misanthropist (*Le Misanthrope*, in *Œuvres complètes de Molière*. Paris: Gallimard, 1971): Molière's often hilarious but sometimes dark comedy can be read in several English editions, including *The Misanthrope, Tartuffe, and Other Plays* from Oxford University Press (2008), translated by Maya Slater.

Missing Person (*Rue des boutiques obscures*. Paris: Gallimard, 1978): Patrick Modiano's novel is available in Daniel Weissbort's translation from David R. Godine (2004).

Mister Venus (*Monsieur Vénus*. New York: Modern Language Association, 2004): Rachilde's erotic novel is available from the Modern Language Association of America (2004) in Melanie Hawthorne's translation.

Moderato Cantabile (*Moderato Cantabile*. Paris: Editions de minuit, 1958): Marguerite Duras's novel has been translated by Richard Seaver and is published by Riverrun Press (2004).

Monsieur Ibrahim and the Flowers of the Koran (*Monsieur Ibrahim et les fleurs du Coran*. Paris: Albin Michel, 2001): Eric-Emmanuel Schmitt's novella has appeared in a translation by Marjolijn de Jager in *Monsieur Ibrahim and the Flowers of the Koran* and *Oscar and the Lady in Pink* (Other Press, 2004).

My Life and My Films (*Ma Vie et mes films*. Paris: Garnier-Flammarion, 1974): Jean Renoir's autobiography has been published in a translation by Norman Denny by Da Capo Press (1991).

Mythologies (*Mythologies*. Paris: Seuil, 1957): Roland Barthes's perceptive and often amusing analyses of various aspects of twentieth-century French society have been translated by Annette Lavers (Farrar, Straus and Giroux, 1972).

Nadja (*Nadja*. Paris: Gallimard, 1963): This surrealist novel by André Breton is available in a Grove Press edition (1994), translated by Richard Howard.

Nausea (*La Nausée*. Paris: Gallimard, 1968): Jean-Paul Sartre's philosophical novel can be read in Lloyd Alexander's translation (W. W. Norton, 2007).

The Nun (*La Religieuse*. Paris: Colin, 1961): Leonard Tancock has translated Denis Diderot's text (Penguin, 1974).

Old Goriot (*Le Père Goriot*. Paris: Magnard, 1985): Honoré de Balzac's novel can be found in a number of translations. Barnes and Noble offers a translation by Ellen Marriage (2005), Cambridge University Press has published David Bellos's version (1987), and Penguin Classics uses the translation by Marion Crawford (1951).

On Monsters and Marvels (*Des Monstres et prodiges*. Geneva, Droz, 1971): Janis L. Pallister is the translator of Ambroise Paré's book from the sixteenth century (University of Chicago Press, 1995).

Ourika (*Ourika*. New York: Modern Language Association, 1994): The translation by the novelist John Fowles of Claire de Duras's influential novel is available from the Modern Language Association of America (1994).

Pantagruel (*Pantagruel*. Paris: Livre de poche, 1994): The Rabelais scholar M. A. Screech has translated both this work and Rabelais's *Gargantua* (Penguin Classics, 2006).

Paul and Virginia (*Paul et Virginie*. Paris: Nizet, 1975): John Donovan's translation of Bernardin de Saint-Pierre's exotic novel is available from Peter Owens Publishers (2005).

Persian Letters (*Lettres persanes*. Paris: Gallimard, 2006): A recent translation of Montesquieu's satirical look at French society is Margaret Mauldon's from Oxford University Press (2008). An older translation by C. J. Betts is published by Penguin Classics (1973).

Phaedra (*Phèdre*. Paris: P. U. F., 1999): There are two readily available translations of Racine's play, Margaret Rawlings's from Penguin (1992) and the poet Ted Hughes's from Farrar, Straus and Giroux (2000).

The Physiology of Taste (*La Physiologie du goût*. Paris: Bonnot, 1968): Brillat-Savarin's exploration of gastronomy can be found in Anne Drayton's translation (Penguin, 1994).

The Possibility of an Island (*La Possibilité d'une île*. Paris: Fayard, 2005): Gavin Bowd has translated Michel Houellebecq's novel (Vintage, 2007).

The Princess of Clèves (*La Princesse de Clèves*. Paris: Imprimerie nationale, 1980): Marie-Madeleine de La Fayette's novel is available in a translation by Terence Cave from Oxford University Press (2009).

The Prospector (*Le Chercheur d'or*. Paris: Gallimard, 1985): This novel by Jean-Marie Gustave Le Clézio can be read in Carol Marks's translation (David R. Godine, 2008).

The Red and the Black (*Le Rouge et le Noir*. Paris: Garnier, 1973): Stendhal's novel about the young Julien Sorel's social ascension and subsequent fall is translated by Burton Raffel (Modern Library, 2003), among others.

René (*René*. Geneva: Droz, 1970): François-René de Chateaubriand's romantic short novel is available, together with his *Atala,* in Irving Putter's translation published by University of California Press (1952).

Reveries of the Solitary Walker (*Rêveries du promeneur solitaire*. Paris: Imprimerie nationale, 1978): Jean-Jacques Rousseau's walks and thoughts are translated by Peter France (Penguin Classics, 1980).

Rhinoceros (*Rhinocéros.* Paris: Gallimard, 1959): Derek Prouse has translated Eugène Ionesco's political allegory in *Rhinoceros and Other Plays* (Grove Press, 1994).

The Romance of the Rose (*Le Roman de la rose.* Paris: Garnier-Flammarion, 1974): Oxford University Press has published Frances Horgan's translation of Guillaume de Lorris's and Jean de Meun's influential medieval allegory (1999).

The Sand Child (*L'Enfant de sable.* Paris: Seuil, 1985): Tahar Ben Jelloun's novel has been translated by Alan Sheridan (Johns Hopkins University Press, 2000).

Satanism and Witchcraft (*La Sorcière.* Paris: M. Didier, 1957): Jules Michelet's classic study is available from Carol Publishing in a translation by A. R. Allinson (1992).

The Second Sex (*Le Deuxième sexe.* Paris: Gallimard, 1949): Simone de Beauvoir's treatise has been published by Vintage Books (1989) in H. M. Parshley's translation.

Short Stories (*Boule de Suif.* Paris: Folio, 1973): A selection of Guy de Maupassant short stories is presented under the title *Best Short Stories* in a Dover edition (1996). A larger collection of stories is available as *A Parisian Affair and Other Stories* from Penguin Classics (2004), translated by Siân Miles.

Simple Passion (*Passion simple.* Paris: Gallimard, 1991): Tanya Leslie has translated Annie Ernaux's novel (Seven Stories Press, 2003).

So Long a Letter (*Une si longue lettre.* Dakar: Nouvelles éditions africaines, 1980): Mariama Bâ's evocation of the life of a modern Senegalese woman has been translated by Modupe Bode-Thomas (Heinemann, 2008).

The Song of Roland (*La Chanson de Roland.* Paris: Hatier, 1967): This founding text of French literature has been translated by Glyn S. Burgess (Penguin Classics, 1990). Penguin also has a translation by the novelist Dorothy Sayers (1957), while Modern Library offers a translation by W. S. Merwin (2001).

Sonnets (*Œuvres complètes de Louise Labé.* Paris: Poche, 2004): Annie Finch and Deborah Lesko Baker have collaborated to produce *The Complete Poetry and Prose of Louise Labé* (University of Chicago Press, 2006).

The Stranger (*L'Etranger.* Paris: Gallimard, 1988): The Vintage edition of Albert Camus's novel is available in a translation by Matthew Ward (1989).

The Testament (*Le Testament,* in *Œuvres de François Villon.* Geneva: Slatkine, 1969): François Villon's poetry is available in Peter Dale's translation from Anvil Press (2004).

Thérèse Desqueyroux (*Thérèse Desqueyroux*. Paris: Grasset, 1970): Penguin offers the Gerard Manley Hopkins translation of François Mauriac's masterful novel (2002), while a translation by Raymond MacKenzie is published by Rowman and Littlefield (2005).

Thérèse Raquin (*Thérèse Raquin*. Paris: Fasquelle, 1970): A number of translations of this macabre novel by Emile Zola are available, including A. Rothwell's from Oxford University Press (1992) and Robin Buss's from Penguin Classics (2005).

Thoughts (*Pensées de Pascal*. Paris: Mercure de France, 1976): Blaise Pascal's fragmentary, posthumous work is available in several editions, including Honor Levi's translation, *Pensées and Other Writings*, Oxford University Press (2008).

Tomorrow's Eve (*L'Eve future*. Paris: Gallimard, 1993): A reprint of Robert Adam's translation of Villiers de l'Isle-Adam's science fiction novel is available from University of Illinois Press (2000).

The Torments of Love (*Les Angoysses douloureuses qui procedent d'amours*. Saint Etienne: Publications de l'Université de Saint-Etienne, 2005): Steven Rendall and Lisa Neal have translated this sentimental sixteenth-century novel (University of Minnesota Press, 1996).

Trap for Cinderella (*Piège pour Cendrillon*. Paris: Folio, 1999): Helen Weaver has translated Sébastien Japrisot's mystery (Penguin, 1997).

Tristan and Iseut (*Le Roman de Tristan et Iseut*. Paris: 10/18, 1981): Joseph Bédier's compilation of the versions by Béroul, Thomas, and others, which gives the reader an overall view of this famous medieval romance, has been translated by Hilaire Belloc and is published as *The Romance of Tristan and Iseult* (Vintage, 1994).

W, or The Memory of Childhood (*W ou le souvenir d'enfance*. Paris: Denoël, 1975): The translation of Georges Perec's novel was done by David Bellos (David R. Godine, 1988).

Waiting for Godot (*En attendant Godot*. Paris: Editions de minuit, 1952): Although there are various translations of this play, a first choice could be Samuel Beckett's own English version (Grove Press, 1994).

Yvain, or the Knight of the Lion (*Yvain ou le Chevalier au lion*. Paris: Livre de Poche, 1994): Burton Raffel's translation of this medieval romance by Chrétien de Troyes is published by Yale University Press (1987).

INDEX

◆ ◆ ◆